Contextual Social Psychology

Contextual Social Psychology

Reanalyzing Prejudice, Voting, and Intergroup Contact

Thomas F. Pettigrew

AMERICAN PSYCHOLOGICAL ASSOCIATION

Published by
American Psychological Association
750 First Street, NE
Washington, DC 20002
https://www.apa.org

Order Department
https://www.apa.org/pubs/books
order@apa.org

In the U.K., Europe, Africa, and the Middle East, copies may be ordered from Eurospan
https://www.eurospanbookstore.com/apa
info@eurospangroup.com

Typeset in Charter and Interstate by Circle Graphics, Inc., Reisterstown, MD

Printer: Gasch Printing, Odenton, MD
Cover Designer: Beth Schlenoff Design, Bethesda, MD

Library of Congress Cataloging-in-Publication Data

Names: Pettigrew, Thomas F., author.
Title: Contextual social psychology : reanalyzing prejudice, voting, and intergroup contact / Thomas F. Pettigrew.
Description: Washington : American Psychological Association, 2020. | Includes bibliographical references and index.
Identifiers: LCCN 2020011354 (print) | LCCN 2020011355 (ebook) | ISBN 9781433832949 (paperback) | ISBN 9781433833182 (ebook)
Subjects: LCSH: Social psychology--Research. | Intergroup relations. | Voting. | Prejudices.
Classification: LCC HM1019 .P48 2020 (print) | LCC HM1019 (ebook) | DDC 302—dc23
LC record available at https://lccn.loc.gov/2020011354
LC ebook record available at https://lccn.loc.gov/2020011355

https://doi.org/10.1037/0000210-000

Printed in the United States of America

10 9 8 7 6 5 4 3 2 1

I wish to dedicate this book to my late wife of 63 years, Ann Hallman Pettigrew, BA, MD, MPH. While engaged in a long and distinguished career in pediatric public health that actually saved children's lives, Ann somehow managed to listen patiently to and improve dozens of my speeches and edit virtually all of my published writings. In the last month of her life, she urged me to write this book.

Contents

Acknowledgments

I wish to acknowledge my former doctoral students, colleagues, and friends who helped me in many ways with the writing of this volume. They contributed many good ideas and references, but the remaining mistakes are my responsibility. First, those who read early drafts and made exceedingly helpful comments: Professor Ulrich Wagner of the Philipps University in Marburg, Germany; Professor Howard Schuman of the University of Michigan; Professor Norman Feather of the University of Flinders in Australia; Professor Heather Smith of Sonoma State University in Rohnert Park, California; Professor Linda Tropp of the University of Massachusetts at Amherst; Professor Christian Crandall of the University of Kansas; Professor Susan Fiske of Princeton University; Professor Craig Reineman of the University of California, Santa Cruz; and three anonymous reviewers. I also thank Kristen Knight of the American Psychological Association Press—an extremely helpful book editor.

Chapters 4 and 5 on statistics and prejudice were influenced heavily by my work with Wagner and Oliver Christ of Fern University in Germany. Professor David Kenny at the University of Connecticut, Professor Charles Judd of the University of Colorado, and Professor Anthony Greenwald of the University of Washington also supplied invaluable advice on these chapters. Chapter 6 on relative deprivation was significantly shaped by my joint research and writing over 3 decades with Heather Smith and Professor Ian Walker of the Australian National University in Canberra, Australia. Chapter 7 on intergroup contact is the latest statement growing out of a 2-decade-long collaboration with Tropp.

In addition, Eric Uslaner, emeritus professor of political science at the University of Maryland, provided vital assistance on the issue of contact's effects on trust. Chapter 8 on right-wing voting was made possible by my partnership with Jasper van Assche of Ghent University in Belgium and Professor Kristof Dhont of Kent University of Canterbury in Great Britain.

My most sincere thanks to them all.

Contextual Social Psychology

INTRODUCTION

Once you become an octogenarian and have engaged in social psychological research and writing for two thirds of a century, you must ask yourself just what it all adds up to in the end. Were there central themes? Was there an overarching perspective that developed over the years? What, if anything, contributed to advances in my discipline of social psychology?

This volume provides my answers to these questions. I have consistently tried, with varying success, to place the psychological characteristics of individuals within their structural, cultural, and normative contexts. In other words, I have long sought to help establish a *contextual social psychology.*

The idea of a contextual social psychology is simple, straightforward, and hardly new. It simply means placing data from one level of analysis within the context of other levels. In what was one of the very first studies in North American social psychology, Norman Triplett (1898), an amateur bicycle racer himself, keenly observed that riders tended to pump harder and race faster when riding with others than when riding alone—a basic contextual result.

https://doi.org/10.1037/0000210-001
Contextual Social Psychology: Reanalyzing Prejudice, Voting, and Intergroup Contact, by T. F. Pettigrew

But advancing the contextual idea is anything but simple. Indeed, social science has wrestled with this problem both theoretically and methodologically throughout its history. This book illustrates how, over the years, slow progress has been made in establishing a theoretically and methodologically sound contextual approach in the discipline. Indeed, recent years have witnessed major methodological and statistical advances that have made contextual research far easier to conduct, more rigorous, and more common. And it is this emergence of contextual research in social psychology that this volume traces and describes, and for which it advocates. I have attempted to write the book so that non–social scientists can easily follow the argument. But it is aimed primarily at social scientists in general and at advanced undergraduates and graduate students in psychology and sociology who wish to learn about these contextual ideas and how they have historically developed.

BOOK SYNOPSIS

Let me first provide an outline of the book's nine chapters so that the reader understands how the book's contentions unfold.

Chapter 1: A Personal Quest

My two thirds of a century of research and writing has been shaped by a desire to see psychological social psychology become a more contextual discipline. This chapter records aspects of my life that contributed to this aspiration. With great good fortune, I benefited from instruction from three inspiring Harvard University professors—Gordon Allport, Samuel Stouffer and Talcott Parsons—as well as from two caring and candid African Americans: Mildred Adams and Kenneth Clark. And my experiences in the courtroom, on racial commissions, and advising school districts and other organizations bolstered further my conviction that a multilevel, contextual approach is essential.

Chapter 2: What Is Contextual Social Psychology?

Just as its name implies, contextual social psychology seeks to place basic psychological phenomena in their social contexts. This procedure typically involves more than one level of analysis. Figure 2.1 presents a simple diagram involving three levels of analysis—the micro-, meso-, and macrolevels—with six causal paths connecting them. The chapter provides examples, both empirical and theoretical, to illustrate each path. This diagram is then used throughout the volume.

Chapter 3: Five Advantages of Contextual Analyses for Social Psychology

This chapter answers the question "Why employ contextual analyses?" by specifying five advantages of the approach.

1. *Contextual analyses offer a rapprochement between social psychologists in sociology and psychology, as well as with the other social sciences.* Examples show how other social sciences, especially political science and economics, have benefited from borrowing social psychological ideas and how social psychology could benefit from their ideas.

2. *Contextual analyses avoid the compositional fallacy, the ecological fallacy, and the single-factor fallacy.* Each fallacy is described, and examples are provided. This is an especially significant advantage because these fallacies are surprisingly common in the social science literature and even more common in popular discussion.

3. *Contextual analyses importantly expand social psychology's explanatory power.* Using the cognitive example of group attribution bias, this section cites the numerous contextual factors that influence the bias.

4. *Contextual analyses help to counter social psychology's so-called crises.* Over the past half century, social psychology has experienced two self-inflicted "crises." The first was the crisis of relevance. During the 1960s, many social psychologists worried that the discipline was drifting from its roots as a change-oriented field. The second crisis is currently a crisis of method, concentrating on "false positives" and replication failures. Both concerns have been overblown, but this latest crisis has led to greater methodological and statistical rigor. Contextual analyses aid the corrections for these related issues.

5. *Contextual analyses generate results that more easily influence public policy.* Social policy largely operates at the macrolevel. Policymakers, who are often lawyers, cannot easily use social science findings at micro- and mesolevels, levels at which social psychologists typically work, but contextual findings that use the macrolevel readily translate into policy terms.

Chapter 4: Statistical Advances Enable and Encourage Contextual Analyses in Social Psychology

This chapter traces the development over the past half century of advanced statistics that both enabled and encouraged the use of contextual analyses. First came *structural equation modeling* and related methods. Then Blalock (1984) published his *explicit analysis of contextual effects models*. Next came simple and direct methods for uncovering *mediating and moderator effects*. Then *meta-analysis* offered a standardized and systematic method for combining the results of multiple studies. Finally, *multilevel analyses* were introduced—the most valuable method of all for contextual analyses. Indeed, this volume describes one multilevel analysis study after another to establish how important this statistical advance is for the contextual approach.

Chapter 5: Applying Contextual Analyses to Intergroup Prejudice

Chapters 5 through 8 demonstrate how predictors of an important phenomenon are found at the micro-, meso-, and macrolevels. Prejudice correlates at the microlevel include authoritarianism, social dominance orientation, openness to experience, agreeableness, need for closure, and deprovincialization; at the mesolevel, intergroup contact; and at the macrolevel, restrictions on intergroup contact (e.g., segregation), discriminatory norms, and difficult economic times.

Chapter 6: Applying Contextual Analyses to Relative Deprivation

Relative deprivation also has correlates at all three analysis levels. The microlevel has political alienation and inefficacy, age, and education; the mesolevel has differences in economic well-being in the immediate environment; and the macrolevel has cultural and normative differences in individualism and collectivism and has economic differences between nations.

Chapter 7: Applying Contextual Analyses to Intergroup Contact

Again, critical correlates of this central phenomenon emerge at all three levels. The microlevel has the usual suspects—authoritarianism, social dominance orientation, sensitivity to threats, empathy, perspective taking, insecure attachment, and the Big Five traits of Agreeableness and Openness to Experience. The mesolevel has prior intergroup experience, situational threat, equal-status and common goals of groups in the situation, and intergroup cooperation. The macrolevel has cultural and normative differences in egalitarian values and authority support.

Chapter 8: Applying Contextual Analyses to Far-Right Voting Patterns

This chapter records the remarkable similarities at all three analysis levels in extreme right-wing voting in the United States, the United Kingdom, and continental Europe. At all levels, the predictors of voting for Trump and other nationalists are much the same as those for positively predicting prejudice and those negatively predicting intergroup contact. The microlevel has authoritarianism, social dominance orientation, prejudice, and relative deprivation; the mesolevel has lack of intergroup contact; and the macrolevel has the rapid recent arrival of immigrants in the area.

Chapter 9: Looking Ahead

The final chapter summarizes various implications of the contextual approach for the teaching of social psychology at the graduate and undergraduate levels, as well as the proposal for concepts that span all three levels of analysis.

From this outline, we turn to the details of my long experience in the discipline that led me to become an ardent advocate of contextual analyses of social psychological phenomena.

1 A PERSONAL QUEST

Allowing for the distortions of memory while looking back over a long life, I can trace how I came to focus on contextual effects that included both structural and cultural factors as well as purely psychological factors. Indeed, it became a personal quest.

INITIAL INFLUENCES

Standing up in class and calling your seventh-grade history teacher "a bigot" was not regarded as acceptable student behavior at my junior high school in Richmond, Virginia, in 1944. My only defense was that the epithet was richly deserved. Miss Prentiss daily disparaged African Americans and even claimed that Hitler was not all bad—"look what he did with the Jews." I was promptly expelled, but my mother and grandmother, both fiery Scottish

Some of the passages in this chapter have been reprinted or adapted from "In Pursuit of Three Theories: Authoritarianism, Relative Deprivation, and Intergroup Contact," by T. F. Pettigrew, 2016, *Annual Review of Psychology*, *67*, 1–21. Copyright 2016 by Annual Reviews. Reprinted with permission.

https://doi.org/10.1037/0000210-002
Contextual Social Psychology: Reanalyzing Prejudice, Voting, and Intergroup Contact, by T. F. Pettigrew

immigrants, were at the school to protest within the hour. I was readmitted the next day.

I recall this intense incident because it made me aware of the power of social norms as well as the intense prejudice of some individuals operating and supported within those norms. In racist Richmond of 1944, Miss Prentiss felt she could safely express her prejudices because they received at that time substantial local normative social support. I recall feeling sorry for the school's principal, Mr. Mellis, as he endured the unrelenting wrath of my family. He felt he had to defend his staff member and be cognizant of the prevailing norms, although he obviously did not share the teacher's strident views.

MY FIRST MENTOR OF AMERICAN RACE RELATIONS: MISS MILDRED ADAMS

I also greatly benefited from firsthand instruction on what it was like to be an African American in the Richmond of the 1930s and 1940s. Miss Mildred Adams became my family's housekeeper when I was 5 years old in 1936. Her role within the family was a mixed one between Southern tradition and full acceptance as a member. As immigrants, my mother and grandmother did not possess the typical White Southern view of race.[1] In fact, my grandmother felt a deep resentment of English discriminatory treatment of the Scots and perceived a loose link between this treatment and American racial discrimination. And although a fourth-generation Scots American, my father grew up in the Allegheny Mountains of Virginia where there were virtually no African Americans or strict racial norms. Yet some southern proprieties of the time persisted. Adams did not stay in the home at night; she had only 1½ days off each week from her job; her pay was low, although above that of other servants in the neighborhood;[2] and she did not eat at the table with

[1] Years later, I was proud of my mother for legal action she undertook for Adams. Richmond decided to have a federal highway run through the city to help suburbanites ride quickly into the city. As in Buffalo, New York, and other American cities, the new road ran straight through a major Black neighborhood, splitting it in two, as it was the cheapest land to obtain. Adding to the residents' misery, the disrupted homeowners were offered compensation far below market value. Incensed, my feisty mother hired a lawyer and threatened to take Adams's case to court. Knowing they were almost certain to lose, the highway authority settled immediately, and Adams received as compensation a nicer home in North Richmond.

[2] The U.S. government did not open up Social Security benefits for domestics until 1954—19 years after its original enactment—an openly discriminatory ruling that especially affected African Americans.

the family. The motion picture *The Help* captures this situation accurately (Taylor, 2011).

I have dedicated several of my books to Adams, for she is responsible for my lifelong focus on intergroup relations. Unlike most adults, she took children seriously; she gently step by step introduced me to a world about which most White Americans know almost nothing. Gradually, she allowed me to glimpse into Black life and sense how White supremacy limited the life chances and choices of Black Richmonders in the 1930s and 1940s. While my family was economically struggling, like most middle-class White families during the Great Depression, I slowly began to understand that my white skin bestowed upon me special privilege that Adams could not share. These insights fired me early with indignation over racial injustice.

Wednesday afternoon was wash and ironing day. I learned to attend regularly her quiet seminars on race in the basement of our home. She patiently and gently described her life—its harsh beginnings in poverty, a scant 6 years of racially segregated education, and never knowing her Native American father. Later, hoping to escape the South's all-encompassing racism, she migrated with an older cousin to New York City. She soon learned that the northern metropolis in the 1930s was different from the South but hardly much of an improvement. She and her cousin ventured out one night to a nice restaurant in Times Square. They secured a table, but then they had to sit there for hours, never to be served. Obviously, African Americans were not welcome, but there were no signs saying so as in Richmond.

Adams's cousin had her own story. She had majored in Latin at Virginia Union, Richmond's predominantly Black university, but she could never obtain a position as a Latin teacher in Virginia's tightly segregated schools. So she, too, worked as a housekeeper and even regularly tutored her employer's children in Latin.

Years later, when I told this all-too-true story to friends in the Senior Common Room of Harvard University's Dunster House, my listeners rolled their eyes in disbelief. They obviously did not believe a word of it. This was motivated disbelief. My colleagues simply did not want to accept that an African American Latin scholar was working as a housekeeper and teaching Latin only to the children of her employer. This taught me how extremely reluctant even well-meaning White Americans are to accept how racism severely disrupts individual Black lives. This insight led me to begin all my undergraduate courses on race relations (1956–1998), as well as my 10-part educational television series, *Epitaph for Jim Crow* (Pettigrew, 1964a), with a detailed analysis of the well-documented, if ghastly, phenomenon of racial lynching. This horrible stain on American history had to be believed, and it established the needed context for the rest of the race relations course.

Racial incidents in the New York City of the 1930s continued relentlessly for Adams and her cousin—frequent refusal of service, empty cabs that would not stop for them, store detectives following them, and so on—all with no signs or clear norms as in Richmond. Being a shy person who avoided confrontations if possible, Adams ultimately decided in 1936 to return to Richmond, where the norms were patently clear. Ambiguity and uncertainty can be more debilitating than overt discrimination.

In later years, Adams introduced me to her all-Black neighborhood—with the approval of my parents. Here I met people whom I knew only in their "racial roles" when dealing with Whites. For example, our postman, Mr. Anderson (I knew him only by his last name), was an entirely different person when I encountered him one Sunday as the expansive, handsomely dressed chief layman at his Baptist church. The difference between the two racial contexts was astounding. When I later read W. E. B. Du Bois's (1903/1994) description of "double consciousness" among African Americans, I knew exactly what he meant. One side knows yourself as a distinctive individual, the other side looks at yourself through the eyes of stereotyping Whites. When Whites were not around, Anderson could be his true extroverted self. Two decades later, I tried to capture this phenomenon with the concept of "racial roles" (Pettigrew, 1964b).

Two memorable experiences revealed what Adams was describing to me on wash days felt like in real life. Indeed, if anything, she was softening the cruel reality of racism for my young ears. On many nights, there was recurrent screaming from one of her neighbors, who was seriously mentally ill. Although the screams often occurred in the middle of the night, the neighbors tolerated the many piercing interruptions. Not to do so meant that she would be institutionalized at the segregated state facility for the Black "insane" in Petersburg, Virginia. "That's a snake pit," explained Adams. "The neighborhood just couldn't do that to her." Thus, I learned early how segregation at the institutional level directly and negatively impacted the everyday lives of African Americans in many direct and indirect ways at the individual level.

Adams was an early fan of Humphrey Bogart. At that time, movies took almost 2 years to reach Richmond's segregated "Black" theaters. So when a new Bogart movie—*The Maltese Falcon*—came to the "White" Loew's theater in 1941, Adams was eager to attend. She dressed in an all-white uniform to make it abundantly clear that she was a servant escorting me. But the attempt completely failed. The theater staff flatly and angrily refused to admit her, even threatened to call the police.

Years later she told me that I had made a loud scene of protest, although I do not recall these details. I have just remembered for 8 decades having a front-row seat to witness the cruel injustice dealt to someone I cherished. The event has been seared into my memory for a lifetime. The only reason for denying Mildred Adams entry was raw, vicious, unadulterated racism supported by racist state law. These events, by the time I was 10 years old, ensured that the many psychological and cultural defenses that blind most White Americans to the racial injustice that surrounds them were no longer available to me.

The Forbidden Subject

Adams's instruction was especially valuable for me because racial discrimination and racial matters generally were virtually forbidden topics in the Richmond of my childhood. Slavery was never once discussed in my 11 years of public schooling (then-impoverished Virginia did not offer the now-standard 12 years), nor did anyone ever tell me that my family lived on the very street—Richmond's Franklin Street—where large slave trading establishments were centered before the Civil War (Dew, 2016; Pettigrew, 2017a). Abraham Lincoln was mentioned by a teacher only once to my memory; the heroes were Generals Robert E. Lee, Thomas "Stonewall" Jackson, James Ewell Brown ("Jeb") Stuart, and other high-ranking Virginian officers of the Confederate army. My father actually taught me to read with a short biography of Confederate Brigadier General James Johnston Pettigrew—our distant family connection with the "War between the States," as it was politely called.

Then I began reading on the subject of race. Two leading books impressed me in particular (Pettigrew, 2016). Gunnar Myrdal's (1944) 1,500-page *An American Dilemma* provided a sociological perspective on the South's racial situation. I was attracted to the tome because the local racist newspapers routinely and ferociously attacked the pro-integrationist Myrdal—usually referring to him as "the socialist Swede." I reasoned that if the local papers despised him, Myrdal must be a great man.[3] Surprisingly, the city's public library had a copy I could borrow.

[3] I was right in my assessment. Three decades later, I had the wonderful opportunity to get to know Myrdal well when we cotaught a graduate seminar at the University of California, Irvine in the winter of 1975–1976. He did not disappoint me.

Later, I began to study *The Authoritarian Personality* (Adorno et al., 1950). It provided quite a different psychological perspective. Although Myrdal's tome accurately reflected my experiences growing up in racially segregated Richmond, the theory of the authoritarian personality seemed incomplete to me. I knew many Virginians—foremost among them my soft-spoken, equalitarian father—who largely conformed to the region's racial norms but did not at all fit the authoritarian mold.[4] *The Authoritarian Personality* contained no Southern samples and simply assumed that greater authoritarianism explained the White South's elevated racism. This early observation of the importance of conformity became the basis of my doctoral thesis at Harvard University years later. Indeed, I suspect many theories of social science similarly spring from such personal experience.

Something important was missing when authoritarianism theory was applied to the White South. The answer was supplied by Myrdal's landmark volume. The South's tortured history—slavery, a lost war, poverty, and intense racial segregation—had shaped discriminatory norms to which Southerners of both races had to conform for decades. And social psychology has long shown that behavior can powerfully shape attitudes through cognitive dissonance processes (Stone & Fernandez, 2008). To be sure, authoritarianism plays a role as Miss Prentiss had clearly demonstrated for me. But so did conformity to entrenched racially discriminatory norms that characterized Southern society. My former history teacher and junior high school principal were reflecting this tragic history that was still vibrant in the Richmond of the 1930s and 1940s, eight decades after the Civil War.

STARTING MY CAREER

My discovery of social psychology remains a vivid memory. It was a crisp February morning in 1951 when I began an introductory course on the subject at the University of Virginia. There were no social psychologists in the department at that time; the field was still regarded by the dominant experimental psychologists as questionable science at best (Pettigrew, 2016). Nevertheless, the course was ably taught by a leading expert on hearing—Willard Thurlow.

[4] Having grown up in the mountains of Virginia without established racial norms, my Scottish American father easily violated the South's racist norms when his actions were out of the purview of other Whites. And he never questioned my efforts to combat racial discrimination; he only cautioned me, wisely, to be "careful."

The course text was the venerable *Theory and Problems of Social Psychology* (Krech & Crutchfield, 1948). It featured two intriguing chapters on prejudice—one on racial prejudice, and a second on "how to eliminate this prejudice among our people." Because of my deep concerns about Southern race relations, this subject was of enormous interest to me. As my first professional ambition to be an architect had not worked out (I could not draw!), I knew immediately that I had found the field in which to specialize.

I majored in psychology, but, influenced by Myrdal, I minored in the University of Virginia's then small sociology department. And the well-taught sociology courses reinforced my awareness of macrofactors. The psychology department gave me the chance to be a course assistant in the introductory psychological course as a junior and senior—a great opportunity that led me to decide firmly that I wanted to become a university teacher.

I am also grateful to the University of Virginia for recommending me for a Rockefeller Foundation Graduate Fellowship that paid for my 1st year of graduate work. To be nominated for the needed grant, I had to face a stern interview with a select committee of three senior and politically conservative professors from the university's history and English departments. I worried that they might not take too kindly to my ambition to venture north to Harvard University to study Southern racism. But, as luck and Southern culture would have it, the committee was primarily interested in my name. Did I know about the Confederate General Pettigrew? Was I kin to him? Did I know what he did at the critical Battle of Gettysburg? Because my father had taught me all about the general years before, I was able to answer at length their Civil War questions. I later wondered if I had obtained the scholarship more because of my name and the general than of my graduate plans!

Graduate Training

My interest in both psychology and sociology led me to apply to Harvard University's Department of Social Relations, where I could once again major in social psychology and minor in sociology. Somehow, Thurlow knew that Gordon Allport was writing a book on prejudice and recommended that I apply to Harvard. Such timely mentoring can redirect your life, and I remain appreciative for Thurlow's guidance. Innocently unaware of how arrogant it appeared, I mentioned in my Harvard application that I wanted to work with Allport on race relations, otherwise I was not interested in attending Harvard. Fortunately, Allport was in charge of graduate admissions, and my naive impertinence did not prove fatal (Pettigrew, 2016).

The social psychology doctoral program accepted me and gave me the extraordinary opportunity to work with Allport, a warm mentor and legendary psychologist (Pettigrew, 1969, 1990, 1999, 2015a), as well as Samuel Stouffer (Pettigrew, 2015b), an inspiring sociological social psychologist who specialized in national surveys. Years later, I annually cotaught a graduate course with Talcott Parsons, a confident macroscale theorist of sweeping scope whose work was dominant in the sociology of that period. Repeatedly hearing his lectures year after year furthered my interest in social structure.[5]

Stouffer was an exciting but unorthodox teacher; he could not have been more different in style and manner from either the socially shy, circumspect Allport or the expansive Parsons (Pettigrew, 2015b, 2016). Instruction from him was invariably informal, detailed, and empirical. Intensely engrossed in his work, Stouffer taught by example. You followed him from office to computing room and back, absorbing as best you could his excitement and "feel" for survey analysis. To this day, I have never lost the sense of excitement and curiosity in analyzing new survey data instilled by these memorable occasions. If a member of his graduate seminar on survey analysis offered an interesting hypothesis, he would leap up at once and exclaim, "Let's test it!" Then he would lead the class to the machine room and start stuffing hundreds of survey data cards into the old IBM 101 counter, sorter, and printer.[6]

In 1952, race relations was not a favored specialty. I was the object of concern among my fellow doctoral students. They urged me to choose another specialty, as race relations offered few jobs and little research support. But my Southern experiences with racial injustice had sparked my desire to be a social psychologist, so these concerns seemed irrelevant. The scene changed in 1954 when the U.S. Supreme Court ruled that racial segregation in public schools was unconstitutional. It overturned an 1896 high court decision that had established what was erroneously termed "separate but equal" schools (although all-Black and all-White schools had never been truly equal in resources). Suddenly, my peers became interested in the topic, and their kind worries about my future diminished.

---

[5] While I was listening to Parsons's lectures, my physician wife was studying for her MPH at Harvard's School of Public Health. I became intrigued by her statistics textbook. It was unlike any psychology statistics text I had ever seen. Given the particular concerns of public health, her text provided multiple examples of how to analyze macrolevel (water systems, medical laws, etc.) influences on microlevel phenomena (individual health). These simultaneous influences—Parsons's lectures and public health's statistical methods—made a lasting impression on me.

[6] Dreeben (2019) speculated that colorful Stouffer stories could fill a whole magazine. My retelling of some of them can be found in Pettigrew (2015b).

A Simple Contextual Thesis

On the basis of my earlier concerns about how authoritarianism could not explain the South's heightened racial prejudice, I planned a basic contextual doctoral thesis. Both Allport and Stouffer encouraged me to pursue this topic. It was an exciting time to be working with them. Not only was Allport (1954, 1958) writing his classic book on prejudice, but Stouffer was developing his important work on American attitudes toward the fierce Wisconsin senator Joseph McCarthy—*Communism, Conformity and Civil Liberties* (Stouffer, 1955). McCarthy had attacked political liberals, even political moderates (including Parsons and Stouffer, a registered Republican), as Communists aiding the then Soviet Union. Stouffer's massive surveys showed that the senator had far less public support than had been supposed—a finding that aided his rapid downfall soon after. Stouffer's (1955) book on McCarthy remains to this day one of the best step-by-step introductions on how to analyze survey data.

Each of these volumes influenced me greatly. I almost committed Allport's (1954) *The Nature of Prejudice* entirely to memory. I was especially captivated by two chapters in particular—one on conformity, which I regarded as central to much of White southern behavior, and the other on the potential of intergroup contact to diminish prejudice. Indeed, this was the start of my lifelong fascination with intergroup contact theory, which is considered in detail in Chapter 7 of this volume.

Both Allport and Stouffer and their writings shaped my doctoral thesis (Pettigrew, 1958b, 1959). From Allport, I learned how to cast my contentions in sharper conceptual focus. From Stouffer, I learned how to test them on probability samples with survey methods. In the summer of 1955, I set out with Charles Lamont, my undergraduate assistant and undaunted friend, to sample door-to-door White racial opinions in small towns in the South and North in order to make a rough regional comparison. To deter trouble, I put Virginia license plates on my old two-door Chevrolet, and Stouffer got official interviewer certification papers from a national survey agency for us to identify ourselves with local police departments.

In the most Deep South community sampled—Moultrie, Georgia—the tension was palpable. In May 1955, just before we arrived, the Supreme Court had undercut its historic desegregation ruling with a new and vague "all deliberate speed" order. The White South, quite deliberate but rarely speedy, interpreted this order as a sign of weakness. This second decision had the unfortunate, if unintended, consequence of heightening opposition to the original decision. Resistance groups called White Citizens'

Councils—basically middle-class Ku Klux Klans—soon mobilized in such towns as Moultrie.[7]

So the survey schedule had to minimize recognition of its purpose. Following Stouffer's shrewd advice, we asked the White respondents what they considered to be the most important problem facing the nation. With the school desegregation issue so salient, most respondents named it as the most important. If they did not, we asked for the second most important problem—if need be, the third most important. By then, the entire sample had named racial issues. Then we introduced the racial attitude questions as a subject they themselves had introduced.

As predicted, the mean levels of authoritarianism were not significantly different between the southern and northern samples. And the authoritarian scores predicted anti-Black attitudes equally well in the two regions—showing the measure's validity at the individual level of analysis. But at the macrolevel, authoritarianism could not begin to explain the great difference in racial prejudice between the regions. Thus, historical, cultural, and normative contextual factors are needed to explain the far greater racial prejudice of my native South.

At the University of Wisconsin, Russell Middleton (1976) followed up this work with an intensive analysis of a 1964 national probability survey. Using a far more adequate and extensive probability sample, he both replicated and extended my earlier results. Unsurprisingly, his southern White respondents revealed far greater anti-Black prejudice than the northern White respondents, but the two regional subsamples differed only slightly in anti-Semitism, anti-Catholic prejudice, and authoritarianism. Also, the regional difference in anti-Black attitudes could not be accounted for in terms of degree of urbanization, socioeconomic status, or ethnic composition. Middleton interpreted this strong contextual effect as supporting a subcultural interpretation consistent with my earlier conclusions.

A Visit to a Second South

In 1956, Allport obtained a small foundation grant for me to accompany him for a half-year visit to a social science center in Durban, South Africa.

[7] White Citizens' Councils sprung up all over the South in opposition to the 1954 Supreme Court's public school desegregation decision, especially in such small towns as Moultrie. Even Atticus Finch, the fictitious name Harper Lee (1960) gave her father who was the hero of her beloved novel and the movie *To Kill a Mockingbird*, was a member of the White Citizens' Council of Monroeville, Alabama—as later revealed in Lee's (2015) *Go Set a Watchman*.

I initially hoped to repeat my thesis study in this new setting. Although I could obtain only all-White university student respondents, I did manage to replicate the American results with one important difference. Afrikaners *were* more authoritarian as well as more prejudiced against Black Africans than other White South Africans. Nonetheless, conformity to rigorously enforced racist norms remained central (Pettigrew, 1958a).

These and other results have led me to embrace normative theory throughout my career (Pettigrew, 1991b). So, I am pleased to see that psychological social psychologists are now paying far greater attention to normative factors (e.g., Cialdini & Trost, 1998; Crandall et al., 2000, 2002; De Tezanos-Pinto et al., 2010; Gelfand et al., 2017; Kahneman & Miller, 1986; Legros & Cislaghi, 2020; Mortensen et al., 2019; Paluck, 2009; Schultz et al., 2007, 2018; Stephens et al., 2019; Tankard & Paluck, 2017; Zitek & Hebl, 2007).

Consider a surprising finding by Crandall and his colleagues (2020). They secured prejudiced ratings by university students on 115 groups collected 11 years apart. They discovered that those stereotype groups whose prejudice ratings had the largest variances in 2007 tended significantly to yield the largest reductions in prejudice between 2007 and 2018. In other words, large variances in 2007 indicated emerging normative shifts that were reflected in the reduced prejudice for those particular stereotypes years later.

This renewal of attention to norms, returning at last to Sherif's (1936) emphasis, is helpful in two ways. First, because normative and cultural differences are major contextual entities, this trend will result in more contextual findings throughout social psychology. Second, an emphasis on norms forms a tie with the extensive literature on norms in sociological social psychology. Yet another concept that has proven highly useful among colleagues in sociology—social roles—has yet to obtain major usage in psychological social psychology. It, too, would prove useful, especially if it were employed in research and theory now focused on the popular concept of identity.[8]

While in South Africa, Allport and I also conducted two perception studies—a favorite area for Allport since his Gestalt days in Germany on a Sheldon Fellowship in the 1920s. First, we tested South Africans of all four racial groups on binocular resolution (Pettigrew et al., 1958). African, Colored, Indian, and White (Afrikaners and English) adult subjects viewed

[8] Role and identity are closely intertwined. A lifelong occupation, for example, typically becomes a central component of one's identity. Just how tightly role and identity are tied together becomes apparent upon retirement. One's identity is altered when a lifetime occupational role no longer anchors one's place in the world.

photographs of members of all four groups in a stereoscope that mixed the dual pictures of the groups systematically. They were asked to determine the group membership of each picture. Afrikaner subjects in particular tended to report either pure European or pure African for the mixed pictures involving one White and one African. This strong bifurcation tendency is consistent with authoritarian rigidity and greater apprehension regarding race relations.

Next, we tested young 1998 children from a rural "reserve" with Ames's trapezoidal window illusion and discovered a strong cultural context effect (Allport & Pettigrew, 1957). The Ames Window, observed frontally, appears to be a window when in fact it is a trapezoid. When rotated vertically under slightly limiting conditions,[9] subjects tend to view "the window" as swinging back and forth in a 180° arc when it is actually swinging all around in a 360° arc. The standard explanation was that Western subjects assume right angles from growing up all their lives with right-angle windows, doors, and other everyday items.

But we wondered about people whose experience had few objects with right angles. South Africa's Zulus offered the perfect culture to test the standard explanation. Their culture values round objects—in their art, in their huts (*rondavels*), in their windows and doors, and throughout their environment (Doob, 1957). Right angles were rarely found in the rural parts of Zululand in 1956. Do they "see" the trapezoidal illusion like Westerners? The answer is no—not nearly to the same degree as others. Thus, the rural Zulu children were *more accurate* in their perception of the "window." The right-angle explanation is supported further in that Zulu children who lived in cities witnessed the illusion at approximately the same rate as Westerners.

Return to the South

Following 4 years away, I returned to the South in 1956 as an assistant professor of social psychology at the University of North Carolina in Chapel Hill. It was here I devised a test measure of Bruner's ingenious concept of category width—that individuals tend to exhibit relatively consistent widths of categories of all types (Pettigrew, 1958a). The Category Width Scale confirmed Bruner's contention and found it to be positively correlated with mathematical ability (Pettigrew, 1982). Those subjects who received a high

[9] The illusion appears with one-eye vision at a distance of 3 m or more, or with both eyes at 6 m or more.

score on a standard math test tended to exhibit broader categories of many different types.

Returning to my native South following 5 months of living in South Africa renewed my interest in the study of American race relations. There are many close similarities between the two regions once you allow for about a 3-decade lag of the American South's history in South Africa—from poverty and a lost war to racial segregation. I came back to Harvard as an assistant professor of social psychology in 1957 determined to dig deeper into the study of prejudice from a contextual perspective.

But as soon as I arrived in Cambridge, the Little Rock, Arkansas, school desegregation crisis broke out. The Arkansas governor, Orval Faubus, defied a federal court school desegregation ruling and refused to allow the city's all-White high school to admit just nine brave Black American students. Reluctantly, the conservative president Dwight Eisenhower sent in American troops to allow the court-ordered desegregation to proceed. This action marked the first explicit action in the South to counter the Supreme Court's 1954 desegregation ruling.

With characteristic decisiveness, Stouffer sent Ernest Campbell, a Southern sociologist who was visiting Harvard, and me off to study the disruption at close hand. "You two are the Southerners around here," he barked. We chose to focus on the one White group in Little Rock that one would expect to be under cross-pressures over the conflict—the White clergy.

Our major finding was that only eight of the city's White ministers actively participated in efforts for school desegregation. Their White congregations were uniformly opposed to the racial change. Thus, for all but eight valiant White ministers, concern over the possible loss of members and support overcame their religious values (E. Q. Campbell & Pettigrew, 1959a, 1959b; Pettigrew, 2015b; Pettigrew & Campbell, 1960).

MY SECOND MENTOR OF AMERICAN RACE RELATIONS: PROFESSOR KENNETH CLARK

The first social psychologist to make a decisive impact on the nation's social policy, Kenneth Clark, became well known for his central role in the U.S. Supreme Court's 1954 *Brown v. Topeka* public school desegregation case (Benjamin & Crouse, 2002; J. M. Jones & Pettigrew, 2005). Recommended to them by Otto Klineberg, Thurgood Marshall and his Legal Defense Fund staff based their argument on Clark's contention that segregation caused psychological damage to African American children.

Clark worked through the Society for the Psychological Study of Social Issues to secure many of the nation's leading social psychologists to testify in the original school desegregation cases that were later combined to form the final Supreme Court case. A prime list of the discipline's members answered the call—Jerome Bruner, Isadore Chein, Stuart Cook, Otto Klineberg, David Kretch, and Brewster Smith. It was largely they that the high court referred to as "modern authority."

Different as our lives were, Clark and I shared four things. We were both confirmed racial integrationists who were willing to defend our views against formidable opposition.[10] We were also confirmed social psychologists. And we both benefitted from having strong mothers who made sure that we received optimal educational opportunities. Clark was fond of telling the story of how his mother successfully battled New York City's Board of Education to keep him from being channeled into a vocational high school and placed instead into the college-oriented George Washington High School.

We also shared a religion; we were both raised in the Episcopal Church, with Clark becoming an acolyte. This connection led to our first meeting in 1961. The head of the American Episcopal Church, Bishop Arthur Lichtenberger, decided to form a Presiding Bishop's Advisory Commission on Race Relations. He named us as chair and vice-chair of the commission together with several equally pro-integrationist members. Two were well-known Southern White liberal authors—Virginia's Sarah-Patton Boyle (1962) and Mississippi's "Uncle" Will Campbell (1986).[11] We were to review how the denomination fared in its racial practices throughout the nation. The only explanation for why the Presiding Bishop would bring together outspoken advocates of racial integration to do this task is that he apparently was under the mistaken impression that the Episcopal Church was doing quite well in this domain and would receive a "clean bill of health" from the commission.

What we found was actually worse than what we expected. Individual church memberships were overwhelmingly racially segregated throughout the country—not just in the South. Private Episcopal preparatory schools

---

[10] Clark lived his beliefs and repeatedly personally broke the "color line." He was the first Black American to earn a doctorate in psychology from Columbia University, to become a tenured member of New York's City College system, to be elected to the New York State Board of Regents, and to be elected president to both the American Psychological Association and the Society for the Psychological Study of Social Issues.

[11] For examples of the "tell it like it is" speeches of these two leading Southern White liberals, see Houck and Dixon (2006).

were also routinely racially segregated; even Martin Luther King's children were denied entry in Atlanta. Predominantly Black Episcopal colleges were grossly underfunded.[12] Episcopal hospitals typically refused Black patients; one African American man died of a heart attack on the steps of an Episcopal hospital near Harlem after being refused help. On and on, we uncovered and recorded the Church's racist practices that mirrored those of the larger American society of the 1960s.

Clark anticipated what happened next. The report was never released or acted upon. Indeed, looking back 6 decades later in the files of the denomination on the web, I could not find a single mention of our advisory group or its report. It is as if the commission had never existed. The practical message is clear. Large macroinstitutions can use their power to retard social change in order to maintain its position with its subunits while publicly hiding its actions with counter-rhetoric.[13]

With our friendship forged in this telling episode, Clark and I continued to work together. He came to Harvard to give the first Allport Memorial Lecture. I regularly did advisory work for his Metropolitan Applied Research Center. We often gave joint lectures. We cried together over the phone at the news of the assassination of Martin Luther King.[14] I routinely sought his counsel before serving as an expert witness in school desegregation cases. I regret that my move to California in 1979 restricted our continued interaction.

Clark, my second race relations mentor, provided an invaluable education for me. Following up on the teachings I had gleaned about the segregated life of Black Southerners from Mildred Adams, Clark introduced me to the world of Black American leadership. I met King, Bayard Rustin, Julian Bond, Thurgood Marshall, and many other African American leaders through

---

[12] Not surprisingly, one of the three predominantly Black colleges that were affiliated with the Episcopal Church—St. Paul's College in Lawrenceville, Virginia—closed its doors in 2013.

[13] Note that after this period, the Episcopal Church in the United States witnessed major changes in its practices. Spurred on by movements such as the Episcopal Society for Cultural and Racial Unity, the Church became a leader among denominations in breaking down sexual and gender barriers. Racial segregation of parishes, however, remains largely intact.

[14] Clark and other African American friends were not the only phone calls I had that fateful night of April 4, 1968. A young woman, who lived two houses away from me throughout my childhood in Richmond, also called me from Virginia. She was celebrating the murder of King with a big party of friends and wanted to let me know that she was sorry that I was not in attendance. Nothing in the decades I had known her prepared me for this truly heinous expression of racism.

Clark. And I was able to get a sense of their concerns and burdens. They all were under great stress to succeed against formidable opposition—not to mention concern over continuous death threats (Pettigrew, 2018b).[15]

But Adams's and Clark's experiences were not totally different. Clark, too, had been refused service in New York's restaurants earlier in his life, just like Adams in the 1930s. In fact, all these leaders had experienced in their own lives some of the racist incidents Adams had faced—empty cabs that would not stop for them, store detectives following them, and so on. The depth of American racism ironically served as a valuable asset for these leaders; they could identify easily with less fortunate African Americans for whose rights they fought.

Making My Case Against Racist Beliefs

In the midst of the racial turmoil of the early 1960s, I wrote my second book, *A Profile of the Negro American* (Pettigrew, 1964b). In it, my physician wife and I attempted to use the then-available biological and psychological evidence to answer directly the widely held racist beliefs concerning health, intelligence, crime, and the very concept of race itself. The book's timing was fortuitous. It appeared just as the civil rights movement was gaining momentum and the nation was belatedly starting to question the long-entrenched myths surrounding the subject. The book led to invitations to speak at predominantly Black universities—although the students at these institutions were often surprised, even a wee disappointed, to learn that I was a White Southerner.

Governmental Consulting

During the 1960s and early 1970s, I concentrated on the racial desegregation of the nation's public schools. In addition to conducting research on the subject, I gave numerous public speeches, wrote popular articles on the subject, and held various roles in the so-called Coleman Report on school desegregation (J. S. Coleman, 1966). But I learned the most from consulting with both the U.S. Commission on Civil Rights (1966–1971) and the U.S. Office of Education (1966–1968).

---

[15] As the psychologist in the group, Clark served for many of these leaders, especially King, as a comforting clinician.

A Peek at the Macrolevel of Power

In 1966, I was appointed a member of President Lyndon Johnson's White House Task Force on Education. Chaired by William Friday, then president of the University of North Carolina, the five-person group began its work just as the tragic Vietnam War was heating up to full intensity. Consequently, the group's recommendations for educational change—including racial integration—had little chance of being implemented. There was not enough federal money for both "guns and butter," as the then current phrase described it. But the assignment gave me a rare opportunity to witness how power at the highest level was wielded.[16]

The Role of Values in Social Science

One could reasonably ask if my particular life experience and my concerns about American racism have not necessarily biased my research. My answer is shaped by Gunnar Myrdal's (1944) insightful position on values in science. He held that values are inherent in social science. Be aware of your values, he urged. Struggle against their biasing effects and alert your readers to them (as I have in this book). Objectivity becomes, then, a sought-for goal that can never be fully satisfied. This does not exclude social commitment. But such commitment must be combined with an equally strong commitment to competent research. Science and values need not conflict. Donald Campbell (1959) argued that strong motivation can lead to a greater investment in tracing an accurate map of reality. Indeed, I have endeavored to employ the most rigorous methods possible to understand better what the most effective remedial actions are for combatting racism and other societal ills. And I believe that this is true for the vast majority of social psychologists.

A prime example of this view of values in operation is provided by Janet Schofield, holder of a 1972 PhD in social psychology at Harvard, in her Allport Intergroup Relations Prize–winning book *Black and White in School* (Schofield, 1982). A firm believer in racially desegregated education,

[16] Contact theory worked for me. I came away from this experience with a far more positive view of Johnson and his staff (especially Joseph Califano). Crude as he could often be, I became convinced that Johnson was truly committed to advancing the rights of American minorities. And I was surprised how much he understood about them based largely on his contact with poor Mexican Americans early in his life. The negative depiction of Johnson in the movie *Selma* (DuVernay, 2014) is pure fiction. I have now lived long enough to see how history gets rewritten, even reversed, years later to fit present-day biases and circumstances.

Schofield studied a middle school in Pittsburgh for 3 years as it struggled to establish racial integration. She uncovered the problems and difficulties involved in the process and recommended ways to improve on how school desegregation can be better achieved. Her values led her to the subject; her training as a social psychologist led her to conduct a solid ethnographic study and to uncover the problems and needed remedies. Rather than blinding her to the many problems of implementing the racial desegregation the schools, Scofield's values impelled her to understand the process as fully as possible. Her book deservingly won scientific prizes and was cited by the U.S. Supreme Court.

SUMMING UP

My life has indeed been privileged. I have benefitted from valuable educational experiences from my boyhood to the present. Egalitarian parents; racial education from Adams and Clark; social scientific training from Allport, Parsons, and Stouffer; a supportive wife who shared my values and beliefs; and a myriad of experiences from around the world all served to shape and reinforce my quest for a wider contextual social psychology.

But what is contextual analyses? The next chapter takes up this question in detail.

2 WHAT IS CONTEXTUAL SOCIAL PSYCHOLOGY?

In 1988, a group of social psychologists at Germany's University of Würzburg conducted an ingenious laboratory experiment (Strack et al., 1988). They showed how facial activity actually influences affective feelings. Subjects held a pen in their mouths so as to either inhibit or facilitate the facial muscles associated with smiling without being required to pose with a smiling face. The subjects then viewed humorous cartoons. Those subjects in the facilitating facial condition found the cartoons considerably more amusing than those in the inhibited facial condition. Thus, Strack and his colleagues found strong evidence for the facial feedback hypothesis.

Complications arose, however, when replications of the experiment were attempted. As part of the Registered Replication Report Project, 17 studies repeated the experiment. When their results were combined, there was no effect whatsoever (Wagenmakers et al., 2016). Did that mean that the original Würzburg findings had to be rejected? Or were the 17 repeated studies not true replications?

Subsequent work by Israeli social psychologists supplied the answer (Noah et al., 2018). They noted that the supposed replications had filmed

https://doi.org/10.1037/0000210-003
Contextual Social Psychology: Reanalyzing Prejudice, Voting, and Intergroup Contact, by T. F. Pettigrew

the subjects, and the original Würzburg study had not. Being observed altered the participants' behavior. When filming occurred, the facial feedback effect disappeared; when there was no filming or any other observing, the effect emerged. In other words, *the situational context* of the experiment led to sharp differences at the individual level.

This experiment highlights the essence of contextual social psychology. An effect at the microlevel of individual subjects is sharply modified by a mesolevel contextual condition—whether or not the subject is being observed. Placing phenomena at one level of analysis in the context of another level is the core operation of contextual social psychology. It sounds easy and straightforward, but I show that in practice it often poses complex issues. For example, the clever Würzburg contextual study highlights the difficulty of obtaining precise replications—a critical issue discussed in Chapter 4. This smile example is just a recent illustration of a long history of large contextual effects in psychology following the aforementioned Triplett (1898) bicycle study. Equally striking contextual effects can be found beyond the experimental laboratory—as noted throughout this book.

DIFFERENT TYPES OF CONTEXTUAL ANALYSES

Thus, in the broadest terms, contextual analysis in all its forms studies a given phenomenon at two or more levels of analysis. It places lower level phenomena in their situational, structural,[1] and institutional contexts. Two such forms of analysis are of particular concern to social psychology: (a) microindividual data in the context of mesosituational data and (b) both microindividual and mesosituational data in the context of such macrolevel data as cultural, societal, and institutional measures. Figure 2.1 helps to specify the various types of contextual analyses.

Six paths connect the three basic levels of analysis: micro-, meso-, and macro. Microlevel variables include the data of individuals from the biological level and such personality domains as traits. Mesolevel variables involve face-to-face interactions of individuals, such as with intergroup contact. Macrolevel variables encompass such cultural and social structural variables as social norms.

Placing such personality variables as authoritarianism and social dominance orientation in their situational contexts is a prime example of

[1] For the purposes of this book, *social structure* is defined as relatively persistent social and organizational patterning.

FIGURE 2.1. Six Causal Paths From Three Levels of Analysis

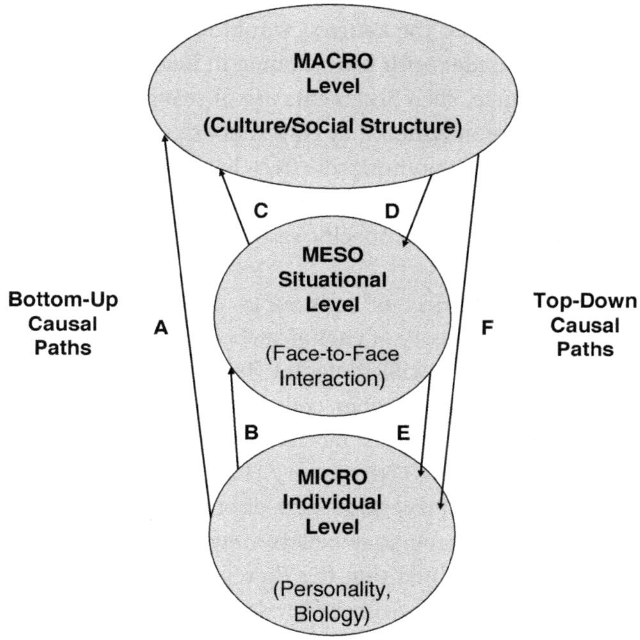

From "Personality and Social Structure: Social Psychological Contributions," by T. F. Pettigrew, in R. Hogan, J. A. Johnson, and S. R. Briggs (Eds.), *Handbook of Personality Psychology* (p. 419), 1997, Academic Press/Elsevier (https://doi.org/10.1016/B978-012134645-4/50018-4). Copyright 1997 by Elsevier. Adapted with permission.

contextual analysis (Paths B and E); this effort has been a growing trend over recent decades in both personality and social psychology (Cacioppo et al., 2000; S. T. Fiske, 2000; Fleeson, 2012; Pettigrew, 2019; Reis & Holmes, 2012). With interactions of personality and situation (Paths B and E) commonplace now, this book concentrates in particular on Paths A, C, D, and F, which have received far less attention in psychological social psychology. These paths link the micro- and mesolevels with the broad macrocontexts that are the foci of the other social sciences—not just sociology but economics, political science, and anthropology as well. Consider examples of each of these various paths.

Path A

Path A—causation from the micro to macrolevel unmediated by the mesolevel—is often involved in popular discussion. For instance, take the sweeping "great man" theories of history. Such loose contentions have put these unmoored arguments in disrepute. Had Napoleon not lived, goes the counter, who is to say that the *Zeitgeist* would not have produced a similar charismatic French leader with little change in history? At this gross level of contention, of course, such arguments are of scant value.

Yet it has been demonstrated that Path A does occur when the measures at both levels and the hypothesized effect have been carefully specified. Actually, even laboratory research supports a narrowed version of the great man theory when placed in the specific setting of small task-oriented groups (Borgatta et al., 1954).

Path A has been a subject of continuous debate in social theory. Max Weber's (1930) famous theory of capitalism constitutes a classic Path A link between personality and social structure. In his text *The Protestant Ethic and the Spirit of Capitalism*, Weber countered Karl Marx by holding that such microphenomenon as beliefs, motives, and values could independently shape macrostructure. With 17th-century Hollanders particularly in mind, he explained why ascetic Protestant sects often met with economic success even though their strong religious beliefs viewed wealth as dangerous for their souls. Weber maintained that the Protestant ethic, epitomized in the anxiety-arousing Calvinist doctrine of predestination, explained the riddle. A self-denying, frugal, and work-oriented routine in busy preparation for final judgment led to accumulated wealth.[2]

Later work expanded Weber's theory. Historian Simon Schama (1987) considerably extended the discussion of how the "Golden Age" Dutch managed their embarrassment over their accumulated wealth. They simply saw their gains as evidence that God looked down upon them favorably. The French social psychologist Serge Moscovici (1993) further strengthened the Path A argument of psychological causes of macrophenomena. He held that the minority status of the Dutch Protestants was just as important as their religion for their development of capitalism. They threw over the past and were separated from and stigmatized by the Roman Catholic majority. Protestant theology, argued Moscovici convincingly, was thus both a cause and a result of the ethic that Weber made famous (Paths A and F).

[2] Weber was aware of both top-down and bottom-up causal paths, for he also allowed that social structure could shape personality (Paths D, E, and F). But his theory remains one of the most famous prototypes of Path A.

Also building on Weber's thesis, personality psychologist David McClelland (1955, 1961) posited that the link between the Protestant ethic and capitalism was generated by the achievement motive at the microlevel. Fostered by child-training practices consistent with the Protestant ethic, the need for achievement, he maintained, is both challenged and satisfied by entrepreneurial activity that characterizes capitalism at its early stages. Both high-need achievers and entrepreneurs are independent minded, relatively autonomous, and strivers for success. The fundamental situational mediation McClelland specifies is that such people seek out situations in which they can feel personally responsible for clearly measurable results of their efforts (Atkinson & Hoselitz, 1958).

Carrying his analysis to the macrolevel, McClelland (1961) attempted to show that the achievement motive played a significant part in the rapid economic growth of the Western world—a pure Path A contention. He emphasized cross-national and longitudinal relationships between levels of the achievement motive and a variety of measures of technological growth.

Psychohistorical biographies of such famous society-changing figures as Luther and Gandhi (Erikson, 1958, 1969) offer additional examples of such sweepingly extensive Path A theories. But research that is more delimited in scope and more differentiated in prediction is more convincing. A study of change in a prison brought about by the prisoners themselves found that contrasting personality styles of the prisoners acquired greater salience at different times in propelling the process of organizational change (Gluckstern & Packard, 1977).

Paths B and C

For Paths B and C, the upward causal effects of the microlevel are mediated by the mesosituational level of analyses. While emphasizing Path A, Weber clearly understood that the Protestant ethic's influence on capitalism could be mediated by family, work, and other face-to-face situations—classic B and C paths.

Path F

For Path F, the downward causal effects of the macrolevel on the microlevel go unmediated by the mesolevel. Many of the major social theorists have fashioned concepts and developed hypotheses about Path F. These efforts often center on the presumed negative effects on individuals caused by the decline of traditionalism and the rise of modern institutions. Hence, for Emile Durkheim[3] (1897/1951), the decline of religious institutions and political stability caused personal isolation and depression, whereas for Gustave LeBon (1896) these changes allowed the ugly, irrational side of humanity to burst forth in the crowd. For Karl Marx (1964), the new technology and property relations led to worker alienation from their work. For Max Weber (1968), the growth of bureaucracy foretold dehumanization and depersonalizing outcomes. Even the increase in equality in modern times for Alexis de Tocqueville (1835–1840/1945) could lead to envy and resentment. And for Sigmund Freud (1930), modern life at the macrolevel deepened the conflict between an individual's impulses and their repression.

It remained for the German social psychologist and philosopher Georg Simmel (1955) to see any good in the momentous structural changes taking place around these 19th- and early 20th-century theorists. He noted that the social differentiation that characterized modern institutions at the macrolevel made it possible at the micro- and mesolevels for individuals to develop "a web of affiliations" in nonascriptive groups. This "web," argued Simmel, ran the risk of role conflict, even social marginality, in its newly differentiated and cross-cutting social relationships. But it also made possible the individualization of personality and the recognition of personal uniqueness. In other words, the macrochanges sweeping Western society at the time were beginning to free individuals from the shackles of social status at birth and the many other social restraints of earlier times. Note the mediated form of Simmel's contentions: Altered macrostructure leads first to cross-cutting group memberships and face-to-face interactions at the mesolevel (Path D) that, in turn, allow individuation at the microlevel (Path E).

A famous political science study illustrates a direct F path analysis. Almond and Verba (1963) studied five democratic nations with varying political structures. They employed surveys to ascertain each nation's political attitudes, then compared these data with each nation's political institutions. The most pertinent of their contentions concerns their structural explanations for the wide differences they uncovered for the five national populations even after education and other variables are controlled. For example, British respondents evinced considerable confidence in both their administrative and political-legislative officials, Germans revealed particular confidence in administrative officials, Americans in legislative officials, and Italians and Mexicans in neither.

[3] Durkheim is my favorite of the old masters of social theory because he was consistently concerned with issues that are fundamental for social psychology. Psychological social psychologists who have not read Durkheim would find it rewarding.

Almond and Verba (1963) accounted for these aggregated individual differences in terms of the contrasting contextual histories across the countries. Germany had witnessed the establishment of an early and stable bureaucracy but a late and unstable political development. The United States had a reverse history, with a late-developing civil service but an early foundation of its political structure. The United Kingdom had experienced early development of both institutions, whereas Italy and Mexico had suffered late development of both.

But the persistent problem with Path F analyses is that they omit explaining how the macrolevel effect to the individual level is mediated at the mesolevel of analysis.

Paths D and E

For Paths D and E, the macrolevel effects on the microlevel are mediated by the mesolevel. We noted Simmel's carefully mediated argument. The impressive work of Alex Inkeles in six developing nations provides another empirical example of the D and E causal paths (Inkeles & Smith, 1974). He demonstrated that industrialization leads to similar forms of social organization in all six countries. In turn, these modern organizations shape face-to-face situations (Path D) that, in time, produce similar patterns of "modern" beliefs, perceptions, and values (Path E).

The D and E paths were often the focus of early work by the Chicago school of sociologists (Bulmer, 1984). Their detailed ethnographic research in the varied neighborhoods of Chicago during the 1920s and 1930s focused on how social structures and even physical factors shape human behavior. This tradition has been revitalized in recent years (e.g., Sampson, 2019; Sampson et al., 2002). Sampson focused on local neighborhood effects in large cities and showed how these effects influence the microlevel of individuals (Path E) as well as the macrolevel of the metropolitan areas themselves (Path C). Thus, the nation's increasing density of the poor and Blacks into concentrated urban neighborhoods has sharp effects on both crime and individual health.

Chapters 3, 5, 6, 7, and 8 review contextual effects in certain specific domains—group attributional bias, prejudice, relative deprivation, intergroup contact, and right-wing voting. Numerous examples of D and E paths are noted. For instance, social change brought about by legislation at the macrolevel—such as affirmative action laws in the United States—can lead to greater interracial contact (Path D), which in turn typically leads to reduced intergroup prejudice at the microlevel (Path E).

CONTEXTUAL ANALYSIS IS NOT NEW

As these examples make amply clear, the basic idea of contextual analysis is hardly new—even in the 19th-century beginning of modern psychology. Wilhelm Wundt, the German founder of experimental psychology, also helped to develop *Völkerpsychologie*—"a forerunner of today's social psychology" (Klautke, 2014).[4] Indeed, he spent the last 2 decades of his life writing 10 massive volumes on the subject. Although this effort centered on the psychological composition of nations, it provided a means for considering basic psychological ideas in different contexts. Unfortunately, Wundt's doctoral student, Edward Titchener, did not bring with him this early social science side of Wundt when he left Wundt's Leipzig laboratory and came to Cornell University to help establish experimental psychology in the United States.

As outlined by House (1981), the first half of the 20th century witnessed special attention to the relationship between personality and social structure—Paths A, B, and C in Figure 2.1. Quite gross molar conceptions of both personality and social structure characterized these early attempts. Broad Freudian notions prevailed, and whole societies were mistakenly considered to be homogeneous entities. Margaret Mead's (1935/2003) influential and controversial work *Sex and Temperament in Three Primitive Societies* typifies this period.

During World War II, American specialists attempted to contribute to the war effort by advancing sweepingly expansive analyses of the Germans, Japanese, and Russians. The holistic and crude nature of these analyses is illustrated by Gorer's (1943) capsule contentions about Japanese national character as anal-compulsive. He attributed this condition to Japan's early and severe toilet training in childhood. The most successful effort of these activities for the Office of Strategic Services (now the Central Intelligence Agency) involved an evaluation of Adolf Hitler's personality. Three psychoanalysts and Henry Murray correctly predicted that Hitler, when faced with unequivocal defeat, would commit suicide. The most lasting thesis of these national character studies was the analysis of authoritarianism as applied to Nazi Germany (Adorno et al., 1950).

---

[4] *Völkerpsychologie* is today sometimes regarded as simply a Nazi-inspired means for promoting national stereotypes. Klautke (2014) showed that this view is mistaken. This early social science movement long preceded the Third Reich and spread to many countries beyond Germany. It was a forerunner of such current concepts as "national identity" and "national character." But it proved to be easy to combine it with National Socialist views during Hitler's reign (Klautke, 2013).

By 1965, several prominent psychologists in the mental health domain broke away from the traditional models of treating individual patients and advocated a community emphasis (Trickett, 1972). They formed the Society for Community Research and Action—now Division 27 of the American Psychological Association. The research initiated by this organization is necessarily contextual. Borrowing from public health and preventive health doctrines, community psychology stresses a contextual approach that aims to prevent mental illness before any treatment is needed by altering macro- and mesolevel entities that lead to mental illness. This strategy is a straightforward top-down approach—Paths D, E, and F.

As the tools for contextual analysis improved, Ryff (1987) published an influential article. She pointed out that there was a general failure to explicate the *causal* links in the relevant literature that did exist. She decried the relative lack of attention in mainstream psychology to the personality and social structure domain. She was on target on both points. Specifying the causal linkages of Figure 2.1's six paths remains a difficult task, and psychologists were conspicuously absent in contextual research during the 20th century. Most of the names mentioned earlier are sociologists who regarded themselves, at least in part, to be social psychologists—for example, Georg Simmel, Alex Inkeles, James House, and Robert Sampson. Psychologists, I suspect, would be surprised to learn that a sizable number—roughly 10% of the members of the American Sociological Association (ASA)—regard themselves as social psychologists at least in part (personal search of ASA membership data).

The split between social psychologists in the two distinct disciplines is regrettable but understandable. Each could learn much from the other. It is understandable because each must answer to contrasting demands from their major disciplines. Sociological social psychologists feel the need to demonstrate that micro- and mesophenomena are important for the major macroconcerns of their core discipline, largely the bottom-up paths of Figure 2.1. Surprisingly, sociological social psychologists continued to study and stress emotion in the 1970s, when psychological social psychologists were engaging in the "cognitive revolution" and virtually ignoring emotion.[5]

In contrast, psychological social psychologists feel the need to demonstrate that meso- and macroconcerns are important for the microconcerns of their core discipline, largely the top-down paths of Figure 2.1. Note, however,

[5] The "cognitive revolution" describes the shift from attention to emotion and affect to an almost exclusive focus on mental processes throughout psychology.

that mesolevel face-to-face concerns are central mediators for both groups of social psychologists.

It is my strong impression that social psychologists in sociology are far more conversant with the work of their psychological colleagues than the reverse. And they make more efforts to combine the work of the two groups.[6] Thus, the ASA journal *Social Psychology Quarterly* routinely publishes research from both major disciplines. The ASA also publishes a popular magazine appropriately titled *Contexts*. In addition, a small group of us with a foot in each camp persist in calling for more cooperation across the disciplinary boundary—cooperation that would greatly enhance the furtherance of contextual analysis (e.g., C. W. Stephan et al., 1991).

But why conduct contextual analyses? In the next chapter, I turn to answer this blunt question directly by discussing the many advantages of the contextual approach.

[6] Although psychological social psychology could benefit from placing its phenomena in the broader contexts of social structure (the central theme of this book), sociological social psychology could benefit from using more microlevel analyses—especially in such fields as drug addiction (drug specialist and Professor Craig Reineman, personal communication, July 2019).

3 FIVE ADVANTAGES OF CONTEXTUAL ANALYSES FOR SOCIAL PSYCHOLOGY

Contextual analyses possess at least five interrelated and important advantages for social psychology. (a) Contextual analyses offer a rapprochement between social psychologists in sociology and psychology, as well as with the other social sciences. (b) Contextual analyses avoid three common fallacies of social science research. (c) Contextual analyses importantly expand social psychology's explanatory power. (d) Contextual analyses help to counter social psychology's so-called crises. (e) Contextual analyses generate results that more easily influence public policy. Let's consider each of these advantages in turn.

Some of the passages in this chapter have been reprinted or adapted from "The Emergence of Contextual Social Psychology," by T. F. Pettigrew, 2018, *Personality and Social Psychology Bulletin*, *44*(7), pp. 963–971 (https://doi.org/10.1177/0146167218756033). Copyright 2018 by SAGE. Reprinted with permission.

https://doi.org/10.1037/0000210-004
Contextual Social Psychology: Reanalyzing Prejudice, Voting, and Intergroup Contact, by T. F. Pettigrew

CONTEXTUAL ANALYSES OFFER A RAPPROCHEMENT BETWEEN SOCIAL PSYCHOLOGISTS IN SOCIOLOGY AND PSYCHOLOGY, AS WELL AS WITH THE OTHER SOCIAL SCIENCES

Earlier we noted the relative lack of interchange between social psychologists in psychology and sociology. To the extent that psychological social psychologists adopt more contextual analyses that are already more common in sociological social psychology, the chasm between the two groups would necessarily decline. Similarly, the divide between the discipline and the other, largely macrolevel social sciences would also decline.

Such a trend would repair in part the long-standing split between psychological social psychology and the other social sciences. In particular, social psychologists in both disciplines began paying less attention to one another's work while focusing on increasingly different phenomena. This situation did not always exist. World War II brought social scientists of all the disciplines together to work on war-related research. Thus, personality psychologists worked on selecting candidates for pilots and spies, and social psychologists worked on the morale of both the armed forces and civilians. Following World War II, this led to numerous attempts to bring social psychology and the other social sciences closer together on university campuses.

Social psychologists from both core disciplines worked on attitudes during the war. The best known of these efforts is the four-volume series *The American Soldier* (Stouffer et al., 1949). This work also had its lesser known domestic equivalent, *Civilian Morale* (Watson, 1942), to which Gordon Allport contributed a chapter. Other work centered on rumor—a feared and widespread wartime phenomenon: "Loose lips sink ships!" (Allport & Postman, 1947). Such applied wartime projects brought psychologists of all types in close association with one another and with researchers from the other social sciences.

This interdisciplinary contact led to the formation after the war of numerous interdisciplinary institutes and programs in American universities. The Institute of Personality, Assessment, and Research at the University of California at Berkeley; the Institute for Social Research (ISR) at the University of Michigan; and the Department of Social Relations at Harvard University are leading examples of these efforts. Later, the University of Nevada at Reno began a social psychology doctoral program that joined psychologists with sociologists.

Donald MacKinnon, a Henry Murray student, founded the Berkeley effort and brought his teacher's assessment methods to California. Michigan's ISR was founded in 1949. It has greatly expanded over the years and now has become the world's largest academic social science survey and research organization. ISR serves today as the nation's leading institution for bringing social psychologists together with social scientists from a wide variety of disciplines.

Harvard's Social Relations Department represented a sharp division within the university's psychology programs. Founded in 1946, the department initially combined clinical and social psychology with cultural anthropology and sociology (Allport & Boring, 1946; Capshew, 1992). Experimental psychology and physical anthropology remained as separate departments in other buildings. Talcott Parsons was the guiding light and longtime chair of the Social Relations Department throughout its existence. He was joined by Allport, Murray, Robert White, Stouffer, and Clyde Kluckhohn.

Four programs were formed: cultural anthropology (initially directed by Kluckhohn), clinical psychology and later termed *personality psychology* (initially directed by Murray, followed by David McClelland), social psychology (initially directed by Allport, followed by Robert Freed Bales), and sociology (directed throughout the department's existence by Parsons). Doctoral students were required to have some acquaintance with all four fields and to specialize in two as a major and minor. Stouffer was in charge of methodological training and the Laboratory of Social Relations. He enhanced methodological training by hiring Frederick Mosteller to teach statistics and Richard Solomon to teach experimental methods.

The two psychological areas did not form a special axis within this unique arrangement. Rather, social psychology and sociology, on one side, and cultural anthropology and personality psychology, on the other, interacted the most. This somewhat surprising arrangement maximized the opportunity for contextual research, and it reflected the interests of the faculty. Kluckhohn and Murray shared mutual interests in psychoanalysis and in how culture shapes personality. They coedited a popular reader on the subject: *Personality in Nature, Society, and Culture* (Kluckhohn & Murray, 1953).

On the other axis, several sociologists were prominent social psychologists—most notably Stouffer, Inkeles, and the small-group specialist, Bales. Here, too, cross-disciplinary work took place. For instance, sociologist Inkeles and psychologist Daniel Levinson wrote an influential contextual chapter on national character for the first edition of the *Handbook of Social Psychology* (Inkeles & Levinson, 1954).

Even greater blending of sociology and social psychology took place when Bales switched from sociology to the social psychology program and became its director following Allport's death in 1967. As a tireless theorist and experimentalist, Bales (1950, 1970, 1999; Bales & Cohen, 1979) developed an advanced contextual model of how personality and the situation combine to predict behavior in a small-group setting—System for the Multiple Level Observation of Groups (SYMLOG). This singular achievement in empirically combining personality and situational effects was a contextual advance far ahead of its time. And it has not received the recognition it deserves. The best-remembered finding of this work in social science, perhaps, is Bale's useful distinction between task-oriented and socioemotional roles that emerge in small groups. SYMLOG is now recognized largely in business circles as represented by the SYMLOG Consulting Group.

Over its 26 years of existence, the Social Relations experiment in interdisciplinary and contextual scholarship boasted a great variety of major figures in psychology and the social sciences on its staff—from Roger Brown, Jerome Bruner, Erik Erikson, and Ezra Vogel to Jerome Kagan, Sheldon White, David Riesman, and Herbert Kelman. But as the founders aged, the university's administration grew less supportive, and the Social Relations distinctive template was not copied by other universities. Harvard closed its unique department in 1972 over strenuous objections from Parsons, Bales, Kelman, Vogel, and me—three of whom were themselves doctoral products of that department.

A major factor in the demise of these promising attempts at social science unity was the uneven size and resources across the disciplines. Thus, in both the Michigan and Harvard breakups, the dominant size of the psychological components led sociologists to press for new arrangements and close social psychology programs that combined the two disciplines.

So, as the joint programs closed, the post–World War II period marked an era of growing separation between social psychology and the other social sciences. Psychological social psychology narrowed its theoretical focus, broke ties with the other social sciences, focused on laboratory experiments as its prime method, and lost interest in Kurt Lewin's action research. These actions triggered what was somewhat extravagantly termed a "crisis" of relevance in social psychology—to be described later in this chapter.

As these interdisciplinary efforts closed one by one, social scientists scurried back to their departmental fiefdoms. Contextual research of all types necessarily suffered. From the vantage point of contextual social psychology, the discipline could be acting today as a mesolevel link between the microlevel of psychology and the largely macrolevel of the other social sciences. As noted in Chapter 2 of this volume, this focus was certainly a major goal of the founders of the field from Wilhelm Wundt to Gordon Allport, Kurt Lewin, Gardner Murphy, Muzafer Sherif, and Henri Tajfel.

Lewin's classic formula of Behavior = f (Person, *Environment*) was an early statement for contextual social psychology.

Consider the following example of contextual multilevel research that demonstrates the importance of normative climate on a phenomenon of interest to all the social sciences. (I discuss multilevel analyses in detail in Chapter 4 of this volume.) That intergroup climate shapes acculturation preferences among host-majority and immigrant group members has long been acknowledged in the acculturation literature of several social sciences, but only now has multilevel contextual research made it possible to examine this phenomenon directly.

Christ et al. (2013) adopted a multilevel approach to examine the effect of the intergroup norms and climate (the macrolevel of analysis) on immigrants' acculturation preferences (at the individual level of analysis) over and above individual-level predictors of acculturation preferences. The authors employed German cross-sectional survey data and examined the acculturation preferences of members of immigrant groups living in various German districts.

At the macrolevel, they used the mean prejudice and acculturation preferences scores of nonimmigrant German respondents as indicators of the dominant intergroup norms and climates within these districts. Results of their multilevel path analysis revealed that a negative intergroup climate (i.e., a higher amount of prejudice of the German respondents within the districts) was systematically related to a stronger desire for cultural maintenance among the immigrants. When faced with greater prejudice of native Germans, immigrants turned inward and worked to maintain their culture rather than work more actively to adopt their new host culture. In short, hostile intergroup norms led to reduced assimilation efforts. The causality here runs both ways. As the immigrants resist adopting German culture, many native Germans become more threatened by and hostile to the newcomers with their "strange" customs. A vicious circle of conflict can easily develop in such a situation.

How would a rapprochement with the other social sciences benefit psychological social psychology? Ironically, in recent years other fields, such as economics and political science, have been making far more use of social psychology than social psychology has benefitted from their work. In fact, social psychology was found by Boyack et al. (2005) to be a "hub science"—a discipline cited asymmetrically more often by such other fields as communication and management. For example, ever since Daniel Kahneman won the 2002 Nobel Prize in Economic Sciences for his work on human judgment and decision-making under uncertainty, economists have been exploiting psychological ideas and findings leading to the rapid growth of microeconomics. In fact, Kahneman is now sometimes referred to as an economist and the "Godfather of behavioral economics" ("Daniel Kahneman," 2018).

Indeed, sometimes social psychological ideas have been used in economics without acknowledgment. Note the intergroup contact study by Ashutosh Varshney (2002). He found that Indian cities that avoided Hindu–Muslim violence, when contrasted with cities that had such violence, more often had multiethnic associations with common interests and considerable intergroup contact among the Hindu and Muslim elites. But not one social psychological reference to social psychology's intergroup contact theory and research can be found in Varshney's book. In fact, his chief finding had already been uncovered for communities in Northern Ireland by Darby (1986).

One of the most fruitful collaborations across disciplines can be found in political research. Social psychologists, together with political scientists and political sociologists, formed the International Society of Political Psychology in 1978. With a worldwide membership and conferences held globally, the Society publishes its own journal, *Political Psychology*. When you read the journal's articles, the authors' disciplinary affiliations are often not obvious. And examples of contextual analyses abound in its pages.

Social psychologists who belong to this thriving society can testify to the benefits of cross-disciplinary interaction. Work in other disciplines would undoubtedly also set off sparks for social psychologists. Think of the implications of the work of distinguished economist Thomas Schelling, winner of the 2005 Nobel Prize for Economic Sciences. Of particular concern to social psychologists, *Micromotives and Macrobehavior* (Schelling, 1978/2006) is virtually a primer for contextual analyses involving both the micro- and macrolevels. Using his own version of game theory, Schelling was fascinated by situations in which the prior choices of individuals in turn form an influential context for later choices that individuals make. And this can lead to major, unplanned macroeffects. For example, he demonstrated how even slight, but not necessarily malicious, choices by individuals to have neighbors of their own group can rapidly lead to unintended total housing segregation between two groups.

I refer back to Figure 2.1 in Chapter 2 of this volume. Schelling supplied invaluable insights into how microbehavior can have large macroeffects (upward causal paths A, B, and C). Social psychologists concerned with these causal paths will find a host of suggestive ideas in *Micromotives and Macrobehavior* (Schelling, 1978/2006).

CONTEXTUAL ANALYSES AVOID THREE COMMON FALLACIES OF SOCIAL SCIENCE RESEARCH[1]

Contextual analyses directly circumvent three major weaknesses of many social science studies: the compositional fallacy, the ecological fallacy, and the single-factor fallacy (Pettigrew, 2006; Pettigrew & Hewstone, 2017; Robinson, 1950). Let's review each of these fallacies in turn.

The *compositional* fallacy (also called the individualistic fallacy) involves drawing conclusions at the macrolevel of analysis from individual data alone—a problem that all too often arises in psychological and psychiatric theorizing and commentary. Because something is true at the microlevel does not signify that it is true at the macrolevel. Alker (1969) identified this problem and argued that it and the ecological fallacy should be thought of together as problems that arise when research is limited to a single level of analysis.

Examples abound. The classic example involves your sitting in the bleachers at a crowded sporting event. If you stand up, you get a better view of the game. But if the whole crowd stands up, they will not get better views. An extreme illustration is provided by a book written by a psychoanalyst who attempted to provide macrolevel interpretations of violence in American society on the basis of his few patients (Abrahamson, 1970). This is a fallacy because organizations and societies are social systems and as such are invariably more than the sum of their individual parts. Macrounits have unique properties that the macrosocial sciences specialize in studying.

The *ecological* fallacy involves the exact opposite confusion of levels. Here we draw conclusions about individuals from macrolevel data alone. More formally, the fallacy occurs when inferences about individuals are deduced from inferences about the group to which these individuals belong. Put statistically, correlations for the same two variables can be quite dissimilar at different levels of analysis. Selvin's (1958) description is the simplest and most direct: "the invalid transfer of aggregate results to individuals."

The ecological fallacy was identified by Robinson (1950) and named by Selvin. Robinson showed with 1930 U.S. Census data that at the macro-48-state level the correlation between illiteracy and nativity (foreign-born

[1] Some of the passages in this section have been reprinted or adapted from "The Single Factor Fallacy: Implications of Missing Critical Variables From an Analysis of Intergroup Contact Theory," by T. F. Pettigrew and M. Hewstone, 2017, *Social Issues and Policy Review*, *11*(1), pp. 8–37 (https://doi.org/10.1111/sipr.12026). Copyright 2017 by Wiley. Reprinted with permission.

vs. others) was a negative $r = -.53$, whereas at the individual level the correlation was a positive +.12 (but also see Subramanian et al., 2009). This publication had a major influence on how social scientists regarded findings at contrasting levels of analysis.

The ecological fallacy is often discussed in relation to Durkheim's (1951) famous treatise on suicide, first introduced in 1897 (Selvin, 1958). This 19th-century investigation is an important early example of nonexperimental research on a major societal problem. Durkheim gathered data on both religion and suicide from various regions of Europe. He uncovered a striking relationship between the two variables: Heavily populated Protestant *areas* had high suicide rates, whereas heavily populated Roman Catholic *areas* had low rates. Durkheim concluded that Protestant *individuals* were far more likely to commit suicide than Catholic *individuals*. But this commits the ecological fallacy, and the relative rareness of suicide heightens the problem. It could be that the few minority Catholics in the Protestant areas had high suicide rates—perhaps because of religious persecution.

Durkheim, however, was aware of the problem. Because he could obtain only fragments of individual suicide data to test his theory, he did the next best thing. He checked on his findings in increasingly smaller and smaller regions—thus getting closer and closer to the microlevel of individuals. Some small regions had so few Catholics that they could not possibly be causing the high suicide rate. The French sociologist did not eliminate the ecological fallacy, but he did limit it as best his data would allow.[2] By the way, Durkheim was right. Later research with individual data firmly established that suicide *is* more prevalent among Protestants.

Today, the ecological fallacy is often seen in political statements made about individual voters derived from only aggregate voting results. In the 1964 American presidential election, George Wallace, then governor of Alabama, entered the race as a third-party candidate. As a forceful racial segregationist, he sought northern votes with a campaign that combined racism with a social class appeal to White workers. In parts of the industrial Midwest, Wallace received substantial support. Surprised by this, the mass media, using only aggregated voting data, explained Wallace's moderate success by claiming that *individual* White workers had engaged in a "racial backlash." But this claim ignored the fact that the total vote had risen sharply in areas where Wallace received strong support. Without individual data, media analysts thought that Wallace had changed the voting patterns

[2] In limited cases, individual-level data can be recovered from aggregate data (see Iversen, 1973).

of Democratic voters. They largely missed the fact, revealed by election day surveys, that Wallace had succeeded in bringing to the polls *new* White voters attracted by his racist rhetoric. I called it the "out-from-under-the-rocks" phenomenon (Pettigrew, 1964c). In Chapter 8 of this volume, I note that a somewhat similar phenomenon occurred in the 2016 election of Donald Trump as president of the United States.

Group stereotypes offer another example of this fallacy. Traits thought to be common among a certain group are applied to all individuals from that group. Such loose reasoning is clearly wrong. It assumes that all members of a group share the same mean group level of the characteristic with little or no variance. In sum, macrounits are generally too broad to determine individual data, and individuals have unique properties that cannot be inferred from macrodata.

Alker (1969), followed later by epidemiologists (Subramanian et al., 2009), provided strong accounts of how multilevel contextual analyses easily avoid both the compositional and ecological fallacies.

The *single-factor* fallacy is also all too common. This fallacy occurs when social scientists model their applied work largely around a single factor. The problem generally arises either when a highly relevant theory is ignored or when missing key variables distort the results (Pettigrew & Hewstone, 2017).

It is easy to understand how this fallacy occurs. Many social scientists want their theory and research findings to inform social policy. This is especially true of social psychologists. Indeed, the Society for the Psychological Study of Social Issues (SPSSI) and the journals it sponsors are dedicated to this purpose. Moreover, many social scientists have their favorite theories and research findings that they have spent years developing and eagerly wish to apply to social policy. These two inclinations set the scene for repeated and unfortunate occurrences of the single-factor fallacy.

Of course, social scientists are painfully aware that the world is highly complex, that virtually all social phenomena are multivariate and multilevel. Yet, among many researchers, strong beliefs in their own work and the conviction that the variables they prioritize account for a large share of the variance in outcomes of relevance frequently lead to the attempt to build one's applied work largely around a single factor.

Think of the implications of this fallacy for racially desegregated schools in the United States of two well-established theories in social psychology—intergroup contact and stereotype threat. As I detail in Chapter 7 of this volume, positive outcomes of most intergroup contact have now been firmly established through a series of meta-analyses (Beelmann & Heinemann, 2014; Davies et al., 2011; Lemmer & Wagner, 2015; Miles & Crisp, 2014;

Page-Gould & Zhou, in press; Pettigrew & Tropp, 2006, 2008, 2011; Zhou et al., 2019). Literally hundreds of studies throughout the world demonstrate that intergroup contact with many target outgroups—along dimensions as varied as race, ethnicity, sexual orientation, disability status, and so on—typically leads to a host of positive outcomes.

Given such contact benefits, one is tempted to project the results from prior studies onto interracial schools and expect largely positive effects. But this would completely ignore other psychological processes that are equally well established—a classic single-factor fallacy. Research shows that intergroup threat can retard and sometimes even reverse the effects of intergroup contact. As Pettigrew and Tropp (2006; see also Pettigrew & Tropp, 2011, Chapter 12) noted in discussing the results of their meta-analysis,

> Not all contact experiences are positive, of course. Although most of the contact studies in our analysis focused on positive contact outcomes, some recent work has shown that negative intergroup experiences can enhance feelings of anxiety and threat and hinder the development of positive orientations toward the outgroup. (p. 767)

It is hardly surprising that threat is a key factor that can mitigate the positive effects of contact. Think of Steele's (1997, 2010) incisive work on stereotype threat. He and his colleagues have shown that across race, gender, and nationality, people perform less well in settings where the threat of an evaluation is present or at least implied and when the task at hand is associated with a stereotype that their own group will perform worse than others and that their performance might confirm this negative stereotype. Thus, for example, on tests of mathematical ability, women might do less well in the presence of men, African Americans less well in the presence of White Americans, and White Americans less well in the presence of Asian Americans.

Ignoring the intergroup contact research literature and other psychological processes and focusing alone on stereotype threat, one might conclude that desegregated schools across race, gender, and nationality would not be a wise social policy—another example of the single-factor fallacy. Obviously, both phenomena must be carefully considered in designing effective integrated schools. Ways to maximize the benefits of intergroup contact while minimizing stereotype threat must be devised—a far more complex task than simply attending to just one of these concerns. But even this might be merely a two-factor fallacy. We also need to study the larger macrocontext of the school, such as the intergroup diversity of the school's staff, student clubs, sports teams, and other activities.

Working at multiple levels and contextualizing the findings at each level protects against these three common fallacies in social science.

CONTEXTUAL ANALYSES IMPORTANTLY EXPAND SOCIAL PSYCHOLOGY'S EXPLANATORY POWER

Analyses can both broaden and deepen social psychology's explanatory power simply by being contextual. For example, four experiments uncovered large shifts in the judgments of college students about a presidential debate as a function of the context in which they viewed the debate (Fein et al., 2007). These shifts occurred directly as a function of how the audience at the debates responded to the debates—clapping in approval or jeering in disapproval. As the authors concluded, their results demonstrated "the power of social context to strongly influence individuals' judgments of even large amounts of relevant, important information" (p. 165).

But it is less obvious how multilevel research can alter quite basic psychological phenomena operating in contrasting contexts. It often does so by demonstrating how a given phenomenon is impacted by culture, social structure, and norms in addition to psychological factors at the individual level of analysis. This book provides multiple examples of how contextual analysis significantly expands social psychology's explanatory power. This section shows how contextual research greatly enlarges how we think about even such a basic cognitive phenomenon as the intergroup attribution bias.[3]

Intergroup attribution refers to causal attributions people make about the behavior of outgroups as well as their own ingroup. Attribution theory began in the late 1950s and 1960s. Inspired by the innovative writings of Fritz Heider (1958), the initial focus was limited to how individuals causally interpreted the behavior of other individuals. But in the 1970s social psychologists began to consider how causal attributions function at the group level.

The guiding theory for research in this area has been largely structured by the predictions of the *ultimate attribution error* (more accurately described as the *intergroup attribution bias*; Hewstone, 1989, 1990; Pettigrew, 1979b, 2020). Its principal contentions flow from patterns observed in earlier studies that individuals often differentially explain the behavior of outgroups and ingroups. A modest observational study attracted initial attention to the issue. In 1951, Dartmouth College and Princeton University engaged in an exceptionally rough football game. Hastorf and Cantril (1954) then asked students at both schools to evaluate the game. Eighty-six percent of the Princeton students compared with only 36% of the Dartmouth students viewed the aggression as initiated by Dartmouth.

---

[3] This section is drawn from Pettigrew (2020).

It was not until the 1970s that social psychology began to pay full attention to the general area. Several papers during this decade were especially influential. Work by Tajfel and his colleagues (1971), using the minimal group laboratory paradigm, firmly established the operation of a strong ingroup favorability bias—just as Sumner (1906) had claimed 6 decades earlier. Later, the ingroup favorability bias was confirmed with a meta-analysis of 37 tests (Mullen et al., 1992). Ross (1977; Ross et al., 1977) experimentally demonstrated the power and inaccurate overuse of dispositional attributions. E. E. Jones (1976; E. E. Jones & Nisbett, 1972) showed how actors are prone to explain their actions in situational terms, whereas observers (as in intergroup attribution research) are prone to explain the same actions in dispositional terms.

Ingroup protection (explaining away *negative ingroup behavior* as situationally determined—"Given the situation, we had to do it") is typically a stronger effect than ingroup enhancement (accepting *positive ingroup behavior* as dispositionally determined—"As a people, we are kind and compassionate"; Hewstone, 1990). J. G. Weber (1994) studied this distinction directly in two experiments. In Experiment 1, artificial groups of undergraduates, varying in level of intergroup conflict, provided causal attributions for videotaped positive and negative intergroup behavior. Results showed that only protective attributions (e.g., explaining away negative ingroup behavior) increased in response to low-level conflict, relative to nonconflict control groups, and accounted for the observed attribution bias. In Experiment 2, African American and Korean American students were exposed to a conflict or neutral prime in an embedded survey manipulation of conflict. Once again, conflict increased protective attribution for the ingroup's negative behavior, but it did not influence enhancement attributions.[4]

Thus, the theory holds that these group attributions, especially among the highly prejudiced, will be biased for the ingroup and against outgroups. Together with such closely related processes as the fundamental attribution error (Ross, 1977) and actor–observer asymmetry (E. E. Jones & Nisbett, 1972), the intergroup attribution bias phenomenon has proven useful in a variety of applications. Moreover, the intergroup attribution bias serves as an integral component of the multilevel intergroup prejudice syndrome, to be described in Chapter 9 of this volume. The bias especially helps to maintain negative stereotypes of disliked outgroups by explaining away their positive behaviors and exaggerating their negative behaviors.

[4] For an exception to this trend, see Khandelwal et al. (2014).

Moderating and Mediating Factors

But this cognitive bias is not nearly as automatic as first thought. The context in which it occurs is crucial. Researchers began to find significant moderating and mediating factors providing critical context for the intergroup attribution bias. Indeed, this cognitive process is shaped largely by a variety of contextual factors at all three levels of analysis.

National Identification Contexts (A Microlevel Effect)[5]

Doosje and Branscombe (2003) asked national groups to attribute causally the negative historical actions of their own nation with those of other nations. They found that the intergroup attributional bias was more pronounced among subjects who were highly identified with their national ingroup. In an early study, Wang and McKillip (1978) noted that when identification with their ingroup is weak, ethnic attributional bias is also weak. Similarly, Chinese research has also found that the strength of group identification was positively correlated with the bias (Ma & Karasawa, 2006). And a Belgium study showed that French speakers exhibited the bias more if they strongly identified with their linguistic group (O. Klein & Licata, 2001). Thus, the stronger the ingroup identification, the greater the attributional tendency to enhance and especially defend the ingroup.

Emotion (A Microlevel Effect)

M. D. Coleman (2013) conducted an online study to determine whether emotions influence the intergroup attributional bias. He induced two American political groups—Democrats and Republicans—to feel fear, anger, or a neutral emotion. Then he asked them to explain causally the good and bad behavior of both Democratic and Republican politicians. Emotion did not make participants any more or less likely to commit the intergroup attribution bias, but it did change the pattern of attributions made within the bias. Participants experiencing negative emotions made more dispositional attributions for bad behavior and more situational attributions for good behavior than subjects experiencing a neutral emotion.

Another demonstration of attribution bias from political partisanship is provided by Tilley and Hobolt (2011). The authors found that partisan loyalties had strong effects on attributions for who was responsible for national economic trends. Likewise, Northington (2016) had subjects read a

[5] This is a microlevel moderator because it refers to the degree of national identification held by individuals.

hypothetical news article involving a congressperson acting in an antisocial manner. When the actor was listed as being from the subject's opposition party, the poor behavior was attributed as more intentional than when participants read an identical news article involving a congressperson from their own political party. In addition, attributions of intentionality and controllability influenced social judgments and voting intentions both directly and indirectly through anger.

Empathy and Perspective-Taking Contexts (A Microlevel Effect)
Regan and Totten (1975) had their subjects watch a videotape of a "get-together conversation" with instructions to either observe a target in the videotape or empathize with her. As predicted, those subjects who empathized with the target employed relatively more situational and less dispositional attributions than those subjects who acted as standard observers. Other research has also found empathy to be a significant moderator of intergroup bias effects (Boag & Carnelley, 2016; Krumhuber et al., 2015). This result is consistent with a wider research literature that shows how empathy can reduce intergroup prejudice in general (Batson & Ahmad, 2009; Regan & Totten, 1975).

Language as Context (A Microlevel Effect)
The linguistic intergroup bias often accompanies the intergroup attributional bias. Positive ingroup and negative outgroup behaviors tend to be described concretely (Zyzniewski, 2002). Abstract terms, on the other hand, tend to emphasize dispositional attributes of the actor. If one's personal identity is threatened, this language effect is heightened (Maass et al., 1996).

Past Experience and Training as Context (A Microlevel Effect)
The intergroup causal attribution bias can be overcome by training. Stewart et al. (2010) trained White subjects to choose situational over dispositional explanations for negative stereotype-consistent behaviors performed by Black men. In two separate experiments, they showed that extensive training did significantly reduce automatic stereotyping compared with an untrained control group. This situational training works best for individuals high in need for cognition and under conditions of no cognitive load (Latu, 2011).

Gender (A Microlevel Effect)
There are also gender differences. Rosenfield and Stephan (1978) had male and female participants succeed or fail on traditionally masculine and feminine tasks. Male participants made more egotistical, self-serving attributions

than female participants on the masculine task. But on the feminine task, female participants made more egotistical attributions than male participants. These differences were explained in terms of both expectancy for success and ego-involvement in the task.

Intergroup Contact Contexts (A Mesolevel Effect)

Close and extended intercultural contact can reduce the bias not only for the contacted outgroup but also for other uncontacted outgroups. Vollhardt (2010) studied Germans who had hosted non-European exchange students and compared their open-ended attributions with comparable Germans who had volunteered to host such students but who had not yet begun the process. She found that those with the contact, compared with the future hosts, used significantly less internal and more external attributions, as well as culturally sensitive attributions, to explain behavior described in critical and ambiguous intercultural contexts. This contact effect remained even after Vollhardt controlled for perspective-taking empathy and prior intercultural experience. Similarly, in an Indian study of college students, those Hindu participants who lived in mixed Hindu and Muslim neighborhoods were less likely to blame Muslims for interreligious riots (Ruback & Singh, 2007).

Contact even diminishes the intergroup attributional bias among young children. Rutland and his colleagues (2005) studied 3- to 5-year-old children in parts of Great Britain with diverse racial densities. Only children in racially mixed areas failed to show discrimination in favor of the White ingroup on both positive and negative trait attributions.

Cultural Contextual Differences (A Macrolevel Effect)

Some cultures exhibit the intergroup attributional bias far less than others. Research has found repeatedly that some Asian cultures are less prone to dispositional attributions in general and to the intergroup attribution bias in particular (Hewstone & Ward, 1985; Khan & Liu, 2008; Menon et al., 1999; Morris et al., 1995; Morris & Peng, 1994). Maori adolescents in New Zealand even slightly favor the outgroup (Lynskey et al., 1991).

Al-Zahrani and Kaplowitz (1993) tested both Saudi and American university students and found systematic differences. The Saudi students made fewer internal attributions and revealed more intergroup bias—especially more outgroup derogating bias. The Saudis were also more collectivistic than the individualistic Americans, but this difference did not relate to their attributional disparities.

There are also complex interethnic communities where the typical causal attribution bias is turned upside down. Consider the multiethnic northern

Italian province of South Tyrol. Here the stereotypes of the Italian and German speakers are found to be favorable to the ingroup, but their causal attributions are generally favorable to the outgroup as well (Capozza & Rattazzi, 1999).

In sum, we conclude that even such a cognitive phenomenon as the group attribution bias must be viewed as subject to multiple mediators and moderators within a complex three-level contextual framework.

CONTEXTUAL ANALYSES HELP TO COUNTER SOCIAL PSYCHOLOGY'S SO-CALLED CRISES

Every generation or so, social psychologists seem to enjoy experiencing a "crisis." Although sympathetic to the intentions underlying these episodes—first the field's relevance, then the field's methodological and statistical rigor, the term *crisis* seems to me an overly dramatic description.

Placed in a positive light, social psychology's presumed crises actually marked advances in the discipline. The first crisis was triggered by the large-scale entrance into the field of young, politically liberal doctorates who were strongly influenced by the marked changes going on during the 1960s and early 1970s throughout the Western world (Tryon, 1964). (More radical young social scientists, it seems, tended to enter sociology.) This was the largest cohort of new PhDs ever to have entered social psychology up to that point. And those who entered at that fateful time were often disappointed that the discipline was not more active in social change.

Pre-World War II social psychology in North America had addressed social issues far more. Witness the formation of SPSSI in 1936 (Pettigrew, 2011). As we previously noted, sweeping changes in social psychology following the war—a narrowed theoretical focus, an emphasis on laboratory experiments, and declining interest in action research—triggered what was extravagantly termed a "crisis" in psychological social psychology (Pettigrew, 2019). A host of critiques from all directions ensued from established members of the field as well as others who had entered the field during the political turmoil of the 1960s (e.g., Cartwright, 1979; Elms, 1975; Gergen, 1973; Helmreich, 1975; McGuire, 1973; Ring, 1967; Sherif, 1977). Newcomers to the discipline and others seriously challenged the field's relevance.

European social psychologists also participated in this era of critique. Holzkamp's (1971) "critical psychology" garnered considerable attention in Germany. He argued for a psychology for people and not about people, a psychology that considers research subjects as both participants and coresearchers. In the United Kingdom, Israel and Tajfel (1972) criticized American social psychology for its inattention to the cultural and structural context of its phenomena and its greater focus on equity than on equality. The Europeans held the view, as did many of their North American colleagues, that the field had strayed from its purpose to further human betterment, had become too distanced from "real life," too trivial, too reductionist, and too asocial (Greenwood, 2004). Adding to the malaise, ethical concerns were raised about the deceptive methods employed by some social psychological experimenters and typified by Milgram's (1974) famous and controversial study of obedience.

Their efforts succeeded in making applications of social psychology to social policy a central concern. Membership in SPSSI increased, and the organization moved its office from Ann Arbor, Michigan, to Washington, DC, to play the "honest broker" role of supplying social science information to policymakers (Pettigrew, 1967b). Later, SPSSI began publishing two journals that explicitly address social policy—*Analyses of Social Issues and Public Policy* and *Social Issues and Policy Review.*

Numerous outstanding examples of the field's relevance have emerged. Think of the "real-world" example provided by Susan Fiske et al. (1991) in the groundbreaking gender discrimination case of *Price Waterhouse v. Hopkins.* This was the first case in which the U.S. Supreme Court used social psychological research on sex stereotyping. Susan Fiske effectively testified to the antecedent conditions, indicators, consequences, and remedies of stereotyping on the basis of extensive social psychological research. She convincingly managed to place gender stereotype phenomena at the microlevel into the meso- and macrocontexts of the offices of Price Waterhouse, the defendants. Her testimony was cited at length by the trial and appeals courts as well as the Supreme Court. The plaintiff won the case; this episode surely meets the earlier concerns about the field's relevance to the world's problems.

European social psychologists began to use their research findings on intergroup contact and related phenomena to help generate greater acceptance of the enormous flow of immigrants that suddenly reached the continent's shores. For example, when the number of refugees from Syria, Afghanistan, and African states to Germany increased to nearly 900,000 in 2015 alone, Ulrich Wagner at Philipps University in Marburg organized 150 German social psychologists to join together and sign a petition. He sent it directly to the German chancellor, to the Bundestag, and to the state parliaments. They made recommendations based on social psychological knowledge about intergroup relations and contact for a humanitarian political handling of this sudden surge. They urged authorities to make macrochanges that would maximize intergroup contact effects and minimize the threat of new arrivals. Spread the new arrivals around the country, for example, and keep new ghettoes of immigrants from forming.

Although Chancellor Angela Merkel never directly responded, social psychological knowledge did diffuse into the political debate, especially with discussions in the Bundestag and elsewhere of the positive effects of intergroup contact (U. Wagner, personal communication, September 27, 2015).

This notable German effort suggests the need for similar collective responses from North American social psychologists, joined one would hope by other social scientists, especially sociologists and political scientists. We have helpful things to say on bringing together today's sharp political divides as well as improving the acceptance of immigrants. Like our German counterparts, we should address political leaders directly. To the extent that contextual analyses aid such efforts, they help to respond to the relevance "crisis" of the discipline.

The second so-called crisis of method has focused upon *false positives* and replication failures. It, too, is overblown. And a more rigorously applied contextual approach can help ease these issues. The second crisis is a direct consequence in the field's increasing statistical and methodological sophistication. How can that be a dire development? Indeed, this increasing sophistication is a major driving force behind the growth in multilevel, contextual social psychological studies described throughout this book, and it is part of a general trend of major methodological advances throughout the social sciences.

The first focus concerns false positives—incorrectly claiming significant findings. Even if sharply overstated, this focus can potentially be a step forward in statistical practice in social psychology (Simmons et al., 2011, 2018). But it does *not* represent, in the hyperbole of a writer in the *New York Times Magazine*, a "revolution" that could render "vast amounts of research, even entire subfields, . . . unreliable" (Dominus, 2017).

What is distressing about this debate is its personal, uncivil nature (Dominus, 2017). I have long been proud of the professional stance of social psychology. But unrefereed blogs and social media attacks sent to thousands undermines the professionalism of the discipline. Accusing authors of being either stupid or dishonest has no place in social psychology or any other science—save in such fully documented and lamentable situations as the Diederik Stapel affair ("Diederik Stapel," 2020). Stapel simply made up data to support novel phenomena that did not exist.

Yet there are valuable things to be learned in this latest "crisis." Simmons et al. (2011, 2018) proposed six somewhat burdensome requirements for authors to meet in order to reduce the possibility of *p-hacking*.[6] These suggestions deserve thoughtful consideration. Another reaction is to increase power with larger sample sizes. Researchers in social psychology did just that between 2011 and 2016. But Sassenberg and Ditrich (2019) showed that inflating sample sizes costs money and time, and consequently there has been greater use of less expensive but less rigorous online data collection and self-reports to compensate. Thus, there has been a trade-off between sample size and the research method employed—leaving open the question of whether this trade-off actually elevates research rigor.

Yet the term *p-hacking* implies intentional distortion. That this may occur on occasion cannot be denied, yet I am not convinced that it is as widespread as some critics of the field maintain. John et al. (2012) reported that various "questionable research practices" are common in psychology, with prevalence estimates up to 100% (p. 524). Norbert Schwarz (2012), a survey specialist, pointed out that the John–Lowenstein–Prelec survey purporting to show this widespread *p*-hacking suffered from a very low response rate (24%), selective attrition from an extremely high break-off rate, and seriously biased questions—even questions for which *any* answer counted as a "questionable practice."

Moreover, some adjustments to research data are fully justified, and some even raise *p* levels (e.g., removing extreme outliers that favor the hypothesis). These justifiable adjustments should continue, but they need clear documentation to show the reader how they are affecting the *p* level.

Now some psychologists, following earlier writers in other disciplines (e.g., Schmidt & Hunter, 1995), are suggesting either to stop giving special privilege to significance levels (Amrheim & Greenland, 2017) or to reduce the *p* level from .05 to .005 (Benjamin et al., 2018). This last suggestion by Benjamin and 80 colleagues, including Brian Nosek and Anthony Greenwald, immediately raises questions about the large increase in Type II errors that would necessarily occur from lowering the *p* level for significance. They offer an interesting third option—a "suggestive" category for low *p* levels above .005.

These various possibilities seem premature for social psychology at this point, but they are certainly worth debate. Yet, different levels are appropriate for different fields. Physics, with its typically more reliable measures,

[6] The term *p*-hacking, similar to *data dredging*, refers to the gross misuse of statistics to find patterns in the data that are asserted to be statistically significant when in fact there is no real underlying effect. It is basically cheating with statistics. Different types of analyses with contrasting assumptions are tried out until one emerges with supposedly "significant" results, and only this test is then reported.

can easily afford to have more rigorous standards than the social sciences.[7] There may well be differences among the social sciences and even within psychology itself. Adding to this problem, the phenomena studied by social and personality psychology are often extremely sensitive to contextual effects. Contextual analyses could ease but not eliminate this situation.

Taking the broad view, I agree with Fiedler et al. (2012) that *false negatives*—rejecting a finding that is actually valid—may well be a more serious problem in social psychology. And it has been largely ignored with this intense focus on false positives.

It is also useful for the discipline to think more deeply about replications. The publication in *Science* of the replication findings by the Open Science Collaboration (2015) brought on the so-called replication crisis by purporting to show that psychological research in general, and social psychological and personality research in particular, often fails to replicate. D. T. Gilbert et al. (2016, 2017) calmed the waters by showing that this conclusion was simply not justified. They demonstrated that when the Collaboration's analyses are corrected for error, power, and bias, "the pessimistic conclusions that many have drawn from this article—namely, that there is a 'replication crisis' in psychology—are unwarranted" (D. T. Gilbert et al., 2017, para. 3).

The most damaging part of the Gilbert critique was that many of the replication studies were in fact quite different from the original studies. For instance, the replications of two studies conducted in the United States were actually carried out in Italy and the Netherlands. Such extensive contextual differences can be critical—the fundamental point of contextual social psychology. Not surprising, then, these poorly replicated studies turned out to be 4 times more likely to fail to support the original findings. We already encountered this phenomenon in Chapter 2 with the Würzburg smiling experiment. Precise replication is often exceedingly difficult to attain.

The retort to the Gilbert critique did not fully address its claims (C. J. Anderson et al., 2016; D. T. Gilbert et al., 2017). Indeed, it even acknowledged that the opposite conclusion of high reliability in psychological studies could also be inferred from their project's results. Apparently, social psychological studies do replicate at reasonable levels; this finding also counters the claims of John et al. (2012) concerning widespread "questionable research practices." If indeed there are acceptable levels of replication, then *p*-hacking and other questionable practices cannot be as extensive as these authors claim. In any event, the large-scale effort of the Open Science Collaboration has at least served the valuable purpose of renewing attention

[7] For discussion of this critical point, see Sanbonmatsu and Johnston (2019).

to the importance of replications. It must be noted that the incivility that marked the *p*-hacking debate did not occur in this exchange about replication. Gilbert emphasized that no one in the Collaboration was trying to deceive anyone. And a leader of the Collaboration, Brian Nosek, actually made useful suggestions to D. T. Gilbert and his colleagues (2017) for their rebuttal.

The discipline's major studies, upon which much of its basic theory is based, have been successfully replicated repeatedly—a fact that is forgotten in much of the replication discussion in social psychology. Recall the influential experiments of Solomon Asch (1955, 1956) on conformity and Stanley Milgram (1974) on obedience. Asch carefully repeated his conformity experiment over and over, constantly testing rival explanations for his surprising results. Milgram, who had studied with Asch, did the same thing with his unanticipated obedience results. Indeed, Milgram (1974) carried the replication one step further by varying the physical context of his famous experiment. He worried that the prestige of Yale University, where his experimental laboratory was located, might have influenced his dramatic results. So he repeated the experiment in a run-down location in a nearby industrial city. The same results emerged.

Consistent with the findings of the reproducibility study (Open Science Collaboration, 2015), these legendary studies had strong effects initially—the primary predictor of reproducibility. Each of the Asch and Milgram tests not only replicated their original findings but tested a different explanation for their unexpected results. Thus, this careful work also avoided the single-factor fallacy (Pettigrew & Hewstone, 2017). Moreover, in personality psychology, Soto (2019) found an 87% replication rate of studies that linked personality traits to various life outcomes.

Meta-analysis, which personality and social psychology have extensively and successfully employed, also provides evidence that research in the field is not in the dire position that some of its critics would have us believe. As I show in Chapter 7 of this volume, seven different meta-analyses have repeatedly shown that intergroup contact in widely different forms tends to reduce intergroup prejudice.

All scientists favor replications, but the issue is more complex than often presented. Some critics seem to think that replication problems are largely an issue for social psychology. But, of course, replication is important for all empirical sciences. The hard truth, we repeat, is that thorough, pinpoint replications are extremely difficult to attain in general and in social and personality psychology in particular. Even changes in the computing software can make it mistakenly appear that there has been a failure to replicate (Epskamp, 2019). Indeed, the critics of the discipline do not seem to appreciate fully the difficulty of precise social replications. And imprecise replications can cause serious "confusion" and must "be held to high standards of rigor" (Sundie et al., 2019, p. e1).

Here is where multilevel analyses can be of the special value. By carefully duplicating the cultural, normative, and other social contexts in the replication, major reasons for the failure to confirm the original findings can be sharply reduced. Greenfield (2017) extended this key consideration. She noted that cultures change over time, so failures to replicate may simply reflect this change. Greenfield's point can be extended to dissimilar contexts in general. In social psychology, as D. T. Gilbert and his colleagues (2016, 2017) emphasized, disparate contexts of the experiments can easily lead to differential results—the core consideration of contextual analyses. A study done in the United States may not replicate in Switzerland because of cultural differences between the two nations affecting the phenomenon under study. Studies of crowding and personal space in spacious regions of North America may not replicate in Tokyo, the densely populated Netherlands, or the even more densely populated German state of North Rhine-Westphalia.

Narrower contexts can also disrupt replications. For instance, college campuses vary widely in the composition of their student bodies from which many social psychological experiments draw their subjects. Thus, replicated results from studies conducted on a broad variety of campuses are likely to be more firmly grounded.

Survey research also needs to be carefully replicated. It is often too expensive to repeat large surveys, but a simple, if somewhat crude, method with large surveys is available but rarely employed. Multiple random subsamples can be tested to see how closely their results align with those of the total sample.

CONTEXTUAL ANALYSES GENERATE RESULTS THAT MORE EASILY INFLUENCE PUBLIC POLICY

Yet another advantage of contextual analyses is that their findings are more directly relevant to public policy and more easily understood by policymakers. Those charged with governing often do not have the time, training, or patience to pursue social science journals and books relevant to their work. Moreover, the public policy relevance of findings at the psychological levels of analysis is rarely obvious. Policymakers work largely at macrolevels. And in the United States, they are likely to be lawyers whose training, given the law's adversarial system, contrasts sharply with that of social scientists in many ways (Pettigrew, 1979a).[8]

Think of intergroup contact theory in this light. It has been strongly and publicly advocated for as a means to achieve better intergroup relations by social psychologists in Germany, the United Kingdom, the United States, and other countries (Pettigrew, 2018a; Pettigrew & Hewstone, 2017). But contact theory is largely a mesolevel proposition. Policymakers deal in macrolevel policy and need to know how best to alter institutions so that more optimal conditions for beneficial contact can occur. Consequently, contextual models encompassing these macrolevels are far more likely to be understood and acted upon by policymakers.

Social scientists can also shape policy in the courts. But having served as an expert in four school racial desegregation cases (Springfield, Massachusetts; Norfolk and Richmond, Virginia; and Los Angeles, California), I can testify personally about the difficulty of this activity. Social science and the courts have fundamental differences (Pettigrew, 1979a, 2004a). The adversarial system could hardly be more different from science. Legal logic is not the same as scientific logic. Even the same terms, such as *evidence* and *expert*, can have vastly disparate meanings. Thus, the criteria for what is considered "expert testimony" in American courts can be surprisingly low. A few social scientists have made careers of repeatedly testifying for racially segregated education and are readily accepted as "experts" although they have never conducted intergroup research nor ever taught or published in the race relations field (Pettigrew, 2004a).

Courts seek the specific, and social science seeks the general. In every case in which I participated, something like this cross-examination occurred:

1. The expert cites a general conclusion relevant to the point at issue.
2. The examiner asks for the evidence that supports such a conclusion.
3. The expert describes a number of studies.
4. The examiner then asks *where* these studies were conducted.

[8] The United States is unusual among the world's democracies in its heavy reliance on lawyers in its government even when compared with other English-speaking governments. The percentage of lawyers in the U.S. Congress over recent decades ranges between 40% and 60% compared with about 25% of the Australian parliament and about 15% of the Canadian parliament. In 2013, 41% of the U.S. Congress were lawyers; thus, members were 68 more times likely to be a lawyer than in the American adult population (Measure of America, 2013). Only occasionally has a psychologist or sociologist served in the U.S. Congress.

5. The expert, a bit surprised by the question, cites the many areas sampled by these studies, none of which include the city involved in the case.
6. The examiner now has what she or he wanted. "So, Dr. Jones, *none* of these investigations were actually conducted here in Centerville. There is no reason to believe, then, that the findings of these studies hold true for *our* children here in *our* schools."

The examiner has a narrow point, of course, in arguing that the special context of Centerville could alter the conclusions of research done in multiple areas throughout the nation. It also hints at the fact that the experts are not from Centerville—so how could they possibly know about "our schools?"[9] Although this argument is a long stretch without evidence to support it, it still remains an acceptable argument for American courts.

Adding to the problem is that right-wing judges, even on the U.S. Supreme Court, can be openly hostile and dismissive of social science evidence—especially when it does not support their political beliefs. Even a Chief Justice, John Roberts, seemed to reveal his strong bias against social science when he described evidence showing extreme partisan gerrymandering in Wisconsin as "sociological gobblygook" (Tropp et al., 2007).[10]

Consider, too, when a five-judge majority held narrowly tailored desegregation plans of two school districts—Seattle, Washington, and Jefferson County, Kentucky—to be in violation of the Equal Protection clause of the Fourteenth Amendment (Tropp et al., 2007). They arrived at this conclusion, the majority opinion argued, because a few White children had been denied access to the schools of their choice in order to further racial desegregation and because prior state de jure segregation was not directly involved. This sweeping ruling prohibited assigning students to public schools solely for the purpose of achieving racial desegregation and declined to recognize

[9] Once this tactic backfired when I testified for racial school desegregation in my hometown of Richmond, Virginia. The cross-examining lawyer did not realize I was a native Richmonder. Because he was not from Richmond, I was able to turn the argument against him. I rattled off the names of the city's schools I had attended and further details only a native could know, while making it clear that as an outsider he could not be expected to know these things. Even the presiding federal judge laughed out loud.

[10] Roberts was dismissing an elegant algorithm that produced a simple number as to the number of seats switched as a function of a given gerrymandering of a state's congressional districts. The high court had previously called for just such an indicator. Roberts is obviously a highly intelligent man who can easily understand such an indicator without statistical or social science training. And he did not object to the use of similar methods to construct the gerrymander in the first place. Thus, his partisan bias seems obvious.

racial balancing as a compelling state interest. Earlier, four lower federal courts had consistently upheld these plans to be constitutional; but these rulings were abruptly overturned.

Such decisions drastically undercut *Brown* and other school desegregation rulings. But Justice Clarence Thomas in his concurring opinion and Justice Stephen Breyer in his dissenting opinion both used social science evidence. Indeed, the high court cited social scientific research in these cases "to an extent perhaps never seen before" (Tropp et al., 2007, p. 94).

Justice Breyer cited social science evidence appropriately in his dissent; he carefully mentioned studies that reached conflicting conclusions. By contrast, Justice Thomas repudiated the same evidence that did not support his position by simply raising the bar to unattainable heights. He demanded *full* agreement from *all* social scientists before a finding could be held valid—a hurdle that the high court itself rarely meets, not even in this five-to-four case. He emphasized that there was a divergence of opinion among social scientists when there must be unanimous agreement.

In short, Thomas required entirely conclusive evidence before he would accept social science evidence that contradicted his position. In his opinion, he stated, "Furthermore, it is unclear whether increased interracial contact improves racial attitudes and relations." Apparently, he found inconclusive the findings of the seven meta-analyses detailed in Chapter 7 of this volume. My meta-analysis with Tropp was included in at least two amicus briefs submitted to the court by the American Psychological Association and the American Educational Research Association (Pettigrew & Tropp, 2006).

Such problems make the legal achievement of S. T. Fiske and her colleagues (1991) in their equal employment rights suit described earlier all the more impressive. They proved that it could be accomplished despite the many barriers between the law and social science.

THE IMPORTANCE OF STATISTICAL ADVANCES

As documented throughout this volume, contextual analyses are now emerging far more frequently in psychological social psychology than in the past (Pettigrew, 2018a). This rise is attributable in large part to the introduction of new statistical tools to conduct such analyses. Although contextual analyses have many advantages, they would not have been possible had many exciting new developments in statistics not been made during the past half century. Chapter 4 provides a brief history of this progress that has benefited social science generally and contextual analyses in particular.

4 STATISTICAL ADVANCES ENABLE AND ENCOURAGE CONTEXTUAL ANALYSES IN SOCIAL PSYCHOLOGY

Major statistical advances relevant to social science research have been made over the past half century or so (Glaeser, 2017). Leading statisticians, such as William Cochran, Frederick Mosteller, and John Tukey, turned their full attention to the needs of medicine and social science. Virtually all of the social sciences and their applied fields have greatly profited from their work and the work of others. Contextual analyses especially have benefitted from these advances.

RAPID STATISTICAL ADVANCES AID CONTEXTUAL ANALYSES

My crude thesis method for contextualizing psychological phenomena by comparing two different macrounits (South vs. North) is still in wide use even though far more advanced methods are now available. Often, however, it is the only approach available given the data. For instance, D. Cohen (1996) compared the South and West of the United States to see if regional cultures and past history with or without slavery were associated today with current violence and related social policies. He found that both regions

https://doi.org/10.1037/0000210-005
Contextual Social Psychology: Reanalyzing Prejudice, Voting, and Intergroup Contact, by T. F. Pettigrew

favored individual violence for self-protection. But the South's legacy of slavery did relate to more acceptance of violence used for coercion and punishment as reflected in laws related to spousal abuse, corporal punishment, and capital punishment. Moreover, the South's legacy of slavery still shapes the region's far-right voting (Acharya et al., 2018).

But now, contextual social psychology has far more effective methods to employ when the required data are available. Moore's law—that the speed and capacity of computers would double every 2 years—has proven to date to be surprisingly accurate. And this rapid growth in computer power opened the door for more sophisticated statistical methods. This development of more complex statistical tools was part of similar upgrading throughout the social sciences. To quote Glaeser (2017), "progress is still being made at a ferocious pace, and the contours of [the social sciences] are rapidly evolving" (p. 78).

The advances most relevant to contextual analyses emerged over the past half century. First, *structural equation modeling* (SEM) and related methods came into social science. Later, Blalock's *explicit analysis of contextual effects models* drew attention directly to contextual analyses. Then, direct methods for ascertaining *mediating and moderating effects* became popular in psychology. Next came *meta-analysis* that allowed for more accurate means of combining the results of multiple studies. Finally, the most helpful method of all for contextual analyses—*multilevel analyses*—became available. Each of these interrelated statistical advances enhanced the use of contextual analyses.

STRUCTURAL EQUATION MODELING

SEM fits networks of constructs to data. It involves a wide range of interrelated statistics including path analysis, confirmatory factor analysis, partial least square path modeling, and latent growth modeling. Its particular value to the social sciences is its ability to impute links between latent variables (unobserved constructs) from observable variables, and this feature is of special significance for contextual studies generally. One caution, however, is always worth remembering: SEMs involve models that convey causal *assumptions*—not necessarily models that denote validated causal conclusions.

It took a half century for SEM methods to enter the social sciences.[1] Sewall Wright (1921, 1960), a biological statistician, developed path analysis

[1] For an extensive treatment of the history and development of SEM, see Westland (2015).

in 1921 as part of his groundbreaking work on theoretical population genetics. Wright's work first migrated into economics as a means of clarifying traffic issues. But econometricians were generally reluctant to adopt the method (Goldberger, 1972).

Interest in Wright's work outside the study of genetics increased sharply once computer power greatly expanded in the era of the 1950s to 1970s. Four works were of special importance in ushering in SEM's belated entrance into social science. First, Otis Dudley Duncan (1966, 1975), a highly regarded methodologist in sociology, published a seminal paper on path analysis followed by a book, and he provided sociological examples. Next, Arthur Goldberger (1972), a leading econometrician, published a major paper in *Econometrica*, which he described as a survey that "attempts to redress economists' neglect of the work of Sewall Wright."

The next major influence involved computer programs that made it easier to use SEMs, such as LISREL and EQS. Karl Jöreskog, a Swedish statistician, together with others developed LISREL and released it in 1972 (Jöreskog & Van Thillo, 1972). Social psychologists were slow to adopt LISREL, but that changed with the later introduction of EQS. This influential program and publication was especially important for psychologists because it was written by Peter Bentler (1985), a well-known University of California, Los Angeles psychologist who used psychological examples and wrote in statistical terms more familiar to psychologists.

My adoption of SEMs followed closely this line of development. When I read Duncan's SEM paper in 1966, I was intrigued by the possibilities that path analysis held for a more advanced means of analyzing contextual data sets. My first meager attempt to test this hope involved a study of the acceptance of racial school desegregation across the 187 counties of Texas (Pettigrew & Riley, 1972). Robert T. Riley and I were able to provide a modest path model that indicated that the attitude climate of the counties mediated the effects of two structural variables (retail sales and population growth) in predicting the slow unfolding of school desegregation across Texas counties.

To be honest, I found the early versions of LISREL difficult to use. But Bentler's EQS package proved far easier to employ. And this encouraged me to make SEMs a standard tool for numerous attempts to further my contextual analyses (e.g., Pettigrew et al., 2010). The popularity of EQS is attested to by the fact that Bentler has more than 200,000 citations listed by Google Scholar, and this volume documents the extensive use of SEMs in contextual research.

For example, Wagner et al. (2003), using EQS, were able to explain persistent differences in prejudice between the macrounits of East and

West Germany using individual differences in intergroup contact. They found that the greater prejudice in East Germany was largely a result of East Germans having had far less contact with minorities than West Germans enjoyed. Although previously the East German government had often invited diverse visitors from other Communist countries (e.g., Cuba, North Korea, and Vietnam), it had routinely kept them sealed off in segregated areas, thus greatly restraining intergroup contact.

Once I retired in 1994, my understanding and use of structural equations and other statistical advances were greatly furthered by my repeated visits to the psychology department at Philipps University in Marburg, Germany. Working with Professor Ulrich Wagner and his talented (former) graduate students—Frank Asbrock, Oliver Christ, Gunnar Lemmer, Jost Stellmacher, Rolf van Dick, and Andreas Zick—was not only a great pleasure but highly instructive.

BLALOCK'S EXPLICIT ANALYSIS OF CONTEXTUAL EFFECTS MODELS

Blalock (1984), an influential methodologist, published a widely read chapter that explicitly examined contextual analyses. As a sociologist, he primarily focused on path F—the top-down link between the macrolevel and microlevel. He emphasized that there were many forms of contextual effects, discussed both the statistical and theoretical problems involved with each form, and urged attention to the factual adequacy of key assumptions underlying all contextual analyses. His chapter not only formalized contextual research but also drew widespread attention throughout the social sciences to contextual analyses generally.

MEDIATING AND MODERATING EFFECTS

Two years later, contextual analyses were further enhanced by Baron and Kenny's (1986) influential publication. Their work delineated moderators from mediators and provided straightforward testing procedures for each. Methods to assess moderators and mediators have since been updated (see Fritz & MacKinnon, 2007; Hayes, 2013; Kenny et al., 1998; Krull & MacKinnon, 2001). But Baron and Kenny's original article's focus on multiple predictor variables marked a breakthrough contribution for contextual analyses.

This one article has had a major influence in the analyses of both experiments and survey research. The authors' cogent presentation persuaded many researchers to check for additional factors in their applications. By 2020, Google Scholar had listed more than 90,000 citations to Baron and Kenny's important article. In fact, Google Scholar shows that it is by far the most cited publication ever to appear in the *Journal of Personality and Social Psychology*. The article especially influenced both social and personality psychologists to adopt contextual approaches to their data using Paths B and E in Figure 2.1. Social psychologists began to use more personality variables as possible moderators or mediators of their mesolevel findings, and personality psychologists began to use more situational variables in their analyses of microlevel phenomena (S. T. Fiske, 2000; Fleeson, 2012; Pettigrew, 2019; Reis & Holmes, 2012).

META-ANALYSIS

This approach combines the results of multiple studies so as to improve the estimates of the effect under study, increase power, and resolve conflicting results across investigations. The basic tenet is that the pooled estimate from the combined studies will better approach the unknown true relationship.

This promise of combining results across many studies has long been understood. More than a century ago, the eminent British statistician Karl Pearson (1904) merged the findings of several studies to test the effects of typhoid inoculation. To this day, the use of meta-analysis is especially popular in medical research. But its use in psychology was delayed in part by its misuse. Research summarizers have sometimes let their biases shape their conclusions by cherry-picking the cases to be considered. Gene Glass (2000) singled out Hans Eysenck's summaries of research that aimed to disparage psychotherapy as a stunning case in point. Having benefited from psychotherapy himself, Glass found Eysenck's negative reviews to be arbitrary, idiosyncratic, and high-handedly dismissive. So he began to review the research on psychotherapy systematically and found Eysenck's negative conclusions to be wrong (Glass, 1978; Glass et al., 1981).[2]

[2] Glass's meta-analytic findings led to yet further controversy. Although he found beneficial effects of psychotherapy generally, he did not uncover meaningful differences between different types of therapy. Thus, instead of being reassured by his overall result, strong proponents of various types of psychotherapy were upset that he had not shown their favored type of therapy to be superior.

The term *meta-analysis* was coined by Glass in his 1976 presidential address to the American Educational Research Association (Glass, 1976, 1978; Glass et al., 1981). Glass's advance led to two major contributions. One was to start to shift psychological evaluation to effect sizes rather than *p* values. For this reason alone, noted psychological statistician Jacob Cohen (1990) proclaimed that "meta-analysis makes me very happy" (p. 1310). The second contribution was Glass's insistence on including poorly conducted studies as well as well-conducted studies. Many writers have thought it best to look at only "good" studies, but various researchers have somewhat different ideas about what constitutes a "good" study. More important, including all studies regardless of their quality provides important information that often helps to explain wide variability in results across studies. Following Glass, a host of others—many of them psychologists—have further refined meta-analytic statistics and procedures (e.g., Douglas Bonett, Jacob Cohen, Larry Hedges, Ingram Olkin, Robert Rosenthal, Frank Schmidt).

Meta-analyses are necessarily dependent on published studies combined with as many unpublished studies as can be collected. Consequently, publication bias is a potentially major weakness of the method. Studies with the most positive results may well get published more often than studies with negative or no results. Indeed, research into various areas have shown this bias to be operating (e.g., Dickersin et al., 2005; Dickersin & Min, 1993).

Rosenthal (1991) popularized the term *file-drawer problem* to describe how studies yielding essentially no effects might often be stored away and never submitted for publication. He proposed a fail-safe index to indicate how many samples with no effect whatsoever would have to exist to erase the significance of any particular obtained effect.

Light and Pillemer (1984) introduced the funnel test that consisted of plotting sample sizes against the effect sizes. The more stable large studies show less scatter and appear at the top of the funnel plot, but smaller studies are highly informative. If the effect sizes of these studies are not skewed, it indicates that there is little or no publication bias. If they are skewed to one side of the plot, publication bias is indicated. In other words, when there is no link between the standard errors and effect sizes, publication bias is not a problem. Many ingenious techniques based on the funnel test have been proposed to test further for publication bias.

As with other advances, we now have widely distributed computer programs for meta-analyses—especially the popular *Comprehensive Meta-Analysis* (Borenstein et al., 2009). This program and others, such as *RevMan* and *Stata*, have led to a marked increase in published meta-analyses—especially in social psychology, as well as in education and medicine. It has also led to higher quality and greater uniformity in procedures across various meta-analyses.

As part of this trend, I have published with colleagues meta-analyses of intergroup contact effects (Pettigrew & Tropp, 2006, 2008), memory for schema-relevant information (Rojahn & Pettigrew, 1992), and relative deprivation effects (H. J. Smith et al., 2012). In each case, important contextual variables emerged as a moderator, such as minority versus majority status for contact effects, type of test used for memory of schema-relevant information, and Asian versus Western cultures for relative deprivation.

Notice that the special importance of meta-analysis for contextual research is that it easily uncovers moderation effects. Once the data are assembled, it becomes clear that certain effects vary sharply from the principal effect, and informative moderators thus emerge.

MULTILEVEL ANALYSIS

Multilevel analysis (also called hierarchical models, mixed models, and nested data models) and its various embellishments (e.g., multilevel SEM) were late in development because they had to wait for sufficient computing power to become widespread. Working at two or more levels, this method analyzes individual data distributed ("nested") in groups. Thus, this approach is made to order for contextual analysis—but it is by no means the only way contextual effects can be uncovered. A solid introduction to this ideal multilevel approach is supplied by the Dutch psychologist and statistician J. J. Hox (2010). See also two tutorial articles by Judd et al. (2012) and by Brauer and Curtin (2018). For a sampling of how it is being used in social and personality psychology, see Christ et al. (2012).

But there is a potential limitation to using this approach when it is used in multilevel studies cited throughout this book.[3] There must be a substantial number of group-level cases—say, 50 or more (Feskens & Hox, 2011)—for multilevel analysis to be safely applied. With small numbers of groups, statistical tests for contextual effects can be quite unreliable (Meuleman & Billiet, 2009). Rarely are laboratory experiments going to meet this stringent requirement for multiple groups, so necessarily the book's examples using this method utilize large surveys ranging across such multiple units as nations and provinces.

[3] For other purposes, smaller numbers of groups are sufficient. See Kenny et al. (2002).

This requirement could be a major impediment to the use of multilevel methods. Fortunately, however, statistical methods are being developed to overcome this limitation (Feskens & Hox, 2011; Meuleman, 2011). These procedures, often using bootstrapping and jackknifing techniques, involve resampling as is generally the case when dealing with small sample issues (Yung & Chan, 1999).

Many of the studies employing multilevel analyses to be discussed throughout this book combine the strengths of multilevel SEM and SEM and use tests for moderation, mediation, moderated mediation, and mediated moderation. Vanderbilt University's Kristopher Preacher has been a leader in this development that importantly benefits contextual analyses (e.g., Preacher et al., 2007, 2010, 2016). Usually in science, both physical and social, advances in method soon lead to advances in theory. This method-to-theory sequence seems to be the case here, for these statistical advances helped to develop vastly expanded and improved social psychological theories, such as intergroup contact theory (see Chapter 7, this volume).

Longitudinal analyses are also important and can be usefully used together with multilevel methods to determine causal links. Growth modeling is becoming increasingly popular, and prime examples are provided in later chapters (see *Growth Modeling* by Grimm et al., 2017).

Overtime approaches go hand in hand with contextual approaches. Not only do they check on changes across time, but they augment the search for contextual effects that may themselves change overtime. Looking back on social psychology's history, one is reminded of an often-overlooked feature of Muzafer Sherif's classic experiments (Pettigrew, 1991a). Sherif correctly argued that the social psychology of his time focused far too much on static, isolated effects rather than dynamic, cumulative effects. His most famous findings are cumulative. They emerged because he persisted in repeating the measurement of the dependent variable over many trials. The major results of both his autokinetic (Sherif, 1935, 1937) and Robbers' Cave (Sherif, 1966) studies were *cumulative effects*. Early changes in the situation altered the context for later renderings of the dependent measure.

Although these statistical advances have been extremely important, contextual analysis is not limited to them. We saw in the Würzburg smiling experiment (Chapter 2 of this volume) that it can also be important for laboratory experiments. It can also be important for qualitative research. One of the most ambitious attempts to apply social psychological principles to a major social problem is Herbert Kelman's efforts to ease Middle Eastern tensions through carefully constructed problem-solving workshops (Kelman & Fisher, 2016; Pettigrew, 2010b). Explicitly using contextual principles,

Kelman managed to employ the small group as (a) a microcosm of the larger macrosystem, (b) a laboratory for creating inputs to the larger macrosystem, (c) a setting for direct interaction of significant members of each side of the conflict, (d) a coalition across the conflict lines, and (e) a nucleus for a fresh new relationship between the conflicting parties. Kelman's ambitious efforts provide a useful model for similar efforts in other conflict arenas.

We turn now to applying contextual analyses to four specific content areas: prejudice, relative deprivation, intergroup contact, and right-wing voting.

5 APPLYING CONTEXTUAL ANALYSES TO INTERGROUP PREJUDICE

Gordon Allport was fundamentally a personality psychologist. Indeed, his classic volume *Personality: A Psychological Interpretation* (Allport, 1937) helped to establish the field of personality as a lasting component of the psychological discipline in the United States (Pettigrew, 1990). But in the 1930s, 1940s, and 1950s, personality and social psychology had not yet structurally differentiated (Pettigrew, 2019). So he was also a social psychologist and the longtime editor of the *Journal of Abnormal and Social Psychology*, which combined the two fields.

It is hardly surprising, then, that Allport took a deeply personality approach to the subject of prejudice in his masterpiece, *The Nature of Prejudice* (Allport, 1954, 1958). Twenty-one of the initial edition's 31 chapters are directly focused on the individual. Drawing on his early experience in Germany with Gestalt psychology, Allport anticipated the later

---

Some of the passages in this chapter have been reprinted or adapted from "In Pursuit of Three Theories: Authoritarianism, Relative Deprivation, and Intergroup Contact," by T. F. Pettigrew, 2016, *Annual Review of Psychology*, *67*, pp. 1–21 (https://doi.org/10.1146/annurev-psych-122414-033327). Copyright 2016 by Annual Reviews. Reprinted with permission.

https://doi.org/10.1037/0000210-006
Contextual Social Psychology: Reanalyzing Prejudice, Voting, and Intergroup Contact, by T. F. Pettigrew

"cognitive revolution" in psychology by stressing cognitive factors. To be sure, he carefully noted in Chapter 13 that other levels of explanation were important, such as historical, sociocultural, and situational factors. And he mentioned "the structural argument" in the final chapter. But his principal emphasis throughout was centered on the individual level of prejudice.

The book's strong personality preference accurately reflected the author's viewpoint. Once I coproduced an ecological analysis of the spread of public-school desegregation across the South (Pettigrew & Cramer, 1959). It revealed that a few variables from U.S. Census data could predict surprisingly well the slow adoption of racial desegregation over time across southern counties within states—namely, a negative predictor (the African American percentage of the county's population) and two positive predictors (the county's economic prosperity and the percentage of White women in the county's labor force—a reverse measure of traditionalism). I proudly showed the analysis to Allport. He was singularly unimpressed. "But how about the brave mayor and the wise judge in bringing about racial change?" he asked. I argued that such mayors and judges were far more likely to be located in the optimal ecological counties. Allport remained unconvinced; causation for him basically emanated from individuals.

The Nature of Prejudice inspired and shaped the study of prejudice in social psychology for decades. At the personality level of analysis, the book's principal contentions have been supported astonishingly well, as shown in the review volume celebrating the 50th anniversary of the publication of Allport's work (Dovidio et al., 2005). Chapter by chapter, the chapters' authors reviewed Allport's contentions in every part of his classic work. Repeatedly, they found that Allport's claims had been largely supported as well as advanced further by the research of the intervening 5 decades.

More recent research on prejudice, however, has pushed the boundaries of our understanding of prejudice to a greater extent. In particular, the past 2 decades have witnessed further advances on all three of our major levels of analysis—micro, meso, and macro. Actually, these multilevel advances suggest that we should now consider *prejudice as a multilevel syndrome.* I follow up on this possibility in Chapter 9 of this volume.

MICROLEVEL ADVANCES IN UNDERSTANDING INTERGROUP PREJUDICE

By far, the greatest amount of research on intergroup prejudice has focused exclusively on predicting prejudice among individuals. And this has led to a great expansion of predictors of varying depth.

Distinctive Types of Prejudice

Over the years, different types of prejudice that vary in their depth within the bigot's personality have been proposed. This expansion is one of the major changes in the study of intergroup prejudice since Allport's classic volume appeared.

When social psychology began studying prejudice, primary attention was focused upon blatant, traditional forms of the phenomenon. At that time, such open expressions of bigotry were more normatively accepted both in Europe and North America. The major advance on blatant forms of prejudice has involved the concept of *dehumanization*.

Leyens and his Belgian colleagues (2000) experimentally demonstrated the phenomenon with the differential attribution of emotions to outgroups and ingroups. Racists view their ingroup as more "human" than outgroups. This research distinguished "primary emotions" (e.g., joy, guilt) from "secondary emotions" (e.g., hostility, jealousy). Primary emotions are instinctive responses. Thus, if threatened, we feel fear. Secondary emotions are experienced in response to other emotions. Primary emotions are shared with animals, but secondary emotions are thought to be uniquely "human." This research shows how these particularly human emotions are less often ascribed to outgroups than to ingroups.

There are two types of dehumanization (Haslam, 2006). *Animalistic* dehumanization denies the rejected outgroup human attributes, whereas *mechanistic* dehumanization simply views the outgroup as mere objects. Among racists, dehumanization becomes an everyday social phenomenon rooted in ordinary cognitive processes. This explains how Southern slaveholders could sell off faithful Black servants without regret (Dew, 2016; Pettigrew, 2017a).

Harris and Fiske (2006) went further, to show differential neuroimaging responses to extreme outgroups. Using the stereotype content model (S. T. Fiske et al., 2002), the low-competence, low-warmth type (e.g., drug addicts) is especially disparaged. The disgust elicited by this type of outgroup activates the left insula (related to disgust), as well as the amygdala (related to fear). This outgroup category is most likely to endure dehumanization (see also Nier et al., 2013).

By 1970, however, more subtle forms of prejudice were uncovered internationally and variously labeled. In France, it has been called "under-the-skin racism" (Freriks, 1990); in Germany, "latent" prejudice (Bergmann & Erb, 1986); in the United Kingdom, "the new racism" (Barker, 1984); in the Netherlands, "everyday racism" (Essed, 1984); in Western Europe generally, "subtle prejudice" (Pettigrew & Meertens, 1995); and in the United States, "aversive racism" (Dovidio & Gaertner, 1986; Gaertner & Dovidio, 1986; Kovel, 1970), "symbolic racism" (Sears, 1988), or "modern racism" (McConahay, 1983; Pettigrew, 1989).[1]

The common theme across all these forms is that they are covert means of expressing outgroup prejudice that are far less direct than the old-fashioned forms. Otherwise quite diverse conceptualizations emerged. Thus, Essed (1984) emphasized the commonplace quality of the phenomenon, Kovel (1970) viewed it as a defense against recognizing one's own bigotry, Gaertner and Dovidio (1986) regarded it as a means to avoid contact with outgroups, McConahay (1983) saw it as an attempt to attribute outgroup disadvantage to causes other than discrimination, and Sears (1988) traced it to early socialization. All these claims have some degree of empirical support.

Yet a broader conceptualization with a psychometrically adequate measure that could be used across cultures was needed. My Dutch colleague—Professor Roel Meertens at the University of Amsterdam—and I attempted to meet this need using data from the European Community's Euro-Barometer Survey No. 30, collected in 1988 from Great Britain, the Netherlands, France, and West Germany (the wall with East Germany had not yet come down; Meertens & Pettigrew, 1997; Pettigrew & Meertens, 1992, 1995, 2001; Reif & Melich, 1991). We constructed two 10-item scales in four languages to measure both blatant and subtle prejudice for the 3,800 respondents. Both scales proved reliable and similarly correlated with predictor variables in all seven of the samples across the four nations. Thus, both the Blatant and Subtle Prejudice Scales correlated positively with measures of ethnocentrism, approval of racist movements, political conservatism, group relative deprivation, and age and correlated negatively with education, interest in politics, and intergroup friends.

Blatant prejudice was defined as the traditional type of outgroup prejudice—hot, close, and direct. Two subscales emerged: (a) perceived threat from and rejection of the outgroup and (b) opposition to close contact with the outgroup. Sample items are "West Indians have jobs that the British should have" and "I would not mind if a suitably qualified West Indian person was appointed as my boss" (reverse item).

[1] Many social psychological studies show that subtle prejudice is matched by equally subtle interracial behavior. Whether Whites help Blacks behaviorally depends heavily on the *social context*. Compared with helping Whites in the same situations, Whites discriminate more against Blacks when helping is more time-consuming, riskier, more difficult, or in more effortful situations and when they are farther away from the Blacks in need of help (Saucier et al., 2005).

Subtle prejudice is the newer form—cool, distant, and indirect. Three subscales emerged: (a) defense of traditional values, (b) exaggeration of cultural differences, and (c) the denial of positive emotions. Sample items are "West Indians living here teach their children values and skills different from those required to be successful in Britain," "West Indians living here are very different in their religious beliefs and practices from other British people like yourself," and ". . . never have felt sympathy (or admiration) for West Indians living here."

These last items—lacking sympathy or admiration for the outgroup—proved especially diagnostic. Subtle prejudice, unlike blatant prejudice, does not emphasize negative emotions, such as outgroup hatred, so much as it does a withdrawal of positive emotions. The blatant–subtle prejudice distinction is confirmed not only throughout Europe and the United States but also in Argentina using the same scales to tap attitudes toward that nation's indigenous people (Ungaretti et al., 2018) and in Chile to tap attitudes toward immigrants (Vargas-Salfate et al., 2020).

Moreover, the subtle prejudice phenomenon coincides with other extensive survey and laboratory experimentation. Abelson et al. (1982), using data from American surveys, found that positive and negative feelings toward politicians were almost independent of each other. Moreover, they found these affect reports to be less semantically filtered and less subject to consistency pressures than trait judgments. These findings suggest that reports on feelings, such as the lack of admiration and sympathy, can more easily act as covert indicators of subtle prejudice.

Other laboratory studies, using White American college subjects, found no differences in the ratings of Black and White on such negative attributes as "lazy" (Dovidio et al., 1989; Gaertner & McLaughlin, 1983). But they found systematic biases favoring Whites on such positive attributes as "ambitious."[2] Seemingly, for these students, "Blacks are not worse, but Whites are better" (Dovidio et al., 1989, p. 88). Note the role of norms here. Negative racial stereotypes on American college campuses are now commonly frowned upon; the absence of positive stereotypes, however, is generally not covered by modern norms.

Other research employing different methods supports this finding. Bergsieker and her colleagues (Bergsieker et al., 2012) repeated for the

[2] These results cannot be explained by self-presentation—that somehow these college subjects consciously withheld their racial biases for the negative traits. Gaertner and McLaughlin (1983, Studies 1 and 2) carefully employed a highly indirect measure of bias using reaction times.

fourth time a study of group stereotypes held by Princeton University students. The first studies had been carried out at Princeton in 1932 (Katz & Braly, 1933), 1950 (G. M. Gilbert, 1951), and 1967 (Karlins et al., 1969). By the 21st century, norms and the student body of Princeton had changed sharply.[3] And the 84 adjectives to be assigned to the 10 groups that "seemed typical" changed too. Negative stereotypes had declined markedly, whereas neutral and positive stereotypes remained relatively constant. In addition, the researchers showed that this reduction in negative stereotypes was driven by self-presentation concerns. The researchers called this phenomenon "stereotyping by omission."

How the Subtly Prejudiced Differ in Attitudes Toward Remedies

The most important result of the analysis of the blatant and subtle prejudice scales in Europe emerged when the respondents were asked about remedies for discrimination (Meertens & Pettigrew, 1997; Pettigrew & Meertens, 1992, 1995, 2001). Three types were formed by splitting the blatant and subtle prejudice scale scores at their logical midpoints: The *egalitarians* were low scorers on both scales, the *subtles* were low on the blatant but high on the subtle scales, and the *bigots* were high on both scales.[4]

When asked about improving the rights of minorities in their country, statistically significant results were found in all samples of the four nations. As expected, the egalitarians were disproportionately in favor of extending rights, and the bigots were disproportionately in favor of restricting the rights of minorities further. The subtles assumed a straddling, ostensibly non-prejudicial position. More than either the egalitarians or bigots, they simply wanted the issue to remain as it is.

When asked about immigration policy, bigots again took the extreme position: Send all immigrants back to where they came from, or send back those immigrants who were not born in the country or not contributing to the economy. Only egalitarians in any number rejected sending all the immigrants back to their native countries. The subtles required some justification for exclusionary policies. Overwhelmingly, they favored sending back immigrants if they had committed serious crimes or did not have their proper immigration papers.

---

[3] Earlier, Princeton was all-White male and drew much of its student body from the southern United States.

[4] Less than 2% of the 3,800 respondents fell into the fourth "error" category—low on the subtle measure but high on the blatant measure.

Finally, egalitarians favored prosecuting racists in the courts and making naturalization easier, whereas bigots strongly opposed such remedies. Once again, the subtles straddled the divide. They tended to oppose such strong measures and favor instead "soft remedies" that do not directly involve them, such as promoting tolerance in the schools and expanding international exchange programs for young people.

More recent research has investigated subtle forms of prejudice from several perspectives. There is general agreement that these forms tend to be ambiguous, automatic, and ambivalent. The relative rise of subtle forms of prejudice and the concurrent decline in blatant prejudice throughout Western Europe and North America during the late 20th century reflected the microlevel effects of such macrolevel and mesolevel changes as affirmative action in employment, school desegregation, and greater contact between majority and minority groups. But, as I discuss in Chapter 8 of this volume, regarding right-wing voting, the upsurge of racist nationalism at the macrolevel context has made blatant forms of prejudice more normatively acceptable again in both Europe and North America. Far-right leaders openly model the blatant forms of racism and prejudice that had been declining for decades.

The Implicit Association Test

Digging even deeper than Likert-scale measures of subtle prejudice can go, the Implicit Association Test (IAT) has received considerable attention as well as controversy since its introduction in 1998 by Greenwald et al. (1998). Widely used in social psychology, the IAT has also spawned extensive applications in clinical, cognitive, and developmental psychology. And beyond psychology, the technique is now commonly employed in business, law, criminal justice, medicine, education, and political science (Greenwald & Lai, 2020).

The IAT grew out of an earlier paper by Greenwald and Banaji (1995) that held that the well-established differentiation of explicit and implicit memory should also apply to social constructs. The IAT requires subjects using a computer to classify exemplars of two concept categories (e.g., flowers and insects) and two attributed categories (pleasant and unpleasant), each represented by words or pictures. When the same key must be used to identify two associated categories (flowers and pleasant), the response is faster than when the two categories are not associated (e.g., insects and pleasant). The difference in speed between the "combined task" pairings serves to measure the strength of the associations of the concepts to the attributes.

The idea underlying the IAT is that traces of past experience will mediate the positive or negative feeling, thought, or action toward the social objects (e.g., race, gender). The reader is encouraged to take the test to appreciate fully how it operates. The IAT is available at https://implicit.harvard.edu/implicit/takeatest.html.

Many IAT forms now exist for various social categories—race, gender, obesity, suicide risk, political preferences, and so on. The test's popularity derives from the promise that the IAT can avoid the social-desirability bias that bedevils widely used explicit measures of attitudes, particularly those involving attitudes toward stigmatized groups. Consequently, the IAT has become the dominant measure of implicit attitudes.

Critics of the method challenge just what the IAT actually measures, its reproducibility, and other concerns. Some argue that it is merely measuring familiarity, cultural knowledge, or attribute salience independent of any personal preferences or attitudes. Some of these criticisms, such as the measurement of cultural knowledge and attribute salience, could be quite valid yet still not disrupt the focus of the IAT assessment. Numerous misreadings of the IAT and popular claims by nonpsychologists have also led to specious criticisms. For the reader who wishes to better understand the debate between those who defend and those who attack the method, Jost (2019a) provides a good starting point. An attempt to combine the criticisms of implicit bias measures with the available evidence has been provided by Gawronski (2019).

How well does the IAT predict prejudice? The results of an initial study of internet-administered attitude and stereotype measures with more than 2.5 million subjects were promising (Nosek et al., 2007). The study uncovered a marked difference between the IAT and parallel self-report measures. The IAT scores tended to be more extreme, and they revealed a much larger degree of White preference than the explicit scores.

Later, three meta-analyses attempted to answer our question. The first meta-analysis reviewed 122 research reports boasting 184 samples with 14,900 subjects. Here we report the meta-analytic estimates of the positive correlations between the IAT or self-report measures predicting various criterion measures. This first study found an IAT average of +.27 for all types of psychological measures (Greenwald et al., 2009). This compared with +.36 in 156 of these samples for self-report measures. More to the point, for the 32 samples involving just Black–White interracial behavior, the IAT significantly outperformed the self-report measures—+.24 to +.12—when compared against criterion measures of intergroup behavior. In other words, as predicted, the IAT measure did better than the usual type of self-report measure when attitudes of a stigmatized group are involved.

When both the IAT and self-report measures are used, the two measures together rendered the strongest prediction of all. The more highly IAT and self-report measures were intercorrelated, the greater was the predictive validity of each. For all samples, the two types of measures correlated +.214; for just the 30 samples testing racial attitudes, they correlated less (+.114).

Four years later, another meta-analysis conducted by critics of the test came to different conclusions (Oswald et al., 2013). It used 46 studies with 86 samples measuring implicit and explicit interracial and interethnic bias. The authors concluded that IATs were generally poor predictors and at their best did not outperform such explicit measures as the Modern Racism Scale. In a later article, the same authors became more adamant in their judgment (Oswald et al., 2015): "IAT scores are not good predictors of ethnic prejudice or racial discrimination, and explain, at most, small fractions of the variance in discriminatory behavior in controlled laboratory settings" (p. 562).

Why the difference in results between the first two meta-analyses? The major reason is that the second meta-analysis employed a smaller and somewhat different sampling of studies to test. What you put into a meta-analysis obviously determines what you get out of it. The Oswald study was the smallest of the three studies and the most selective of studies to be included.

The third meta-analysis 6 years later improved on the earlier attempts in several ways (Kurdi et al., 2019). With 36,999 subjects from 217 research reports, it is far larger and more inclusive than the previous analyses. Moreover, it employed structural equation modeling. The structural equation models revealed modest but significant unique contributions of both implicit and explicit measures. But the IAT data varied sharply as a function of purely methodological factors. Thus, using standard IATs rather than variant measures, two categories under test rather than just one, and other stronger methodological features raised the IAT's relationships with criterion measures of intergroup behavior. When all the meta-analyses are considered, a summary conclusion can be broached (Greenwald & Lai, 2020, p. 25–13): Both implicit–explicit and implicit–criterion correlations are consistently moderate to small and are lower when the target is socially sensitive (as with race).

We conclude that the IAT offers an additional measure of prejudice (and many other phenomena) to social psychology's methodological arsenal. For example, IAT measures revealed special liking of ingroup members who are comfortable with intergroup interaction—a subtle finding best uncovered with an implicit test (Jacoby-Senghor et al., 2019). Throughout the book, other IAT studies are reviewed.

Authoritarianism

When Allport wrote his volume in the early 1950s, the principal micro-theory of prejudice was authoritarianism as advanced by Adorno et al. (1950). Allport himself had published earlier research on the phenomenon (Allport & Kramer, 1946). He devised an item that later proved to be at the central core of authoritarianism: "The world is a hazardous place in which men are basically evil and dangerous" (Allport, 1954, p. 407).

Few relationships in social science are as stable and virtually universal as the link between authoritarianism and outgroup prejudice. This is not to claim that the relationship is invariant. Social contexts, as usual, make a difference. As I review, situational and normative variables can substantially moderate the link (Pettigrew, 1958b, 1959; Reynolds et al., 2001; Sales, 1973).

The authoritarian personality is a psychological pattern of traits that correlates so highly and consistently with outgroup prejudice that the sweeping claim can be made that, to my knowledge, no study yet has failed to find a positive relationship between the two variables. This holds true even for the many varieties of prejudice just mentioned. For example, Rattazzi et al. (2007) found that even their short Italian scale measure of authoritarianism correlated highly with both the blatant and subtle forms of prejudice (Pettigrew & Meertens, 1996).

Authoritarianism was initially measured by a Likert scale—called the *F-Scale* for fascism—that inspired massive attention (Adorno et al., 1950). The problem was that it seemed at first to correlate with everything![5] I published a scale to measure Jerome Bruner's concept of category width, and tongue-in-cheek I boasted that it was the rare measure that did *not* correlate with the F-Scale (Pettigrew, 1958a). The situation recalled St. Augustine's frustration with the complex concept of time: "Oh, God, I can measure it, but what it is that I measure I do not know!"

Nazi Germany inspired the first conceptualizations. Hitler's vote was concentrated among the lower middle class, not the poorest of German voters (King et al., 2008). The Frankfurt School, combining Marxism, psychoanalysis, and sociology, introduced the concept to explain the special popularity of Hitler among working-class Germans. An early formulation appeared in Erich Fromm's (1941) *Escape from Freedom*.

[5] Now we know why the old F-Scale was such a catch-all instrument. Its items included what we would now consider both authoritarian and social dominance scale items.

American social psychologists soon demonstrated the phenomenon in the United States. In 1950, the major publication *The Authoritarian Personality* appeared. The product of two European refugees (Theodor Adorno and Else Frenkel-Brunswik) and two American social psychologists (Daniel Levinson and Nevitt Sanford) at the Berkeley campus of the University of California, this publication firmly established the concept throughout the social sciences, especially in political science as well as in social and personality psychology. The volume offered both clinical and questionnaire evidence. But it was the easily administered F-Scale that led to an explosion of more than 2,000 research papers on authoritarianism during the 1950s.

Critics immediately disparaged the work on political, methodological, and theoretical grounds (e.g., Christie & Jahoda, 1954). Right-wing detractors questioned the finding that political conservatives averaged higher scores on the F-Scale. They argued that there was widespread authoritarianism on the left as well. To be sure, all the Berkeley investigators were politically liberal, and the personality type does indeed exist on the political left. But later research has repeatedly shown that authoritarianism is preponderantly found among those on the political right throughout the world. Indeed, a modern measure is simply called the Right-Wing Authoritarianism (RWA) Scale (Altemeyer, 1981, 1988, 1996).

Methodologists unearthed a host of problems (Christie & Jahoda, 1954). For example, the clinical evaluators were not blind to the F-Scale scores of their interviewees. Consequently, their assessments were not independently derived. No probability samples of respondents were tested, only unrepresentative samples of convenience (usually college students). The F-Scale itself has problems. All the items are worded positively so that agreement indicates authoritarian tendencies. This allows response sets to invalidate some scores, because some respondents just agree or disagree with all the items regardless of the item content—the so-called yea-sayers and nay-sayers.

The Authoritarian Personality also provoked theoretical criticism. Its Freudian foundation is difficult to test directly. Many objected to its nominalist approach—the use of extreme categories with the highest fourth of F-Scale scores labeled "authoritarians" and the lowest fourth labeled "equalitarians." But the F-Scale did not yield a unidimensional version of authoritarianism. The Berkeley coauthors virtually ignored the middle half of their subject distribution, and later work rarely found the middle two quartiles to fall in the center of other correlates to form a linear relationship.

From the perspective of this book, the most important theoretical objection concerned the 1950 study's nearly total neglect of the social context. For instance, *The Authoritarian Personality* (pp. 130, 171, 267) recorded its highest F-Scale average in an infamously harsh California state prison without considering the authoritarian context in which the inmates were taking the measure. For these imprisoned respondents, some of the items were literally true—for example, "Most people don't realize how much our lives are controlled by plots hatched in secret places" (Adorno et al., 1950, p. 257).

Many of these criticisms have merit. Nonetheless, research throughout the world with a variety of measures shows that authoritarians reveal similar traits (Duckitt & Sibley, 2007; Sanford, 1973; Strong et al., 1992). In particular, high scorers are more likely than others to exhibit prejudice against outgroups and to favor extreme right-wing politics, as Chapter 8 in this volume reveals.

Interest in authoritarianism waned during the 1960s and 1970s in the midst of the cognitive revolution in psychology. But throughout these decades I continued to include a measure of authoritarianism when studying prejudice of all types in the United States, South Africa, and Western Europe. And it never failed to be a major predictor of prejudice at the individual level of analysis. Conformity to prejudiced norms, my original focus, offers an microlevel explanation for why some areas—such as the southern United States and South Africa—have extremely high levels of intergroup prejudice. Authoritarianism offers a microlevel explanation for prejudice throughout the world.

Finally, in the 1980s, Altemeyer (1981, 1988, 1996) renewed attention to authoritarianism. He simplified the domain by concentrating on three personality traits in particular: *deference to authorities*, *aggression toward outgroups*, and *rigid adherence to cultural conventions*.[6] Thus, authoritarians hold a rigidly hierarchical view of the world. Altemeyer's RWA Scale focused on these three traits and offered a somewhat better measure than the old F-Scale even though it reused some of the old F-Scale items. But, like the F-Scale, it also fails to yield a unidimensional measure of authoritarianism.

In the years since the introduction of the RWA, a number of shorter versions of the scale have been published in German, Italian, and Spanish, as well as English (e.g., Ávila-Batista et al., 2019; Beierlein et al., 2015;

[6] Of these three components, the aggression component correlates the strongest with support for antidemocratic policies that target outgroups (Dunwoody & Plane, 2019). This same component of authoritarianism also best predicted Trump support in the 2016 presidential election (Womick et al., 2019).

Dunwoody & Funke, 2016; Rattazzi et al., 2007). The Very Short Authoritarianism scale by Bizumic and Duckitt[7] (2018) is especially promising, as its balanced six items correlate strongly with the full RWA measure (+.86). For a review of the various short scales of authoritarianism, see Bizumic and Duckitt (2018).

Additional Issues

Despite its many conceptual and methodological problems, authoritarianism has proven to be a durable and indestructible theory. But several central issues remain. First, the original F-Scale and later RWA Scale contain blatantly political content. Does this not confound the results with political conservatism as critics claim? Second, how does authoritarianism develop? And how does it relate to other established personality syndromes? Third, what is the role of affect in authoritarianism? Many studies emphasize the importance of fear, threat, and anxiety. Finally, why is authoritarianism so universal in its strong predictions of prejudices of many varieties in culturally diverse nations around the globe? Let's review work that sheds light on each of these concerns.

Political Confounding

Given the overlap of the F-Scale and RWA Scale with political conservatism, critics justifiably challenge the finding that authoritarianism routinely correlates highly and positively with conservatism. Purely personality measures of authoritarianism are needed to complement these political attitude assessments. This would eliminate the political content of the RWA scale and address the debate between those who view authoritarianism as a personality syndrome and others who view it as a political ideology.

Yet there is no necessary conflict between these two perspectives. Authoritarianism begins early in life as a personality orientation that later typically leads to a particular type of political ideology. Moreover, just because situational and societal contexts influence authoritarianism, this does not mean

[7] I regard John Duckitt, a leader in the social psychological study of prejudice and authoritarianism, a true kindred spirit. He was born in South Africa in 1940 and did not immigrate to New Zealand until 1995. He not only lived through the worst racist years of Afrikaner nationalism but also grew up as a rare minority English South African in a predominantly Afrikaner nationalist area of the Western Cape. Little wonder that Duckitt became interested in prejudice, racism, and authoritarianism. Like myself, he experienced them all up close and personal in early life.

it cannot be considered a personality variable. Other prominent personality syndromes are also contextually sensitive.

The elimination of political content would clarify this debate. Duckitt and Sibley (2010, pp. 1864–1866) made a strong case for treating the factor as an ideological trait. But their supporting evidence uses only Altemeyer's RWA Scale, which, like the old F-Scale, is infused with political content. The use of purely personality measures that relate to prejudice just as strongly as RWA could settle this argument. At this point, I believe it best to think of authoritarianism as it was originally advanced—a personality trait. But it can easily become an ideological trait when measured with politically charged content.

Oesterreich's (2005) authoritarianism measure addresses these issues. By using directly opposed statements (e.g., "I like changes" vs. "I don't like changes") as options from which to choose, Oesterreich balanced his scale. Yet Oesterreich's authoritarianism measure has been rarely used, and its relationship with the RWA is not known. What is known is consistent with the findings of other measures of authoritarianism. Thus, it significantly relates to right-wing extremism and prejudice against both immigrants and women. It also correlates with the Big Five personality factors just as the RWA Scale does (Oesterreich, 2005).

The 23-item scale attained an .84 alpha with a large representative sample of German voters. These items cover a range of the personality characteristics shown previously to be often found among authoritarians—insecurity ("I feel uncomfortable in new and unfamiliar situations"), conformity and submission ("I have no problems following orders, even when I am not convinced of their necessity"), a focus on strength and weakness ("I admire dominant people"), a need for closure ("I am irritated by people who call well-established things into question"), and resistance to new experience ("I don't like to be confronted with new ideas"). Clearly, this purely personality measure deserves more research attention.

Political scientists have also taken an interest in authoritarianism. And they introduced another measure of the variable that also avoids political confounding. This scale asks about what respondents think is more important for children—respect for elders more important than independence, obedience more important than self-reliance, to be well behaved more important than being creative, and to have good manners more important than to be curious (Feldman, 2017; Feldman & Stenner, 1997). The first choice for each of these questions taps authoritarianism. But, unfortunately, this scale lacks strong psychometric properties. It correlates with RWA at only +.64, and its few items do not form a single dimension (Bizumic & Duckitt, 2018).

Altemeyer and other social psychologists prefer items that hark back to such old F-Scale-like Likert items as "The authorities should be obeyed because they are in the best position to know what is good for our country" and "Obedience and respect for authority are the most important virtues children should learn." Note how the RWA and Oesterreich's measure overlap in their attention to basic values. It is methodologically useful and important to have quite different measures of authoritarianism that intercorrelate highly and relate to other variables in similar ways.

Early Development of Authoritarianism

Twin studies have repeatedly revealed some degree of heritability in authoritarianism (Lewis & Bates, 2014; Ludeke et al., 2013; Ludeke & Krueger, 2013; McCourt et al., 1999). This finding is consistent with similar findings of a genetic base for such related variables as ingroup favoritism (Lewis & Bates, 2014), Social Dominance Orientation (SDO; Stössel et al., 2006), political conservatism (Alford et al., 2005; Lewis & Bates, 2014), and obedience to traditional authority (Ludeke et al., 2013).

These genetic findings may surprise you, but they are consistent with similar twin studies conducted on a wide range of psychological processes.[8] Yet the century-old technique of contrasting dizygotic (DZ—nonidentical fraternal) twins with monozygotic (MZ—nearly identical) twins has its problems and is not without its severe critics (e.g., Joseph, 2013; Schönemann, 1997).

The leading contentious issue involves the method's necessary assumption of "equal environments"—namely, that both types of twins share equally identical environments. This assumption is invalid so much as MZ identicals tend to experience somewhat more similar environments than DZ nonidenticals. Critics such as Joseph thus claim that the entire method is therefore seriously flawed and not to be trusted. Certainly, the estimates of heritability are likely to be somewhat inflated and both the environmental and Genetic × Environmental interaction terms likely to be seriously underestimated. Supporting this conclusion, estimates of heritability using molecular-level data are generally considerably lower than the corresponding estimates from twin studies (Felson, 2014).

Nonetheless, it seems likely that there is at least a small genetic factor in authoritarianism and similar phenomena—not as much as sometimes claimed, but a definite factor. I conclude this for four reasons. First, there is strong evidence that political attitudes close to authoritarianism vary with

[8] Physical characteristics—height, weight, and so on—tend to yield the largest heritability estimates followed by psychological characteristics.

physiological traits. Individuals with measurably higher physical sensitivities to sudden noises and threatening visual images are more likely to favor such right-wing causes as defense spending, capital punishment, patriotism, and the Iraq War. Individuals with lower physical sensitivities favor such left-wing causes as pacifism, foreign aid, and gun control (Oxley et al., 2008).

Second, some work suggests that violation of the equal environments assumption does not cause as large an effect as critics have claimed (Felson, 2014). Third, it is impressive that so many twin studies have shown similar heritable effects for so many diverse variables that are all part of what I label a *prejudice syndrome* (see Chapter 9, this volume). For example, a strong negative Big Five correlate of authoritarianism—Openness to Experience—appears to have a strong genetic component. Indeed, it is by far the strongest genetic relationship of the Big Five personality traits (Power & Pluess, 2015). Finally, other work using different methods supports this more modest view. Fraley et al. (2012) noted that temperament ratings of 1-month-old children and their parents' authoritarianism predicted conservatism 17 years later. Altemeyer (1996) also reported strong correlations between the authoritarianism levels of young adults and their parents—most easily explained by both genetic and environmental factors.[9]

But what about the relationships between authoritarianism and other established personality features that could shed light on the early development of authoritarianism? The fact that security issues are critical for authoritarians suggests that there may be important links between authoritarianism and attachment theory. Indeed, numerous investigators have noted this possibility, and its potential importance deserves emphasis.

Hopf (1992) drew explicit links with dismissive-avoidant attachment. Although *The Authoritarian Personality* volume stressed displacement of hostility from a stern father, Hopf noted that seven of the 20 men classified as authoritarian by Frenkel-Brunswik had experienced the death of their *mothers* as young children compared with none of the nonauthoritarians ($\chi^2 = 8.5$, $p <. 01$). In contrast to *The Authoritarian Personality*, Ackerman and Jahoda (1950) emphasized parental rejection and found rejection by one or both parents to be a common experience among their sample of anti-Semites. Hopf (1993) studied 25 lower status German adolescents and determined that those who were high on dismissive-avoidant attachment also articulated the most extreme authoritarian views.

[9] In addition, Bagci and Gungor (2019) demonstrated with Turkish data that parental modeling of intergroup contact directly shapes adolescents' intergroup contact behavior.

Van IJzendoorn (1997) gave a sample of American university students the Adult Attachment Scale and the RWA. Like Hopf, he found that students scoring high on dismissive-avoidant attachment also scored highest on authoritarianism, whereas those scoring high on the secure and anxious attachment dimensions scored lowest on authoritarianism.[10] Other research has also found secure attachment linked with low prejudice (Boag & Carnelley, 2016). In addition, college student avoidants are often seen by their peers as both more hostile and more anxious (Kobak & Sceery, 1988).

Avoidant attachment orientation is one of three delineated by Ainsworth et al. (1978): secure, anxious, and avoidant (see also Mikulincer & Shaver, 2007). These attachment "styles" are best thought of as continuous and interrelated dimensions rather than as exclusive "types" (Fraley & Waller, 1998). In broad strokes, secure individuals neither avoid nor are especially anxious about close relationships. Anxious individuals typically seek close relationships with others but are highly anxious about them. Dismissive-avoidants attempt to avoid close relationships, but they are not especially anxious or fearful about them (Bartholomew, 1990). Prototype items for each style include *secure*—"It is easy for me to become emotionally close to others"; *anxious*—"I worry a lot about my relationships"; and *avoidant*—"I find it difficult to trust others completely."

According to attachment theory, avoidants have suffered a serious loss of or rejection by a primary caregiver in early life. Children respond to this loss in two general ways: Some wish to achieve intimacy but are anxious about another rejection, whereas the avoidants attempt to deactivate their attachment concerns and deny the issue altogether. Both types are distressed, but they handle their discomfort in contrasting ways (Crowell et al., 1999).

Authoritarians will often be deniers—the dismissive-avoidant style. Descriptions of this style often read as if they were direct quotations from *The Authoritarian Personality* volume of 1950. Dismissive-avoidant adults idealize their parents but cannot provide clear, episodic memories to support their unrealistically glowing assessment (Main et al., 1985)—precisely the same description provided by the Berkeley investigators three generations earlier. The "perfect parent" recall of dismissive-avoidants, termed *defensive idealization*, has often been uncovered in research with various measures (Mikulincer & Shaver, 2007).

[10] C. Weber and Federico (2007) reported a rare exception. With an undergraduate convenience sample, they found avoidant attachment associated with SDO but not RWA. Anxious attachment related to RWA in their results. See also Roccato (2008).

Cross-cultural research results are consistent with the link between avoidant attachment and authoritarianism. In India, a study of 400 Muslim teenagers found that parental rejection correlated positively with both authoritarianism and prejudice (Hassan, 1987). In Italy, members of an extreme right-wing political party scored high on measures of authoritarianism, SDO, and avoidant attachment and low on secure attachment (Roccato & Ricolfi, 2005). In Germany, Oesterreich's (2005) authoritarian scale used three items that directly tap dismissive-avoidant attachment: "I don't like to meet new people," "I try to avoid contact with people who are different," and "I feel uncomfortable with people I do not know."

More detailed and longitudinal work on this promising link between authoritarianism and attachment theory is clearly indicated.

The Role of Affect in Authoritarianism

From intolerance of ambiguity to the need for closure, early research on authoritarianism stressed cognitive factors to the neglect of affective factors. This inattention represents a serious omission when one considers how critical emotional factors have been shown to underlie prejudice and intergroup contact effects (Pettigrew, 1997a; Pettigrew & Tropp, 2011; Tropp & Pettigrew, 2004). Indeed, Eliot Smith (1993) defined prejudice as "a social emotion experienced with respect to one's social identity as a group member, with an outgroup as a target."

Threat is typically intertwined with authoritarianism (Dallago & Roccato, 2008; Duckitt & Fisher, 2003; W. G. Stephan et al., 2009). An analysis of a 2004 probability sample of 1,153 German citizens uncovered the links between authoritarianism and two types of threat in predicting anti-Muslim prejudice (Heitmeyer, 2005; Pettigrew & Tropp, 2011). *Individual threat* is measured by four items emphasizing personal feelings: "Foreigners living here threaten *my* personal freedom and rights . . . *my* personal economic situation . . . *my* personal way of life . . . and *my* personal security." Hence, "they" are threatening "*me*."

Collective threat involves the ingroup: "Foreigners living here threaten *our* freedom and rights . . . *our* prosperity . . . *our* culture . . . and *our* security"; in other words, "they" are threatening "*us*." Figure 5.1 illustrates how these threat factors mediate most of the association between authoritarianism and anti-Muslim prejudice in Germany. Although authoritarianism is strongly and positively related to both types of threat, it is the perception of collective threat that is most highly associated with prejudice. Moreover, the effect of individual threat is almost entirely mediated by collective threat.

FIGURE 5.1. Major Predictors of Prejudice

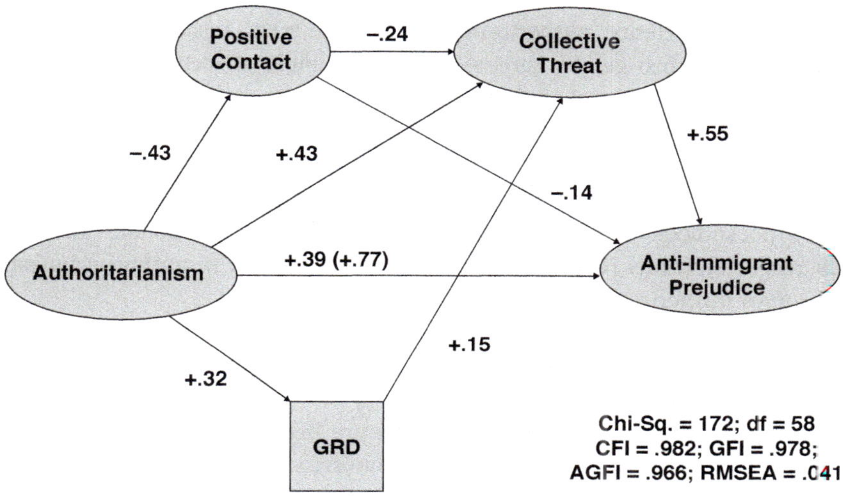

Based on data from the 2004 GRE German probability survey in Heitmeyer (2005).

Figure 5.1's path analysis shows how critical collective threat is in the link between authoritarianism and anti-immigrant prejudice in Germany. Not only is it a major factor in itself, but it also importantly mediates the effects of positive contact (the focus of Chapter 7, this volume) and group relative deprivation (GRD; the focus of Chapter 6, this volume).[11]

That collective, rather than individual, threat drives much of the association between authoritarianism and prejudice is consistent with the emphasis on group identification of both Duckitt (1989) and Stellmacher and Petzel (2005). It is also in line with the findings showing that authoritarianism is strongly influenced by societal-level threat factors (Bianchi et al., 2018; Doty et al., 1991; McCann, 2008; Pettigrew, 1959; Reynolds et al., 2001; Sales, 1973).

Threat also influences gender differences in authoritarianism. In some societies, women are more authoritarian than men; in other societies, men are more authoritarian. Brandt and Henry (2012) used multilevel techniques with data from 54 societies to demonstrate that those societies in which

[11] This particular German data set shows only a weak and indirect effect of GRD on prejudice. But in Chapters 6 and 8 of this volume, I note that GRD often plays a major role in prejudice and right-wing voting in other data sets.

women are particularly authoritarian on average tend to be individualistic cultures with high levels of gender inequality; Morocco, Iran, and Turkey are examples. Hence, authoritarianism in these areas acts as psychological protection against gender threat—another example of Path F in Figure 2.1 uncovered by multilevel analysis.

Fear is also involved. French data reveal that fear predicts far-right political support, and this relationship is mediated by both anger and authoritarianism (Jost, 2019b).[12] Research in France, Germany, and the United States found that "pocketbook anger" was often effectively aroused by nationalist rhetoric in recent elections (P. Marx, 2020). The role of affect in authoritarianism deserves further research attention.

How Does Authoritarianism Influence Such Prejudice-Reducing Remedies as Intergroup Contact?

Many people assume that authoritarians are highly resistant to efforts to reduce prejudice. But consider authoritarianism in the context of intergroup contact. Hodgson and colleagues (Hodson et al., 2009) and others (Dhont & Van Hiel, 2009; Graf & Sczesny, 2019; Pettigrew & Tropp, 2011) have shown that intergroup contact has the potential to significantly reduce prejudice even among high-scoring authoritarians and far-right-wing adherents. This may seem surprising; in fact, it overturns the contrary view of *The Authoritarian Personality* (Adorno et al., 1950, p. 973). But this link fits with an array of findings showing that intergroup contact has the potential to alter numerous factors closely related to authoritarianism and is part of the broad prejudice syndrome discussed in Chapter 9 of this volume.

In *The Nature of Prejudice*, Allport (1954, p. 279) viewed authoritarianism as a barrier to diminishing prejudice with intergroup contact. This conclusion was based on a single study, for Allport had a narrow research base on which to rely in the mid-20th century. Mussen (1950) studied the racial attitudes of White boys at an interracial camp. He found that boys with equalitarian-like traits evinced diminished racial prejudice after their interracial experience, whereas those with authoritarian-like traits had become *more* prejudiced. But this early finding may not be the exception it appears. Mussen did not have direct measures of authoritarianism and contact. Thus,

[12] Although threat typically increases support for right-wing political positions, there are some areas in which threat can stimulate enhanced political liberalism. When Eadeh and Chang (2020) threatened their experimental subjects on three liberal issues—health care access, environmental pollution, and corporate misconduct—support for liberal positions on these three components *increased*.

it is likely the authoritarian White campers were threatened by the presence of the Black campers and simply avoided contact with them.

This is a decisive point. Authoritarianism *is* a barrier to positive intergroup contact effects by restricting the willingness to have the contact in the first place (Pettigrew & Tropp, 2011). Only when authoritarians have the intergroup contact can its positive effects emerge. Attaining the intergroup contact is the problem for authoritarians.

German survey data illustrate the point (Pettigrew & Tropp, 2011, pp. 210–211). Three contact selection processes are delineated. First, 341 of the 1,377 sample members did not live in a neighborhood with foreigners—a 25% drop-off. But the mere presence of foreigners does not guarantee intergroup contact—the second selection process. Indeed, 25% of the German respondents who lived in mixed areas reported no contact at all with their foreign neighbors. Finally, intergroup contact does not ensure that intergroup friendship will develop—and friendships are a major means for contact to diminish prejudice (Davies et al., 2011; Pettigrew & Tropp, 2011). This last selection process removes 18% of the German respondents who have neighborhood contact but no foreign friends.

Regression tests for the predictors of these three processes reveal how authoritarianism consistently blocks intergroup contact at each level. Although age, gender, and prior prejudice are also involved, only authoritarianism is significantly and negatively related to all three processes. Authoritarians are significantly less likely to be living in an area with foreigners, less likely to have contact with them even when they do live in such an area, and less likely to make friends with those foreigners with whom they do have neighborhood contact. Moreover, authoritarians in the survey are significantly more likely to view their contact with the outgroup as superficial, involuntary, and with a resident foreigner of unequal status (Pettigrew & Tropp, 2011).

Thus, authoritarians are careful to avoid resident foreigners at multiple levels. Contact effects can be as successful with authoritarians as others—sometimes even more successful, but authoritarians are less likely to have such contact. This is a critical issue for remedial efforts to combat prejudice. It raises the question: Does intergroup contact theory operate for deeply ideologically intolerant people? Many other means of reducing intergroup prejudice have often failed in practice to dent the attitudes of the hard-core intolerant (e.g., priming multiculturalism, teaching tolerance for diversity). So, is intergroup contact any different?

Gordon Hodson (2011; Kteily et al., 2019) pursued this question directly. He noted that intergroup contact alone among proposed remedies seems to be beneficial for the highly prejudiced—not just in lowering authoritarianism. Chapter 7 of this volume shows that intergroup contact is beneficial for the intensely prejudiced by improving the whole canopy of variables associated with the broad prejudice syndrome—such as reducing anxiety, SDO, and the many different types of prejudice while enhancing empathy.

The practical problem, then, for the remediation of extreme prejudice is "leading the horses to water"—overcoming the resistance of highly prejudiced people and getting them into positive intergroup settings. Three German studies show that those most open to new experience and most extroverted exhibit the most favorable attitudes toward cross-cultural contact (Stürmer et al., 2013).

This issue of avoidance of intergroup contact offers an answer to a pointed question: Why are intergroup conflict and prejudice so intense in the world today when the opportunities for intergroup contact are greater than ever before? Paolini and her colleagues (2018) believe that the basic answer to this question lies in the massive amount of *intergroup contact avoidance* throughout the world. Consequently, they hold that understanding this process of encouraging people to have intergroup contact is the next big task for social psychologists in this area. Adopting the three-level paradigm of Chapter 2 in this volume, they provide a road map for how to foster more intergroup contact at all three major levels of analyses.

Adopt a longer time perspective: Time is on the side of greater acceptance of social diversity. Ramos and his colleagues (2019) pointed out that although humans often react negatively to threats of changes in social diversity in the short term, the initial negative effects are compensated in the long term by the beneficial effects of intergroup contact (see also Tropp, 2019). The timing involved, as we have seen, can be lengthened by any impediments to intergroup contact, such as intergroup segregation and prejudiced modeling by political leaders.

Why Is Authoritarianism so Universal in its Effect on Prejudice?

Authoritarianism predicts prejudice. This consistent finding spans decades of research using a great diversity of respondents, target groups, measures, and nations. Why is this link so strong and ubiquitous? I propose that authoritarianism acts as an "at-risk" personality trait that predisposes people to a wide variety of factors, each of which leads to prejudice.

The remarkable global consistency of authoritarianism results around the globe, despite the problems involved, suggests that the authoritarian personality is a general personality trait with early origins in childhood that center on universal issues of authority. A plethora of theories attempt to define the personality type and its origins. The original Berkeley study viewed it as a personality type with particular characteristics. Relying on psychoanalytic theory, it stressed the effects of a stern father in early life. Later formulations empathize the trait's focus on strength and weakness, its intense orientation to the ingroup, and the importance of modeling of authoritarian behavior by parents and others.

Thus, the authoritarian personality concept is an important tool for social science to understand a range of important social phenomena. For all its problems, it has stood the test of time and an abundance of research. But it operates at the individual level of analysis. Writers often erroneously employ it to explain societal phenomena—yet another example of the compositional fallacy that assumes societal processes are mere composites of individual behavior. However, as later chapters document, when authoritarianism is combined with situational and societal perspectives, it gains explanatory power in accounting for such phenomena as intergroup prejudice and extreme right-wing politics.

Social Dominance Orientation

A half century after the authoritarianism study was published (Adorno et al., 1950), James Sidanius and Felicia Pratto (1999; Pratto et al., 1994) introduced a new theory and a new Likert scale to join with authoritarianism as a powerful microlevel explanation for intergroup prejudice. We have seen that authoritarianism is typically triggered by threat and fear (Duckitt & Sibley, 2010; Feldman & Stenner, 1997; Stenner, 2005), and authoritarians tend to view the world as a very dangerous and threatening place—virtually "a jungle."

SDO relates positively to authoritarianism, but the two are clearly separable (Duckitt & Sibley, 2007; Roccato, 2008; Sidanius & Pratto, 1999). SDO features an individual's preference for the societal hierarchy of groups and domination over lower-status groups. It represents a predisposition toward anti-egalitarianism within and between groups. Those who score high on SDO are typically dominant, driven, tough-minded, disagreeable, and relatively uncaring seekers of power. They believe in a "dog-eat-dog" world, and they report being largely motivated by self-interest and self-indulgence (Levin et al., 2002).

Since SDO's introduction, its emphasis has somewhat shifted (Rubin & Hewstone, 2004). At first, the theory and measure emphasized how people desire social dominance for themselves and their ingroup over other groups. But now it also focuses on nonegalitarian, hierarchical relations between groups. Thus, the SDO measure has two clear subscales. The Dominance subscale contains such items as "Some groups of people must be kept in their place" and "No one group should dominate in society" (reverse scored). The Anti-egalitarianism subscale contains such items as "We should not push for group equality" and "Group equality should be our ideal" (reverse scored).

Research now reveals that SDO not only is partly a group-based phenomenon but also contains an interpersonal dominance component. Thus, high-SDO respondents gravitate toward hierarchy-enhancing jobs and institutions, such as law enforcement (Sidanius & Pratto, 1999). There is also a consistent gender discrepancy: Women as a group score lower on the SDO scale than men.

Values as Predictors of Prejudice

Feather and McKee (2008) conducted research with White Australian university students to uncover the value correlates of prejudice against Australian Aborigines. Using the Schwartz Value Survey (Schwartz, 1992), their path analysis found that authoritarianism (RWA) had positive links with security, conformity, and traditional values and negative links with self-direction and universalism values. Using the SDO measure, the investigators found positive links with power, hedonism, and achievement values and a negative link with universalism values. RWA and SDO mediated the effects of these values on prejudice, just as they also mediate the effects of the Big Five traits.

Similarly, Cohrs et al. (2005), in the aftermath of the horrific 2001 airplane attacks on New York City, revealed that RWA, more than SDO, related to conservative values and threat-related values concerning Muslims. But both RWA and SDO linked equally to self-enhancing values.

Finally, a series of values tapped by a different values test related to Trump support: low on altruism and high on power, commerce, and tradition (Sherman, 2018). Moreover, these results held even after Sherman controlled for political ideology and party affiliation. The results of these three studies suggest that values are especially important predictors of RWA and SDO and through them prejudice. Further value research on prejudice is needed.

The Big Five Personality Predictors of Prejudice

Once factor analysis was introduced in the 1930s, the reduction of human personality traits to a basic minimum became the holy grail for personality psychologists with statistical skills. The quest began with Raymond Cattell.

As a young man, he helped Charles Spearman in the development of factor analysis and other multivariate methods. After immigrating from Great Britain to the United States,[13] Cattell began to emulate Spearman's work with intelligence by applying factor analysis to personality traits. Indeed, he doggedly sought "the primary factors" of personality throughout the rest of his lengthy career and developed numerous editions of his 16PF model of normal personality structure.

Many psychologists have contributed to this effort over the years. Donald Fiske (1949) published an early factor analysis and identified four factors—named social adaptability, emotional control, conformity, and inquiring intellect. In the 1950s, Ernest Tupes and Raymond Christal for the U.S. Air Force Personnel Laboratory further searched for a finite patterning of factors.[14] Starting in 1961, a series of models were advanced by studying relationships between a large number of verbal descriptors of personality traits (e.g., Digman, 1990; Goldberg, 1993; Norman, 1963; Tupes & Christal, 1961). These initial attempts tended to end with five major factors that closely resembled one another although tagged with different trait names.[15] Finally, there was general agreement to settle on the Big Five factors as described by Costa and McCrae (1992a, 1992b). All but one of these five factors relate to one or more of our critical variables—authoritarianism, SDO, and prejudice. The one that rarely relates, Neuroticism, relates to emotional instability—a long-studied temperament trait.[16]

In addition, these five factors are intercorrelated, so two replicable metatraits can be distilled further: *plasticity* (Extraversion and Openness) and *stability* (Neuroticism, Agreeableness, and Conscientiousness; Digman, 1997; Hirsh et al., 2009). It appears that these metatraits relate to engagement and restraint of behavior. I know of no test as yet that has sought to relate these two metatraits directly with prejudice and intergroup contact. But it seems likely that they would relate significantly to both of these variables.

---

[13] Cattell first came to the United States in 1937 to Columbia University at the invitation of Edward Thorndike; later he taught for 3 years at Harvard University at the invitation of Gordon Allport. Finally, he settled at the University of Illinois, where he spent the remainder of his long career.

[14] In the 1950s, major sources of research funding for psychology came from military research centers. The Office of Naval Research particularly supported social psychological research.

[15] A major exception is the HEXACO model, which adds a sixth factor—H for honesty and humility (K. Lee & Ashton, 2013).

[16] There are rare exceptions to this statement: For both the Trump and Brexit elections and for the Trump–Romney vote difference, neurotic traits significantly predict right-wing support (Obschonka et al., 2018).

Indeed, Farmer and Maister (2017) have begun exploring the possibility that the plasticity metatrait could relate to enhanced empathy and decreased intergroup prejudice.

Two of the original five factors seem to be especially important for prejudice: low on Openness to Experience and high on Disagreeableness. Repeated studies have shown that Openness to Experience relates *negatively* to both prejudice and authoritarianism—a finding consistent with authoritarians' vulnerability to threat (e.g., Ackermann & Ackermann, 2015; Butler, 2000; Chirumbolo et al., 2003; Dinesen et al., 2016; Ekehammar et al., 2004; Sibley & Duckitt, 2008).

With an Italian national sample, Dallago and Roccato (2008) showed that perceived societal threat to safety partly mediated the link between negative openness and RWA. In Switzerland, the Openness trait significantly predicted the willingness to allow immigrants to vote (Freitag & Rapp, 2015).

The Big Five inventory measures the Openness trait with such items as "I am full of ideas" and "I am not interested in abstractions" (reverse item). People scoring high on this trait tend to be oriented toward the arts and to be creative, as well as more aware of their feelings. The downside is that high scorers on this trait are more inclined to take extreme risks. Low scores on Openness to Experience reflects a tendency to social conformity—a positive correlate of prejudice emphasized by Allport (1954, Chapter 17) and followed up in later studies (e.g., Pettigrew, 1958b, 1959, 1961).

The other major link emerges with the Disagreeableness trait. This trait consistently relates positively with both prejudice (Ackermann & Ackermann, 2015; Freitag & Rapp, 2015) and social dominance orientation (Ekehammar et al., 2004; Sibley & Duckitt, 2008). The reverse of the Agreeableness trait, Disagreeableness is measured by such items as "I feel little concern for others," "I boast about my virtues," and "I make people feel at ease" (reverse item). The name assigned to this factor does not adequately describe how it is measured. "Empathy" and "no empathy" might be more accurate terms. The Disagreeableness form is a trait quite similar to what was called "tough-mindedness" in the original authoritarianism study (Adorno et al., 1950). This Big Five finding also connects with the tendency of high SDO scorers to see the world in ruthless terms.

As mentioned earlier, another personality trait related positively to prejudice and well as authoritarianism is the need for closure. Although not part of the Big Five, it relates negatively to the Openness to Experience dimension (Chirumbolo et al., 2003; Hodson & Sorrentino, 1999). Need for closure refers to a strong desire for definiteness instead of confusion and uncertainty (Webster & Kruglanski, 1994). It is successfully measured by such items as "I dislike unpredictable situations," "I hate to change my plans at the last minute," and "My personal space is usually messy and disorganized" (a reversal item; Kruglanski et al., 1997). The factor structure of the 42-item Need for Closure scale proved invariant across four cultures—Croatia, Italy, the Netherlands, and the United States (Mannetti et al., 2002).

Roets and Van Hiel (2011) provided a compact 15-item scale and showed that need for closure offers an empirical basis for a general motivated cognitive style that Allport (1954) years earlier had held to be the basis of prejudice. Repeated studies find that need for closure correlates highly and positively with prejudice scales of all kinds—blatant and subtle, explicit and implicit (IAT; Cunningham et al., 2004; Dhont et al., 2013; Van Hiel et al., 2004).

Some studies have also shown weaker ties between Conscientiousness and Extraversion with authoritarianism (e.g., Ekehammar et al., 2004; Sibley & Duckitt, 2008). Ekehammar and his Swedish colleagues offered a tentative causal model for integrating these various results (Ekehammar et al., 2004). They showed right-wing authoritarianism and SDO operating as mediators for the various Big Five traits in influencing a measure of generalized outgroup prejudice. The weakness of their proposal is that it is based on data from a small convenience sample—183 Swedish college students who did not major in psychology. But it merits attention, as its structural equation model is consistent with a wide variety of other studies on the same topics using different samples in various cultures. Indeed, it proved to be a forerunner of the dual process motivational (DPM) model.

The Dual Process Motivational Model

In their seminal article, Duckitt and Sibley (2010) joined together the two leading microlevel predictors of prejudices—RWA and SDO—and offered a DPM model. Although positively correlated,[17] the two factors are seen by the DPM model as basically two different "worldviews" with contrasting

[17] The two scales tend to correlate positively largely because they often share disregard for dissident groups (e.g., atheists; Asbrock et al., 2010) as well as negative relationships with both the Openness to Experience and Agreeableness Big Five factors (e.g., Duckitt & Sibley, 2010; Ekehammar et al., 2004). But, for the most part, they relate in different ways to derogated (e.g., obese people) and dangerous (e.g., drunk drivers) groups as well as to the other Big Five personality factors (Duckitt & Sibley, 2010) and to Schwartz's (1992) value scale.

motivational bases. As we have seen in repeated studies, the RWA Scale taps threat and insecurity, whereas SDO taps self-enhancement and power. Using this fundamental distinction, the DPM then successfully predicts numerous differences in their effects. A 1-year cross-lagged investigation with 112 subjects revealed that the Big Five's Disagreeableness and Extraversion traits predicted change in the motivational goal of SDO, whereas Openness to Experience predicted change in the motivational goal for authoritarianism (Sibley & Duckitt, 2010).

Given their contrasting motivational bases, RWA and SDO tend to be aroused in different situations and target outgroups for different reasons. Those scoring high on RWA tend to target groups that threaten their collective security; we see in Figure 5.1 how collective threat to the ingroup especially arouses their fear and foreboding.

Those people high on SDO, on the other hand, are primarily concerned with ingroup dominance. So they are aroused maximally by competitive situations (Dovidio et al., 2017; Duckitt, 2006). The DPM model also notes that both high RWA and high SDO scorers are often prejudiced against the same groups but for different reasons. Incoming immigrants, for example, may be deprecated by both groups, but high RWAs reject them for security reasons ("Terrorists are among the immigrants"), whereas high SDOs reject them for competitive reasons ("Immigrants will take our jobs"). In this volume, Chapter 8 finds that both authoritarianism and SDO are important for understanding the rise of racist nationalism in both Europe and the United States.

A 6-month longitudinal study with New Zealand undergraduates revealed, as predicted by the dual process model, that RWA linked with prejudice against dangerous groups (e.g., drug dealers), whereas SDO linked with prejudice against derogated groups (e.g., intellectual disability; Asbrock et al., 2010). Both RWA and SDO proved prejudiced against dissident groups (e.g., prostitutes).

In addition, each type of prejudice is likely to have specific beliefs, or fixed "mind-sets," that mediate the effects of authoritarianism and SDO. For example, the firm ideas that immigrants are obligated to assimilate rapidly yet are incapable of assimilating strongly predict opposition to immigration (Madan et al., 2019; Verkuyten, 2011; Verkuyten & Brug, 2004).

MESOLEVEL ADVANCES IN UNDERSTANDING PREJUDICE

Understanding a broad conception of *prejudice* requires that we also check on the mesolevel—the situational context in which individually prejudiced people interact with others. Such interaction can lead to feelings of relative deprivation when one compares one's status with that of others and finds the difference unfair. Chapter 6 of this volume looks at that process in detail. In addition, Chapter 7 demonstrates how authoritarianism, SDO, and prejudice are all firmly relate to intergroup contact.

MACROLEVEL ADVANCES IN UNDERSTANDING PREJUDICE

The macrolevel informs the prejudice syndrome in two basic ways. First, cultures shape the norms and practices of a society and thus provide the background that either nourishes or limits intergroup prejudice and conflict. Second, structural factors shape, encourage, or retard intergroup interaction.

Cultural Effects

Two studies—one in the United States, the other in Italy—found that political ideological cultures sharply moderate the relationship between outgroup size and anti-outgroup opposition. McCann (2009a) discovered that greater threat from ethnic and racial diversity related to an American state harboring *more* explicit hate groups, but only in states with ideologically conservative norms. By contrast, comparable diversity related to *fewer* hate groups in ideologically liberal states. Thus, the dominant political culture of a state shaped its response to ethnic and racial diversity.

Similarly, a multilevel test of a sample of 3,871 people nested in 103 Italian regions revealed that immigrants' group size in each region related positively with greater prejudice against immigrants but *only among right-wing* Italian natives (Russo et al., 2019).

Later, I describe research that shows conclusively that national events have a direct influence on changing norms that, in turn, impact the prejudice syndrome.

Macrofactors Also Shape the Possibilities for Intergroup Contact

Racial segregation throughout the United States has restricted interracial contact for centuries. But historical circumstances have sorted people of various groups in ways that also limit the benefits of intergroup contact. If you are a White American who lives in a small town in, say, Montana, Wyoming, or the Dakotas, you have little opportunity through no choice of your own to meet and thus get to know African Americans. Such White residents rely largely on the mass media for their information about race, and consequently they often acquire sharply mistaken notions about African

Americans, such as grossly overestimating their proportion of the American population.[18] And, as I note in Chapter 8 of this volume, such unintended population patterns played a part in the American presidential election of 2016. Given the importance of intergroup contact for prejudice, the most critical macroeffect of the prejudice syndrome involves restrictions it places on intergroup interaction. The American population is one of the most diverse nations in the world, but patterns of work and residence are not nearly so diverse. Separate "ethnic and racial worlds" are commonplace and serve to greatly restrict intergroup contact. Such programs as Affirmative Action and school and housing desegregation, when effectively administered, break through these barriers and increase intergroup contact leading to the positive contact effects specified in Chapter 7 of this volume.

CONTEXTUAL LINKS BETWEEN THE THREE LEVELS

An extensive research literature has developed to demonstrate a strong connection between the structural macrolevel and the individual microlevel (the downward causal Path F in Figure 2.1 of Chapter 2 of this volume). Mediation of these effects at the mesolevel is highly likely (Paths D and E in Figure 2.1), but these macrolevel studies often cannot test for this possibility.

Stephen Sales (1973) began this line of research by showing that threatening periods in American history (the 1930s and 1967–1970) witnessed increases in authoritarianism compared with more tranquil periods (1920s and 1959–1964).[19] But there are alternative explanations for Sales's finding. Both of his low-threat periods preceded high-threat periods, so differences between them could have simply reflected long-term trends and possibility better record keeping.

Doty et al. (1991) corrected for these possibilities and compared archival data for high-threat (1978–1982) followed by low-threat (1983–1987) periods in the United States. As predicted, most societal attitudinal and behavioral

[18] Americans in general grossly overestimate the Black population of the United States—averaging one third instead of 14% (Carroll, 2001).

[19] The first and most famous archival publication in the prejudice area was advanced by Hovland and Sears (1940). They uncovered a positive correlation between the number of Black Americans lynched in 14 southern states and the price of cotton between 1882 and 1930. Bad economic years witnessed more lynchings, and good years witnessed fewer lynchings. Hovland and Sears interpreted their findings in terms of the then-popular frustration-aggression hypothesis. Hepworth and West (1988) largely replicated the finding using a more adequate time-series approach.

measures revealed declines in authoritarian indicators. Thus, by the middle 1980s, survey respondents reported being far more "satisfied" with the way that things are going. Like Sales earlier, Doty and his coresearchers found that people tended to select dog breeds for power and toughness more in the high-threat era. Distrust of government leadership declined during the low-threat period. Finally, in one of the strongest findings, high school seniors in the low-threat years were significantly more willing to have close contact with members of other races.

Similarly, a study across 28 quite different nations revealed that economic inequality enhanced the wish for a strong authoritarian leader (Sprong et al., 2019). Further archival studies support these results. Padgett and Jorgenson (1982) inspected data from Germany's dark years—1918 to 1940. This period included the massive Weimar inflation when, as German reports claim today, you had to take a wheelbarrow of marks to the market to buy food. As authoritarian theory would predict (Adorno et al., 1950), superstitions rose dramatically during such periods of dire economic threat. Such wildly erroneous beliefs help to alleviate feelings of helplessness and anxiety during unpredictable times (Singer & Benassi, 1981). A comparable phenomenon took place in the U.S. at the close of the Trump presidency with the rapid growth of Q-anon and other extreme conspiracy groups.

Emily Bianchi and her Emory University colleagues found that economic turndowns relate to numerous indicators of prejudice and discrimination against African Americans (Bianchi et al., 2018). Using a variety of measures, they found that economic recessions in the United States were associated with increasing prejudice among White Americans toward Black Americans. They felt "less warmly" toward Blacks, held more negative explicit and implicit attitudes toward Blacks, and more often condoned the use of racial stereotypes. They were also more willing to accept inequality between groups as natural. In addition, Black musicians were less likely to have a hit, and Black politicians were less likely to win a congressional election during difficult economic times.

Apparently, this link between threat and prejudice has surfaced for centuries. R. W. Anderson et al. (2017) checked on varying degrees of the persecution of Jews from 1100 to 1800 in 936 European cities. They found that the expropriation of Jewish property was greatest in colder winters over these years, with the effect strongest in areas with poor soil quality. In other words, it appears that bad weather affected food production that in turn raised prices and triggered more religious discrimination. In addition to these archival studies, numerous laboratory experiments have also shown that threat and economic scarcity increases various levels and types of prejudice (e.g., Krosch & Amodio, 2014; Krosch et al., 2017; Sales & Friend, 1973).

Thus, we can conclude with confidence that authoritarianism—as well as prejudice and discrimination—rises in times of societal threat and recedes in times of calm. Crises invoke authoritarian leadership and encourage even equalitarians to accept such leadership. Future research is likely to use the era of 2016 to 2021 as another example of societal threat and its consequent negative trends.

Positive Intergroup Contact Can Alter Norms

The definitive research demonstrating how normative structures act as critical contextual variables for intergroup contact effects was published by Oliver Christ and his numerous colleagues (2014). They analyzed with multilevel methods seven large-scale European surveys, five of which were cross-sectional and two longitudinal. Most contact studies look for positive contact effects at the level of individuals. But this research specifically also tested for macrolevel effects of positive intergroup contact reducing prejudice in a variety of macrolevel entities—regions, districts, and neighborhoods—and found these effects *larger* than the contact effects at the microindividual level.

In four of the surveys, Christ and his coworkers demonstrated that this significant macroeffect was largely mediated by more *tolerant norms*. Thus, positive contact can reduce prejudice on the macrolevel as well as the microlevel. People are influenced by the behavior of others in their social context, and this process makes it possible for positive intergroup contact to simultaneously impact large numbers of people who are not themselves directly involved in the contact.

This key finding adds a critically significant component to both the theory and empirical support for intergroup contact theory. Note once again that this significant advance could not have been found without multilevel statistical techniques.

The Prejudice Syndrome

Think of all the variables that have been found to relate closely, positively or negatively, to prejudice: authoritarianism, anxiety, biased group attributions, intergroup contact, individual threat, collective threat, meta-stereotypes, SDO, stereotype threat, trust, forgiveness, empathy, perspective taking, group and individual relative deprivation, values of security, power, universalism and benevolence, need for closure, Openness to Experience, deprovincialization, agreeableness, knowledge of the outgroup, ingroup identification, political tolerance, and perceptions of outgroup variability (Pettigrew & Tropp, 2011).

Recall also how these many correlates of prejudice are themselves intercorrelated. This tightly woven network of prejudice predictors strongly suggests that we should consider prejudice as a syndrome of variables operating at all three levels of analysis rather than as simply a characteristic of individuals. Prejudice can also be usefully thought of as a characteristic of situations and even geographic regions. I return to this possibility in Chapter 9.

Some specialists have specifically called for thinking of prejudice as a two-level phenomenon linking the micro- and the mesolevels—Paths B and E of Figure 2.1 in Chapter 2 of this volume (Hodson & Dhont, 2015; Kinket & Verkuyten, 1999). Initial research needed to establish this link firmly has been successfully achieved. For instance, the intergroup evaluations of Dutch and Turkish children in Dutch schools are strongly shaped by the classroom context in which the children are situated (Kinket & Verkuyten, 1999). Less ingroup favoritism formed in classes in which the teacher paid attention to ethnic discrimination and cultural differences.

Building on the Big Five traits, a massive analysis of data from more than 1.5 million subjects attempted to distinguish a basic set of personality types (Gerlach et al., 2018). Recall that both the Openness to Experience and Agreeableness traits consistently relate negatively with intergroup prejudice. And two of the four personality types uncovered by Gerlach and his colleagues are strongly characterized by these two key traits. The *role model type* is high on both of these traits, whereas the *self-centered type* is low on both of them.[20]

Closer directly to prejudice, Jost and his colleagues (2003) meta-analyzed the social cognitive correlates of political conservatism with 88 samples and 22,818 cases across 12 nations. Among the positive correlates of conservatism were dogmatism; fear of threat and loss; and needs for order, structure, and closure. Among the negative correlates of conservatism were openness to experience and tolerance for uncertainty. All these factors relate similarly to prejudice.

[20] Conscientiousness ratings were also high for the role model type and low for the self-centered type. But the relationship of this basic trait with prejudice is not clear-cut. It has diverse relationships with prejudice across cultures and types of prejudice (Sibley & Duckitt, 2008). This diversity may reflect the possibility that this trait relates to following social norms and expectations closely—thus, its link with prejudice would vary with varying norms.

These studies help to initiate work on a prejudice syndrome at the microlevel of analysis. Such work could begin by focusing on the self-centered type who possesses especially strong needs for closure and structure together with how authoritarianism and social dominance orientation mediate the influence of these microvariables upon prejudice. The next empirical step would be to place these microlevel findings within a systematic context of such basic mesolevel variables as intergroup contact and relative deprivation. These mesolevel variables could then be systematically linked with such macrolevel variables as cultural norms and the structural means of influencing intergroup contact. We have seen that most of the relationships between these various factors, even those across levels, have been repeatedly established. Using multilevel methods, the prejudice syndrome could be established using what we already know about intergroup prejudice. I return to this discussion in Chapter 9.

Group Position Theory

A promising theoretical possibility for such a multilevel model of prejudice is to pursue group position theory further. Sketched in outline by Blumer (1958) in an often-cited article of five pages, the theory has been expanded and its contentions made specific and testable by Bobo (1999). The theory's basic claim is that prejudice is grounded in a strong sense of the positional arrangement of groups. Many of Bobo's predictions from the theory have been supported throughout this book. For instance, threat to any shifts in group positions within a society is central to prejudice. Thus, *collective* threat is far more important than individual threat. Moreover, the special impact of *group* relative deprivation, and not individual relative deprivation, in predicting prejudice is made clear by the theory. Prejudice expressions, such as negative stereotypes, are important, but they must be seen within the context of the social status alignments of the groups involved.

Two Different Prejudiced Men

The clear difference between thinking about prejudice as simply an individual trait or as a three-level syndrome is made apparent by comparing two late-middle-aged White male Americans in a hypothetical example. Think of the two men as sharing middle-class status and as having graduated from high school but not having the opportunity to attend college. Imagine further that each scored identically high on measures of authoritarianism, SDO, and prejudice against Inuits (whom they both mistakenly call "Eskimos").

But they do not share the same social context. Man A lives in the Allegheny Mountains of Virginia near Roanoke, where there are no norms concerning Inuits. He never met an Inuk in his life and is unlikely to ever meet one unless he visits Alaska, Canada, or Greenland. He just rejects minorities in general whether or not they threaten him.

Man B lives in Fairbanks, Alaska, and has often encountered Inuit Alaskans—although like many authoritarians he avoids contact with them whenever possible. He differs sharply from most Inuits in his opinions on the future development of Alaska. They generally wish to protect the environment and slow development; he wants to open up Alaska to increased oil drilling to secure greater state revenues and payouts to its citizens.

In regard to intergroup prejudice, should we not think of these two men in quite contrasting ways in spite of their identical scores on social psychology's favorite microlevel measures? Certainly, contextual social psychology forces us to regard them as sharply different. Man A in Virginia walks out of the pages of Allport's (1954) *The Nature of Prejudice*. His bigotry needs no social support. By contrast, Man B's bigotry is closely linked to his social context in Alaska. If their social surroundings changed abruptly, we would anticipate greater effects from Alaska's Man B than we would from Virginia's Man A.

In the following three chapters of this volume, I search for comparable contextual effects regarding relative deprivation, intergroup contact, and far-right-wing voting.

6 APPLYING CONTEXTUAL ANALYSES TO RELATIVE DEPRIVATION

Powerful businesspeople who head major corporations may express unhappiness with their huge annual salaries of tens of millions of dollars or more. At the same time, many workers making just $25 an hour (about $50,000 for a complete year of work) are reasonably satisfied with their pay. Why such a difference?

Clearly, it is not the actual amount received that is crucial. Rather, it involves what comparisons the recipients are using to judge their pay. Corporation executives are typically using as their gauge the pay of comparable executives at similar firms. If these comparison executives are earning significantly more, they feel undercompensated and not fully appreciated although they hardly need more money to live handsomely. The workers are likely to compare their pay with other workers they know who are being compensated with only $15 an hour or even less. Consequently, they feel relatively gratified. Social psychologists try to capture this common phenomenon with the concept of *relative deprivation* (RD).[1]

---

[1] Similar ideas are often referred to as "social comparison" and "inequality" effects. Although it virtually ignores the relative deprivation literature, Keith Payne's (2017) book *The Broken Ladder* provides with a light touch numerous examples of this phenomenon.

https://doi.org/10.1037/0000210-007
Contextual Social Psychology: Reanalyzing Prejudice, Voting, and Intergroup Contact, by T. F. Pettigrew

RD is a social psychological concept par excellence. It postulates a subjective state that shapes emotions, cognitions, and behavior. It links the individual with the interpersonal and intergroup levels of analysis. It melds easily with other social psychological processes to provide more integrative theory—a prime disciplinary need (Pettigrew, 1991c).

Moreover, RD challenges conventional wisdom about the singular importance of absolute deprivation. And it has proven useful in a wide range of areas (H. J. Smith, Pettigrew, & Huo, 2019; H. J. Smith et al., 2012; Tyler & Smith, 1998; Walker & Smith, 2002). Researchers have invoked RD to explain phenomena ranging from poor physical health (Adler et al., 2000; Adler & Stewart, 2010) to who migrates from Mexico to the United States (Stark & Taylor, 1989), who becomes more materialistic (Zhang et al., 2015), who participates in collective protest (Newton, Mann, & Geary, 1980), and who is susceptible to terrorist recruitment (Moghaddam, 2005; Obaidi et al., 2018, 2019). Indeed, the concept has been used throughout the social sciences (Walker & Smith, 2002), from criminology (e.g., Lea & Young, 1984/1993) and economics (e.g., Yitzhaki, 1979) to political science (e.g., Lichbach, 1990) and history (Snyder & Tilly, 1972). Hence, this area offers a prime means for social psychology to connect with other social sciences.

Samuel Stouffer, the survey specialist, introduced the concept at midcentury (Stouffer et al., 1949). He fashioned RD to provide a post hoc explanation for several puzzling findings in his major study of the American soldier in World War II. These puzzles became famous in social science. For example, the military police were far more satisfied with their slow promotions than the air corpsmen were with their rapid promotions. This finding offers an apparent puzzle only if we assume the wrong referent comparisons. Immediate comparisons, Stouffer reasoned, were the salient referents. The military police compared their promotions with those of other military police—not with air corpsmen, whom they seldom encountered. Deprivation alone does not trigger the RD process; the discrepancy has to be recognized and regarded as unfair.

Following Stouffer, relative deprivation can be defined as *a judgment that one or one's ingroup is disadvantaged compared with a relevant referent, and this judgment invokes feelings of anger, resentment, and entitlement*. RD's fundamental feature is that the concept operates at the microlevel of *individuals* with three psychological processes: (a) people first make cognitive comparisons, (b) then people make cognitive appraisals that they or their group are disadvantaged, and (c) these disadvantages are seen as unfair and arouse angry resentment. If any one of these three requirements is missing, RD is not operating (H. J. Smith et al., 2012). Yet many studies in the social science literature claiming to be research on relative deprivation do not meet these three basic criteria (e.g., Gurr, 1970; Useem, 1980). For example, the Yitzhaki (1979) index used in economics as a measure of RD using income data but not how the individuals feel about their income. This and similar weaknesses have delayed the development of RD theory and accounts for much of what has been wrongly considered negative results of RD tests (Pettigrew, 2001, 2015b).

Although my doctoral students and I published regularly on RD from 1967 on,[2] I was disappointed at how slowly the concept came to be employed in social psychology—unlike the rapid spread of intergroup contact theory decades later. Nevertheless, since 1949 the RD idea has slowly but steadily developed into a minitheory that fits snugly with other social psychological theories—from social comparison and attribution theories to social identity theory (Crosby, 1976; Mark & Folger, 1984; Merton, 1957; Olson et al., 1986; Pettigrew, 1967a; Runciman, 1966; H. J. Smith, Pettigrew, & Huo, 2019; H. J. Smith et al., 2012; Suls & Miller, 1977; Vanneman & Pettigrew, 1972; Walker & Pettigrew, 1984; Walker & Smith, 2002). Similarly, RD joins with other social psychological theories to form a broader model of intergroup prejudice. It, too, is one of the many components of the prejudice syndrome mentioned throughout this book.

The military police example just cited is often mentioned in the social science literature. But rarely is it also stated that Stouffer shrewdly asked the soldiers another question concerning how they felt their *branch* was treated in promotions. Two thirds of the military police believed that they did not have as good a chance for promotion as other U.S. Army branches—and this was actually true (Stouffer, 1962, p. 21).

In other words, the military police did not feel individually deprived when comparing themselves with their immediate colleagues in the same branch. But when they considered their group in comparison with other army branches, they did rightly feel deprived. Two levels are involved—the mesolevel of just the military police and the macrolevel of the army and its many branches. Stouffer was acutely aware of contextual effects and

[2] See Gartrell (1987); Pettigrew (1967a, 2001, 2015b, 2016); Pettigrew et al. (2008); Pettigrew and Martin (1987); H. J. Smith and Pettigrew (2014); H. J. Smith, Pettigrew, and Huo (2019); H. J. Smith et al. (2012); H. J. Smith, Ryan, et al. (2018); Vanneman and Pettigrew (1972); Walker and Pettigrew (1984); Walker and Smith (2002); Walker et al. (2001). Joanne Martin, who was a former doctoral student and Merrill Professor of Organizational Behavior, emerita at Stanford's Graduate School of Business, has published 13 RD papers. Chief among them are Martin (1981, 1986) and Martin and Harder (1994).

sought ingenious ways to work at multiple levels before the development of the advanced statistics outlined in Chapter 4, which he would have prized (Lazarsfeld, 1962).[3]

Later, Runciman (1966) made explicit this crucial distinction between individual and group-level types of RD. This contribution proved vital to the concept's development as an important predictor of prejudice. He broadened the construct by carefully distinguishing between egoistic (individual) RD (called IRD) and fraternal (group) RD (called GRD). As with the military police, people can decide whether they are personally deprived or a social group to which they belong and identify is being deprived. Repeated studies show that feelings of GRD, not IRD, directly promote political protest and prejudice (Pettigrew, 1964b, 1967a; Vanneman & Pettigrew, 1972; Walker & Mann, 1987; Walker & Pettigrew, 1984; Walker & Smith, 2002). For instance, in Scotland, GRD—but not IRD—predicts support for Scottish independence (Abrams et al., 2019). In Australia, it is GRD and not IRD that relates to opposition to multicultural policies (Leviston et al., 2020).

Yet researchers often ignore Runciman's critical distinction (Walker & Pettigrew, 1984). For example, many have used interpersonal comparisons to predict collective behavior and prejudice (e.g., Long, 1975; Newton et al., 1980). This confusion of levels explains many of the literature's negative RD results. Feeling deprived can invoke intergroup prejudice, but it does so primarily if one feels deprived on behalf of a relevant and mistreated reference group. The strongest relationships between RD and dependent measures occur when the level of reference for both measures is the same: IRD with variables about individuals, and GRD with broader meso- and macrovariables.

Strong contextual effects are frequently uncovered in RD research. Because choice of comparisons is central to the phenomenon, social contexts often shape the relevant comparisons. If in a hospital all nurses are female and all doctors are male, it is highly likely that gender will be selected for comparisons because gender "fits" both the status and occupational differences. Also, if you are the lone Black or Latinx American in a work situation, ethnicity is likely to become the typical comparison dimension. This "solo role" phenomenon, popularized by Kanter (1977), is a difficult role to play. It often occurs in early situations brought about by affirmative action—and has received social psychological attention (e.g., Lord & Saenz, 1985; Pettigrew & Martin, 1987).

[3] Stouffer died suddenly of brain cancer in 1960—just before the entry of the many statistical advances described in Chapter 4.

META-ANALYTIC RESULTS: THE MANY OUTCOMES OF RELATIVE DEPRIVATION

Social scientists use RD to predict a wide range of significant outcome variables at all three major levels of analysis: willingness to join protests, individual achievement and deviance, intergroup attitudes, and physical and mental health. But the results are often weak and inconsistent, so a comprehensive meta-analysis was needed to sort through the extensive RD research literature. Heather Smith et al. (2012) conducted a full meta-analysis with 210 studies representing 293 independent samples and 186,073 respondents across 38 nations to present a model that integrates GRD and IRD. They found that the most impressive RD studies (a) correctly measure either IRD or GRD, (b) include justice-related affective measures as the response, (c) achieve a "fit" of analytic levels, and (d) use more reliable measures. Studies with these attributes have strong links with a wide variety of dependent variables (H. J. Smith et al., 2019).

IRD correlates highest with individual-level variables involving physical and mental health (e.g., stress, obesity, heart disease) and forms of deviance, escape, and achievement (e.g., aggression, stealing, drug use, academic achievement). In turn, GRD correlates highest with such variables as intergroup behavior (e.g., nationalism, voting intentions, prejudice) and collective behavior (e.g., unstructured and structured forms of collective action and approval of political violence).

A nationwide New Zealand survey confirmed the positive tie between GRD and nationalism (Sengupta et al., 2019). It also found that GRD among White New Zealanders was negatively related to personal well-being, but it determined that nationalism acted to elevate the sense of well-being. Using the same data set, a cross-lagged analysis revealed that ethnic group identification had a stronger positive effect on ethnic GRD than vice versa (Zubielevitch et al., 2019). We are especially focused in this volume on intergroup prejudice, nationalism, and right-wing voting. For these outcomes, GRD captures the appropriate level.

New directions for the study of relative deprivation were discussed in an entire issue of *Social Justice Research* (H. J. Smith & Pettigrew, 2015). Examples of RD's involvement throughout the world were provided for Australia, Canada, the Netherlands, New Zealand, Mongolia, Singapore, and South Africa; these articles give a sampling of how more recent research is expanding RD theory.

Feather (2015) distinguished between deservingness, entitlement, and resentment in reaction to RD. Osborne and Sibley (2015) emphasized the importance of emotions as mediators of GRD's effects on numerous political attitudes—from conservatism to views of the New Zealand government. Van den Bos et al. (2015) showed how culture shapes RD effects in both the Netherlands and Singapore.

Grant et al. (2015) focused on a classic IRD situation and its effects: immigrant Canadians whose skills and foreign qualifications are not recognized in Canada and who must accept lower status jobs. They found that simply perceiving the discrimination does not in itself stir protest. It is the emotional reaction of angry resentment to the perceived discrimination that predicts collective action—as specified in RD theory.

De la Sablonnière et al. (2015) tested with surveys the trajectory of RD's effects on well-being during periods of rapid social change in both South Africa and Mongolia. Their results show that reduced IRD and GRD are both uniformly associated with diminished authoritarianism and prejudice. Klandermans (2015), working with survey data on both Black and White South Africans, checked on the role of grievances at both the individual and group levels. Using comparisons with other people along class and racial lines, he found that Black South Africans were more aggrieved at the individual level (IRD) and White South Africans more aggrieved at the group level (GRD).

The final article in the collection explores *group relative gratification*—the precise opposite of GRD. Group relative gratification involves the experience of attaining far more than you expected. An experiment with Canadian university students revealed that outgroup prejudice increased both when the subjects believed their advantaged status was legitimate and when they thought their privileged status was declining (LeBlanc et al., 2015).

Future research should focus on appropriate and reliable RD measurement, angry resentment, and the inclusion of theoretically relevant appraisals of the situation. Such methodological improvements revitalize RD as a useful social psychological predictor of a broad range of important individual and social outcomes.

A SINGLE-LEVEL INVESTIGATION CHECKING FOR THE RD-PREJUDICE LINKAGE[4]

Out of the hundreds of single-level RD studies summarized in the meta-analysis of Heather Smith and her colleagues (2012), consider one broad study

[4] This section is adapted from "Relative Deprivation and Intergroup Prejudice," by T. F. Pettigrew, O. Christ, R. W. Meertens, U. Wagner, R. van Dick, & A. Zick, 2008, *Journal of Social Issues*, *64*(2), pp. 385–401 (https://doi.org/10.1111/j.1540-4560.2008.00567.x). Copyright by The Society for the Psychological Study of Social Issues. Adapted with permission.

that combined secondary analyses of three European surveys to test for RD's association with prejudice (Pettigrew et al., 2008). The first survey uses the extensive database provided by the European Union's 1988 Eurobarometer 30 survey (Reif & Melich, 1991). This survey drew seven national probability samples from France, West Germany, the Netherlands, and Great Britain and asked 3,796 native adult respondents an array of both prejudice and RD questions.

The second data source is a smaller survey of German youth (Schneider, 1994). It asked 794 East and West German teenagers of varying educational levels both IRD and GRD questions, as well as their attitudes toward immigration and a variety of ethnic groups.

A probability phone survey conducted in Germany in 2002 is the third data source (GMF-Survey; cf. Heitmeyer, 2002). The survey contains data on 2,722 native adult respondents with a varied set of prejudice and RD questions. Marked differences exist between our three data sets in terms of location, time, respondents' age, and items used to test RD and prejudice. Such differences provide a rigorously diverse test.

The Eurobarometer measures GRD by asking, "Would you say that over the last five years people like yourself in Britain have been economically a lot better off, better off, the same, worse off, or a lot worse off than most North Africans living here?" The survey taps IRD with the item "Would you say that over the last five years you have been economically a lot better off, better off, the same, worse off, or a lot worse off than other British people like yourself?" Two scales of 10 items each in the Eurobarometer study assess the blatant and subtle forms of prejudice described previously (Pettigrew & Meertens, 1995).

The German youth study used multiple-item indicators of IRD and GRD styled for its sample of 14- to 18-year-old respondents. Four items tapped the individual form of RD by asking for comparisons with classmates, other Germans, other Germans of their region (East or West), and other German families of their region. Four additional items measured the group form of RD. They asked the young respondents to compare their present ingroup situation with the other region's Germans and German families, as well as with students of a different educational level.

The youth survey used two somewhat different prejudice indicators. A 1-to-10 favorability thermometer tapped feelings toward Turks. Five additional items measured immigration attitudes. The GMF-Survey contains one item each to measure IRD and GRD, respectively. Both questions are directly comparable to those of the Eurobarometer. The Prejudice Scale contains seven items concerning foreigners (e.g., "If jobs become scarce, foreigners should be sent back to their home countries"). These items are similar to the Blatant scale in the Eurobarometer 30 analysis.

Who Are the Relative Deprived?

Popular understanding of prejudice often attributes prejudice to *absolute* deprivation. But we have seen that those who voted for Hitler were not the very poorest Germans but rather lower-middle-class Germans who felt unfairly deprived during the Weimar era (King et al., 2008). And later we will learn that the 2016 vote for Trump in the United States did not disproportionally include the poorest of American voters. This is a common finding in many nations. The lower middle classes throughout the world are squeezed from two directions. They typically aspire to rise into the solid middle class above them and simultaneously fear dropping down into the truly poor and deprived below them. Chapter 8 discusses this same phenomenon operating in the current wave of nationalistic voting in Europe and the United States.

In the Eurobarometer data, both those respondents indicating IRD and GRD are of somewhat lower socioeconomic status, on average. They are less likely to own their own homes or apartments, and they tend to have limited family incomes.

Also, in the Eurobarometer data, older people tend to report more IRD, whereas the less educated report more GRD. These two relatively deprived groups share political alienation and report less interest in politics in general. In addition, both high-scoring IRD and GRD respondents in the Eurobarometer study score higher than others on a scale measuring political inefficacy. Thus, they are significantly more likely than the nondeprived to agree with such items as "Most people in power try to gain something out . . . of you" and "People who run the country are not really concerned with what happens to you." National identity, as indexed by a Eurobarometer item concerning national pride, tends to be lower among those reporting IRD. In addition, thinking of yourself as a European is negatively related with GRD.

Using different predictors, this analysis is repeated for the German youth study. The respondents' gender, which was not a predictor in the adult Eurobarometer sample, rises to significance in this sample; teenage girls report significantly more GRD and IRD than boys. Once again, the relatively deprived tend to be of somewhat lower social status, with such indicators as more persons per room in households and less education of their parents.

As in the German youth study, those reporting GRD in the GMF-Survey are younger, less educated, and more likely to be female. Similar to the Eurobarometer results, both types of deprivation score higher on a political inefficacy scale. Moreover, the high IRD and GRD respondents report more pride in being German but less pride in being European.

In summary, then, the three studies agree that both IRD and GRD are strongest among somewhat lower status respondents. The two adult studies show that both types of relative deprivation correlate with a sense of political inefficacy. But what does this mean for the link between relative deprivation and outgroup prejudice?

RELATIVE DEPRIVATION AND OUTGROUP PREJUDICE

Consistent with the extensive research of the past, it is GRD, not IRD, that is a primary correlate of prejudice (Walker & Pettigrew, 1984). The RD relationships are consistently larger for blatant than subtle prejudice. Controlling for GRD in these three data sets greatly reduces the IRD correlations with the various prejudice indicators; they virtually disappear when social location (e.g., age, gender, education) variables are also controlled.

By contrast, controlling for IRD only marginally reduces the GRD correlations; they remain uniformly significant even after all of the social variables and IRD are controlled. The lone exception to these trends occurs in the GMF survey results. Here the correlation of IRD with prejudice remains significant after controlling for GRD and the social location variables (+.13). But the partial correlation of GRD remains significantly stronger (+.23).

To sum up, these single-level results reveal that GRD typically serves as a proximal correlate of outgroup prejudice and as a mediator of the effects on outgroup prejudice of both IRD and such social variables as social class. In addition, the Eurobarometer 30 data indicated that a significant part of the GRD's enhancement of prejudice is mediated by the denial of discrimination against the outgroup and thus an attribution of intergroup problems to the outgroup itself. In sum, all three surveys indicate that GRD plays a central role in social psychology's understanding of intergroup prejudice.

Using Multilevel Analyses, How Widespread Is This Link Between GRD and Prejudice?

Consistent with intergroup threat theory (W. G. Stephan et al., 2009), we have frequently noted the importance of threat, especially collective threat, in outgroup prejudice. Threat not only induces prejudice but also can fuel extremist violence against the outgroup seen as threatening (Obaidi et al., 2018). But little attention has been given to the role of GRD in generating this threat.

So a group of European colleagues and I set out to examine the association between GRD and ethnic threat systematically across 20 European countries controlling for intergroup contact and value priorities (Meuleman et al., 2020). The probability samples from the seventh round of the European Social Survey included questions assessing 32,813 respondents' feelings of group deprivation compared with immigrants and offered for the first time an opportunity to contextualize the threat-inducing effect of GRD across Europe. The only drawback with these rich data is that they were all gathered at the same time, and without overtime data, we cannot make causal claims.

Perceived ethnic threat was measured using five items. Respondents were asked if they felt that immigrants were a threat to the economy, the labor market, the welfare state, culture life, and religious customs. GRD was measured by a single item that asked the respondents' opinion as to whether the government treated newly arrived immigrants better or worse than members of their own group.

A multilevel structural equation model demonstrates a marked association between the GRD and ethnic threat. The results indicate that GRD is an important mediating factor on both the micro- and macrolevels across the 20 nations. At the individual level, GRD mediates the impact of one's socioeconomic position on the perceptions of ethnic threat. This link is also mediated by the frequency and quality of intergroup contact and such values as universalism and tradition. In addition, people who rate themselves low in social status (e.g., subjective socioeconomic status) are higher in trait aggression even after the Big Five and other personal characteristics are controlled (Greitemeyer & Sagioglou, 2016).

At the societal level, GRD mediates the relationship between the society's economic context and perceived ethnic threat. Indeed, for the 20-nation sample, the aggregated GRD and perceived ethnic threat correlates +.79—accounting for 62% of the variance among the nations' populations sense of threat. Moreover, GRD *fully* mediates the relation between contextual economic factors and ethnic threat. In other words, the effect of a nation's general economic condition has its effect on individuals' degree of threat from immigration entirely through GRD. This degree of threat, in turn, importantly shapes the attitudes toward the new arrivals in their midst.

We noted that *relative gratification* also relates to prejudice; indeed, it has been called "fear of falling." Jetten and her colleagues have shown the existence of a V-curve wherein it is those who feel relatively deprived and those who feel relatively gratified who show the most hostility to immigrants (Jetten et al., 2015, 2017). This result agrees with LeBlanc et al.'s (2015) previously described result on group relative gratification.

THE CULTURAL CONTEXT IS IMPORTANT IN RD

The Meuleman et al. (2020) study found GRD to act in quite similar ways across 20 European nations. But European cultures share many features. A test of GRD across a much wider variety of cultures and situations was now needed. And so it remained for Heather Smith of California State University at Sonoma to organize a massive worldwide test across sharply diverse cultures. Smith and her 37 social psychological colleagues around the globe demonstrated a large cultural contextual effect with two types of studies (H. J. Smith, Ryan, et al., 2018).

First, Smith and her associates used national assessments of power distance, individual-collectivism, and economic inequality from the work of Hofstede (2001, 2017). Power distance refers to the extent to which members of a nation's institutions expect and accept that power in their nation is distributed unequally. So, in high-power distance cultures, power and inequality need less legitimization (Winterich & Zhang, 2014). Smith predicted that members of individualistic cultures are more likely to feel relatively deprived and focus on personal agency than members of collectivist cultures.

The researchers coded 303 effect sizes of relative deprivation studies from 31 countries with 200,578 participants. As predicted, these assessments revealed that RD predicted all types of outcomes more strongly within predominately *individualistic* nations. Australia, the Netherlands, and the United States are prime examples of such individualistic nations; China, Indonesia, and Pakistan are prime examples of collectivist nations.

Next, these investigators employed a survey of 6,112 undergraduate university students from 28 countries that confirmed the importance of cultural differences for RD effects. The range of nations tested is unusually broad and involved national samples rarely included in American research (e.g., Brazil, Chile, Indonesia, Latvia, Malaysia, Pakistan).

The relationship between IRD and different outcomes was again stronger for undergraduates who lived in more individualistic countries. GRD also predicted political trust more strongly for undergraduates who lived in countries marked by lower power distance. Thus, RD effects are culturally bounded. In particular, RD is more likely to motivate reactions within individualistic countries that emphasize individual agency and achievement as a source of self-worth.

Now we turn to one of the most intensely studied phenomenon in modern social psychology: intergroup contact theory.

7 APPLYING CONTEXTUAL ANALYSES TO INTERGROUP CONTACT

Intergroup contact theory is now one of the best-supported theories in social psychology. The theory has a central, straightforward prediction. If it occurs under reasonably favorable conditions, contact between members of diverse groups will result in reduced intergroup prejudice (Allport, 1954; Pettigrew, 1998; Pettigrew & Tropp, 2011). No claims are made that contact alone is by itself a panacea for intergroup conflict (Hewstone, 2003). But it represents social psychology's major theory in the prejudice domain operating at the mesolevel. Recent years have witnessed an enormous extension of this basic idea, which I trace in this chapter.

Some passages in this chapter have been reprinted or adapted from "In Pursuit of Three Theories: Authoritarianism, Relative Deprivation, and Intergroup Contact," by T. F. Pettigrew, 2016, *Annual Review of Psychology*, *67*, pp. 1–21 (https://doi.org/10.1146/annurev-psych-122414-033327). Copyright 2016 by Annual Reviews. Reprinted with permission; and "The Single Factor Fallacy: Implications of Missing Critical Variables From an Analysis of Intergroup Contact Theory," by T. F. Pettigrew and M. Hewstone, 2017, *Social Issues and Policy Review*, *11*(1), pp. 8–37 (https://doi.org/10.1111/sipr.12026). Copyright 2017 by Wiley-Blackwell. Reprinted with permission.

https://doi.org/10.1037/0000210-008
Contextual Social Psychology: Reanalyzing Prejudice, Voting, and Intergroup Contact, by T. F. Pettigrew

Consider the seven meta-analyses conducted on the theory. First, Pettigrew and Tropp (2000, 2006) showed that more than 490 studies found a solid relationship between direct intergroup contact and reduced prejudices of many types. Next, contact studies involving friends led to an even stronger relationship between contact and lessened prejudice (Davies et al., 2011).

Beelmann and Heinemann (2014) demonstrated that structured contact programs promoted positive intergroup attitudes in children and adolescents. Next, Miles and Crisp (2014) analyzed studies of imagined intergroup contact. They uncovered in these studies a significant reduction in both implicit (Implicit Association Test [IAT]) and explicit intergroup prejudice from just thinking about diverse contact. Studies conducted outside the laboratory using direct and indirect contact interventions also significantly reduce ethnic prejudice (Lemmer & Wagner, 2015). This metanalysis used only studies of reasonable quality—a randomized posttest only with control, a pretest–posttest with control, or pretest–posttest single group design. And 85% of their studies had not been included in the original 2006 Pettigrew–Tropp meta-analysis.

Next, Zhou et al. (2019) validated with a meta-analysis the extended contact phenomenon—when just knowing that ingroup members have outgroup friends improves attitudes toward the outgroup. Finally, yet another meta-analysis found positive effects for even impersonal media contact (Page-Gould & Zhou, in press). As just one example of what these meta-analyses were tapping, both direct and extended intergenerational contact markedly improve the attitudes of young people toward the elderly (Drury et al., 2016).

Although there is some overlap in the research included in these seven meta-analyses, together they boast roughly more than 300,000 subjects across more than 800 separate studies in multiple nations throughout the globe. Their summary statistics were significant for both published and unpublished studies and emerged across a broad range of target outgroups and contexts. To be sure, there is a two-way causal problem with many of the studies analyzed in these meta-analyses—that more tolerant people are likely to have intergroup contact and less prejudice. I discuss this important point shortly.

THE RAPID GROWTH OF INTERGROUP CONTACT THEORY

What Allport (1954) had originally called "a hypothesis" has now evolved into a full-fledged major theory within social psychology. To be truthful, although I contributed to this development,[1] I never thought it would advance this extensively so swiftly. The enormous number of full replications of contact's positive effect on reducing intergroup prejudices of many types throughout the world together with the desire by social psychologists to find an effective remedy for intergroup prejudice undoubtedly helped to achieve this rapid growth.

International probability surveys have joined in and tested the theory with success. The Pew Research Center (Gardner & Evans, 2018) asked probability samples of Western Europeans in 15 nations if they agreed with the statement "In their hearts, Muslims want to impose their religious law on everyone else in this country." If they "personally knew a Muslim," 73% of the respondents disagreed with the sharply anti-Islamic statement compared with 48% who did not know a Muslim. The difference emerged in all 15 of the European countries, and this effect was larger than between those European respondents who claimed to know about Islam and those who did not claim to be knowledgeable (25% vs. 4%).

EARLY HISTORY

Contact theory's early history was inauspicious. Long before there was a research base to guide them, 19th-century thinkers regarded intergroup contact as dangerous rather than beneficial. Dominated by Social Darwinist thought and the writings of William Graham Sumner (1906), a Yale University sociologist and an Episcopal minister, intergroup contact was thought to lead inevitably to conflict. Sumner believed that cross-group hostility was simply a certain consequence of each ingroup's presumed sense of superiority. Consequently, intergroup hostility and conflict were considered natural and inevitable outcomes of contact. Some later theories make somewhat similar predictions (Jackson, 1993; Levine & Campbell, 1972).

Twentieth-century White writers continued to speculate about intergroup contact without solid empirical evidence. P. E. Baker (1934) believed that contact between the races, even under conditions of equality, would only breed "suspicion, fear, resentment, disturbance, and at times open conflict" (p. 120). Many of these writers, such as Sumner himself, were delicately

[1] For example, see Pettigrew (1971, 1986, 1997a, 2004b, 2009b, 2016), Pettigrew and Hewstone (2017), Pettigrew and Martin (1987), Pettigrew and Tropp (2000, 2005, 2006, 2008, 2011), Pettigrew et al. (2010), and Tropp and Pettigrew (2004, 2005a, 2005b).

defending the South's then-existing pattern of rigid racial segregation in schools, neighborhoods, and public facilities. But following World War II, many writers became more optimistic. Lett (1945) held that shared interracial experiences with a common objective led to "mutual understanding and regard" (p. 35). Instead, when groups "are isolated from one another," wrote Brameld (1946) ahead of his time, "prejudice and conflict grow like a disease" (p. 245).

Once Hitler had given prejudice an exceedingly evil reputation, a popular crusade formed in America to condemn both racial and religious prejudice. This response, called the Human Relations Movement, sought to end prejudice and correct negative stereotypes. Yet this attempt was as naive as it was well intentioned. The Movement placed its complete faith in educating various groups about one another and countering negative stereotypes. But it avoided controversy by not directly seeking the institutional changes necessary to enhance meaningful intergroup contact and combat discrimination in jobs, housing, and education. Rather, it invested its energies in celebrating Brotherhood Week each February and hosting dinners for all groups to meet once a year.[2]

The Movement, dryly noted Drake and Cayton (1962), was guided by an "almost mystical faith in 'getting to know one another' as a solvent of racial tensions" (p. 281). To be sure, ignorance is a factor in intergroup relations (W. G. Stephan & Stephan, 1984). But ignorance alone does not account for the many situational and institutional barriers that perpetuate prejudice between groups. Moreover, the Human Relations Movement did not grasp the complexity of intergroup contact factors—the focus of the recent surge in research on the topic. Meeting once a year across a dinner table is hardly sufficient.

On the positive side, the Movement helped to inspire early research on contact between groups. During the slow racial desegregation of the merchant marines during World War II, close bonds developed between Black and White seamen on the ships and in the maritime union. They were often facing death together from German U-boat attacks. Brophy (1945) showed that the more voyages the White seamen took with Black seamen, the more positive their racial attitudes became. Of course, their racial prejudice

[2] In the 1950s and 1960s, I attended many of these February Brotherhood Dinners in Boston. The same African American Bostonians were at my assigned table almost each year. And some of the speakers at these events lost sight of the dinner's tone and focus. I recall vividly a Boston Congressman shouting out that he "*hated* people who are prejudiced!"

did not suddenly evaporate with a single interracial voyage. But there was an almost linear effect of change: The more interracial voyages the White seamen took, the less anti-Black prejudice they expressed.

Similarly, White police officers in Philadelphia who had worked with Black colleagues had sharply more positive racial views than other White police (Kephart, 1957). They were more open to teaming with a Black partner, having Blacks join their previously all-White police districts, and taking orders from qualified Black officers.

Allport contributed to this growing literature by testing the effects of equal-status contact on the anti-Jewish attitudes of non-Jewish undergraduates at Dartmouth College and Harvard University (Allport & Kramer, 1946). He, too, found an almost linear effect: The more equal-status contacts these students reported having had with Jewish students, the less they recorded anti-Jewish views.

Field studies of public housing provided the strongest early evidence. This work marked one of the first large-scale field research studies in North American social psychology. Deutsch and Collins (1951) interviewed White housewives across different public housing projects with a quasi-experimental design. Two housing projects in Newark, New Jersey, assigned Black and White residents to apartments in separate buildings. Two comparable public housing projects in New York City desegregated residents by making apartment assignments irrespective of race or personal preference. White women in the desegregated projects reported far more positive contact with their Black neighbors, and they expressed higher esteem for their Black neighbors and greater support for interracial housing.

Further public housing research by Wilner et al. (1955) replicated and extended these positive findings. The authors found that the more intimate the interracial contact, the more favorable the effects. Among those Whites who had just casual greetings with their Black neighbors, only one third revealed more positive attitudes. Among those who had only street conversations with their Black neighbors, half revealed more positive attitudes. And among those who had multiple types of interactions with their Black neighbors, 75% revealed more positive attitudes. Thus, the more the Whites acted like neighbors, the more they felt like neighbors.

These early American studies all focused on White prejudice—which was rightly seen as the basic societal concern. But this raises the question: What were the effects of this same contact on African Americans? Works (1961) supplied the answer. He found that increased equal-status interracial contact in another public housing project in a small midwestern city correlated with more positive feelings and attitudes of the Black residents toward their White neighbors. However, more recent contact research reveals that the positive effects for minorities tend to be somewhat smaller than those for majority participants (Tropp & Pettigrew, 2005b).

EMPIRICAL PROBLEMS OF EARLY INTERGROUP CONTACT RESEARCH

Many of these early studies had their weaknesses—in particular, the problems of self-selection and causal direction mentioned earlier. It could well have been the case that the White seamen, police officers, students, and apartment dwellers in these studies who had intergroup contact were already less prejudiced and that explains why they were the ones having cross-group contact. In other words, the causal sequence could be in the opposite direction from that assumed in this early research—less initial prejudice can lead selectively to more intergroup contact rather than more contact leads to less prejudice.

Later work specifically checked on this causal direction issue. An occasional study found that both directions operate at roughly equal strengths (e.g., Binder et al., 2009). Other research fails to replicate this result (Arnadóttir et al., 2018; Bagci & Turnuklu, 2019; Christ et al., 2008; Pettigrew & Tropp, 2011, Chapter 12). Most of this research has found the contact-to-reduced-prejudice path stronger than the tolerance-to-contact path (Brown et al., 2007; Christ et al., 2014; Dhont et al., 2011; Pettigrew, 1997b; Powers & Ellison, 1995; Wilson, 1996). Obviously, the best means of testing this causal direction issue is with longitudinal data, and these studies find the contact-to-prejudice path to be the primary causal route (e.g., Christ et al., 2014).

THE INITIAL THEORETICAL STATEMENTS

This growing literature led the Social Science Research Council to commission Robin Williams, Jr. (1947), an eminent Cornell University sociologist, to review the race relations research literature. His monograph *The Reduction of Intergroup Tensions* offers 102 testable "propositions" on intergroup relations that included the initial formulation of intergroup contact theory. Williams stressed that many variables were involved in contact's effects. He predicted that contact's positive effects would be greatest when (a) the two groups share similar status; (b) the situation fosters personal, intimate intergroup contact; (c) the participants do not fit their group's stereotype; and (d) the contact activities cut across group lines. Although rudimentary, Williams's astute formulation forecast many of the findings of intergroup research 7 decades later.

Allport (1954) was influenced by and cited Williams's groundbreaking work in his contact chapter in *The Nature of Prejudice*. He was also impressed with Stouffer's famous World War II study of unit desegregation during the desperate Battle of the Bulge in Flanders in the frozen winter of 1944–45.[3] Employing an ingenious quasi-experimental design, Stouffer and his coworkers (1949) demonstrated that the experience of fighting side by side with African Americans greatly improved the racial attitudes of the White American soldiers. These altered attitudes were found among Southerners as well as Northerners, and among officers as well as enlisted men. However, the changes were limited to the combat situation and did not initially extend to such noncombat situations as the army's PX stores.

THE FOUR-FACTORS RESTATEMENT OF ALLPORT'S "CONTACT HYPOTHESIS"

As described in Chapter 2 of this volume, it was this contact chapter that excited me when Allport's important prejudice volume appeared. After all, it was my early contact with Mildred Adams that had set me on the path of studying racial prejudice. Indeed, I became so interested in intergroup contact that I chose to take my doctoral special examination on the subject. The test was administered and graded by Allport himself.

Allport's contact chapter mentions many pertinent points, yet its broad and discursive nature made it difficult to prepare for the examination. So I boiled the text down to four key factors that enabled intergroup contact to reduce prejudice: (a) equal status between the groups within the situation, (b) common goals, (c) cooperation between groups, and (d) authority support for the contact.

Allport approved of my synthesis, and I continued to use it with his endorsement in later publications (e.g., Pettigrew, 1971). These four factors are now routinely cited as Allport's contact theory—although they are not explicitly listed in his chapter. But there are serious limitations to this approach. First, like any list, it does not do full justice to Allport's rich

[3] I know what especially impressed Allport, because I was working at the time as his "go-for"—not for coffee but for books from Harvard's Widener Library.

discussion. Second, it is a "positive factors" approach that research later found to be too narrow. Allport, writing in the midst of the tense McCarthyist and Korean War era, assumed that intergroup contact typically *failed* to reduce prejudice. So he sought to make explicit positive factors that were *necessary* for contact to diminish prejudice.

In turn, this necessary-factors approach led to a third problem (Pettigrew, 1986). During the decades following the publication of Allport's volume, writers added further factors that they presumed to be required for intergroup contact to have positive results. As the laundry list of presumed necessary conditions accumulated, the theory was in danger of becoming meaningless. The ever-increasing list of "necessary" conditions rapidly excluded the vast majority of the world's intergroup situations and began to render the theory trivial. Social psychologists were concentrating too much on avoiding Type I errors (false positives) and ignoring Type II errors (false negatives).

My meta-analysis of intergroup contact effects with Tropp uncovered a fourth limitation of the necessary factors approach (Pettigrew & Tropp, 2006). The four factors thought to be necessary for positive intergroup contact effects proved to be highly facilitating but not absolutely necessary after all.

FURTHER ADVANCES

The 1960s and 1970s witnessed increasing attention to contact theory as its policy implications became more evident. I found it useful as the basis of my expert testimony in support of racial school desegregation in legal cases in Springfield, Massachusetts; Los Angeles, California; and Norfolk and Richmond, Virginia (Pettigrew, 1979b).

In 1998, I published in the *Annual Review of Psychology* a reformulated theory of intergroup contact (Pettigrew, 1998). Figure 7.1 diagrams the article's principal emphases. Note that the schematic outline specifies input from all three levels—micro-, meso-, and macrolevels. Drawing on the then-available contact literature, the chapter urged that broader, multivariate research approaches be undertaken, especially overtime studies that could follow the temporal development of contact's effects—from initial contact on to established contact and finally to a sense of a unified single group. This specified time-sequence follows the three processes proposed by various theorists—decategorization (Brewer & Miller, 1984), salient categorization (Van Oudenhoven et al., 1996), and recategorization (Anastasio

FIGURE 7.1. Reformulated Theory of Intergroup Contact

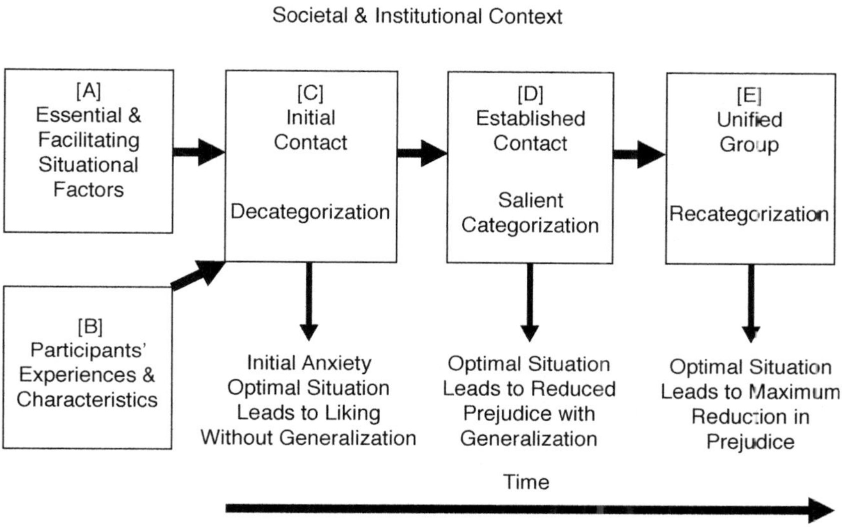

From "Intergroup Contact Theory," by T. F. Pettigrew, 1998, *Annual Review of Psychology*, *49*, p. 77. (https://doi.org/10.1146/annurev.psych.49.1.65). Copyright 1998 by Annual Reviews. Reprinted with permission.

et al., 1997; Gaertner et al., 1993, 1994). Although all three were initially seen as rival processes, this time model held all of them to be operating but at different times in the contact phenomenon.

Other studies using the advanced statistics described in Chapter 4 of this volume have been conducted since 1998, but one-time investigations are still prevalent in the current intergroup contact literature.

It was not until 2015 that MacInnis and Page-Gould (2015) brought the focus back to the time dimension. They proposed an elegant over-time model that reconciled an apparent paradox in the intergroup relations literature. Although intergroup contact research routinely reports mostly positive results (Pettigrew & Tropp, 2006), the largely separate intergroup interaction literature often reports negative outcomes—heightened stress, anxiety, and avoidance (e.g., Shelton et al., 2009; W. G. Stephan & Stephan, 1985; Trawalter et al., 2009, 2012). MacInnis and Page-Gould's temporal model brings the two research literatures together as one process. The model points out that initial intergroup contact is typically awkward and stressful. But as this contact continues, a threshold is passed wherein the initial stress is alleviated in part and positive outcomes begin to emerge.

Brown and Hewstone (2005) advanced contact theory further by providing an intensive review of the many moderating and mediating factors involved in intergroup contact's effects. Over the past 3 decades, these two British investigators have tirelessly contributed significant research and analyses on the theory. And their former doctoral students from around the globe have found intergroup contact to reduce prejudice in their home countries ranging from Italy, Chile, and Cyprus to Pakistan, Australia, and South Africa.

A NEEDED META-ANALYSIS

To focus the theory, I long wanted to review the research on intergroup contact. But for years there were too few studies to analyze and inadequate review methods. By the 1990s, however, the contact literature was expanding and meta-analysis—a vast improvement over qualitative reviews—had been developed. So Linda Tropp (then a doctoral student at the University of California, Santa Cruz and later a professor at the University of Massachusetts at Amherst) and I decided the time had arrived to conduct a thorough review of intergroup contact research (Pettigrew & Tropp, 2000, 2006, 2008, 2011).

As is typical of major meta-analyses, it took years to collect a near-complete collection of the extensive contact-prejudice research. My patient wife thought the task would never end. We uncovered a total of 515 studies with 713 independent samples and 1,351 nonindependent tests that met our inclusion rules. (See Appendix A of Pettigrew & Tropp, 2011, for a complete listing of the studies.) These studies span the years 1941 to 2000 and contain responses from more than 250,000 participants, with half of the samples focused on racial or ethnic target groups.

Our meta-analysis reached several conclusions. First, the average effect for all studies was $r = -.21$ (Cohen's $d = .43$)—a solid, average effect size for most meta-analyses (e.g., Meyer et al., 2001; Zell & Krizan, 2014). Larger effect sizes are rare in meta-analyses because they typically include a wide mix of research formats, analyses, contexts, and subjects.

The average effect size of $r = -.21$ cannot be explained away by participant selection, publication bias, sampling biases, or poorly conducted research. In fact, the most rigorous studies tend to provide the largest effects. This phenomenon is repeated again in 21st-century research. Later research is more rigorously executed and yields larger contact effects than earlier work tested in the meta-analysis (Pettigrew & Tropp, 2006, 2008).

The basic finding is that intergroup contact's positive effects are confined not just to those outgroup members who directly participated in the contact. The primary generalization typically extends from the immediate outgroup members who participate in the contact to the entire outgroup.[4] This effect is enhanced when the contact situation makes participants' group identities salient (Brown & Hewstone, 2005) and when the outgroup members are seen as typical of their group (Brown et al., 2007). Contact's effects also normally extend to situations different from the original contact situation (Cook, 1984; Vezzali et al., 2020). And effective intergroup contact has many positive outcomes in addition to diminishing bias—from supporting prominority social policies to actually participating in collective action on behalf of minority causes (e.g., Selvanathan et al., 2018).

Furthermore, the review uncovered evidence for the apparent universality of intergroup contact phenomena across varied settings, age cohorts, and 38 countries throughout the world. We also found significant contact effects for groups that differ in race, ethnicity, nationality, sexual orientation, and physical and mental disabilities. Of course, there is variability in these effects. For example, the effects for majority groups tend to be larger than those for minority groups (Tropp & Pettigrew, 2005b).[5] Yet the overall positive trend is remarkably consistent. The apparent universality of the intergroup contact phenomenon suggests that there is a basic underlying process. This process undoubtedly reflects the fact that familiarity generally leads to liking—Zajonc's (1968) mere exposure effect.

As mentioned earlier, the most important theoretical finding of the meta-analysis is that the four factors I deduced from Allport's contact chapter were *facilitating* but not *necessary* factors for contact's constructive effects (Pettigrew & Tropp, 2006, 2011). Studies featuring none of the key factors still tend to yield positive effects of contact on prejudice—although smaller than those studies with the key conditions.

---

[4] Think about the enormous generalization leap that this primary step entails. It was logically irrational that my attitudes toward African Americans *as a group* should have been permanently modified by my early experiences with just one person—Mildred Adams. Similarly, it is just as irrational that others develop deep prejudices against *all* African Americans on the basis of a single negative encounter with a single African American. Yet this irrational type of gross overgeneralization, driven by emotions, is common throughout intergroup relations and psychology generally.

[5] There are exceptions to this finding. Some research shows the opposite trend with stronger contact effects for minorities than for majorities (e.g., Wölfer et al., 2016, Study 1).

In the first 2 decades of the 21st century, the research literature on intergroup contact exploded from only 30 publications before 1960 to more than 300 from the years 2000 to 2019—almost 100 of them in the journal *Group Processes and Intergroup Relations* alone (Dovidio et al., 2017, p. 607).

Longitudinal studies provide the most compelling support for the theory (e.g., Binder et al., 2009; Christ et al., 2010; Eller & Abrams, 2004; Levin et al., 2003). Roommate studies at universities have been conducted often on the effects of contact. One such investigation had 1st-year undergraduate students randomly assigned to live either with a same-race or different-race student (Shook et al., 2016). After just one semester, compared with controls, the interracial room participants had significantly lower social dominance orientation (SDO) scores and more positive attitudes toward their roommate's group as well as outgroups different from their roommate—a secondary transfer effect (STE; detailed later in this chapter). Moreover, SDO reduction fully mediated the intergroup contact effect on STEs.

Especially impressive is the longitudinal roommate research conducted by Sidanius and colleagues (2008). This study employed five data points over a 4-year period with more than 2,000 undergraduate students at the University of California, Los Angeles (UCLA). The extensive longitudinal design allowed a direct test of the causal link between intergroup contact and diminished prejudice.

The study also boasted a quasi-experimental design using randomly assigned roommates of diverse ethnicities. Although most contact studies look at only two groups, this work looked at four groups—African, Asian, Latinx, and Whites. Further, the UCLA investigation tested affective, cognitive, and behavioral dependent variables. In short, this study provides a model for future research because it tests for cumulative effects with longitudinal data for multiple groups within a specific macro-institutional setting.

The UCLA investigators found significant reciprocal effects across the 4 years: Interethnic friendships reduced prejudice, whereas initial ingroup bias and intergroup anxiety led to fewer intergroup friends. Those students who had intergroup experience prior to coming to UCLA tended to show the greatest changes revealing the cumulative power of intergroup contact. With one exception involving Asian American students, the randomly assigned roommates from different ethnicities typically decreased their outgroup biases even for outgroups not involved in their roommate relationship—the STE—to which we now turn.

NON-FACE-TO-FACE INTERGROUP CONTACT OF MANY TYPES CAN ALSO HAVE POSITIVE EFFECTS

There are five general types of indirect contact that often diminish prejudice without actually physically meeting, some of them quite surprising: (a) the STE, (b) extended contact, (c) imagined contact, (d) impersonal media contact, and (e) virtual contact through computer-generated communication.

First, there is the STE (Pettigrew, 2009b). This effect occurs when the reduction in prejudice from intergroup contact with one outgroup also acts to reduce the prejudice against other outgroups that did not participate in the original contact. I discovered this effect by following the advice of my old teacher of survey methods, Samuel Stouffer. His constant mantra was "Let the data teach you something!" By this he meant go beyond just testing your theory with survey data; go explore the data thoroughly, and look for patterns that you never expected. This is the exciting part of survey analysis mentioned earlier. And that is how I uncovered the STE.

While analyzing a large four-nation European survey for standard intergroup contact effects (Reif & Melich, 1991), I suddenly noted a consistent and unexpected trend. The data *were* "teaching me something"—just as Stouffer had promised. Contact in each of the nations—France, Great Britain, the Netherlands, and West Germany—was reducing prejudice against not only the contacted outgroup but also outgroups that hardly existed in these countries (Pettigrew, 1997b). For instance, Turks are found in Germany and the Netherlands but rarely in France or Great Britain. Yet significant decreases in anti-Turkish prejudice emerged in France and Great Britain among those who possessed friends of other outgroups. Indeed, this surprising pattern was repeated throughout the data set. Later, I formalized this consistent result as the STE (Pettigrew, 2009b).

An array of follow-up studies has further demonstrated and delineated the effect. Consider a study conducted in Italy. Vezzali and Giovannini (2012) studied 175 high school students. With the effects of prior contact statistically controlled, attitudes toward immigrants improved with contact. And this attitude change generalized to improved attitudes toward people with disabilities and toward gay men and lesbians as well. Intergroup attitudes, intergroup anxiety, and perspective taking all played mediating roles in this secondary transfer finding.

Tausch and her international colleagues (2010) ruled out three alternative accounts of STEs—contact with the secondary outgroup, socially desirable responding, and prior attitudes. They found strong STEs in cross-sectional studies conducted in Cyprus, Northern Ireland, and Texas and a longitudinal study conducted in Northern Ireland. Mediational analyses found strong evidence for attitude generalization as the major underlying process. Consequently, outgroups resembling the contacted outgroup tend to show the largest STEs.

Schmid and her European colleagues (2012) analyzed a cross-sectional sample of 7,042 respondents from eight European nations. They tested for STEs by checking on the links between intergroup contact with immigrants and attitudes toward gay men and lesbians and Jews. Again, via attitude generalization, they uncovered STEs. Those with positive contacts with immigrants became more accepting not just of immigrants but of gay men and lesbians and Jews as well. They also found these effects strongest for respondents who were low in SDO—a microlevel contextual effect.

Questions have been raised about whether intergroup contact phenomena will still operate in situations of intense conflict. There have been consistent findings from repeated studies showing highly positive results from intergroup contact in such embattled areas as Northern Ireland (Hewstone et al., 2006; Tropp et al., 2017), Israel (Shani & Boehnke, 2017), Cyprus (Yucel & Psaltis, 2019), and Southern Africa (Çakal et al., 2011; J. L. Gibson & Claassen, 2010; Tropp et al., 2017). In addition, a study of contact between Roma and non-Roma Hungarians uncovered positive change in a nation intensely hostile to the Roma people (A. Kende et al., 2017).

An Israeli study by Lissitsa and Kushnirovich (2018) went further and tested for STEs. Using an online survey of Israeli Jews and Palestinians, the authors found that the STE among their Jewish subjects with more positive views of Israeli Palestinians spilled over to more positive views of non-Israeli Palestinians. But there was no evidence of the STE for negative contact. Surprising as it may seem, in their meta-analysis of nonlaboratory contact studies, Lemmer and Wagner (2015) showed that such positive results in conflict areas are commonplace. These repeated studies yielding positive results in conflict regions directly refute the charge that intergroup contact theory is applicable only to positive, nonconflict situations.

Second, there is the *extended contact effect* (S. C. Wright et al., 1997). Just having an ingroup friend who has an outgroup friend tends to improve attitudes toward the outgroup. As balance theory predicts, *a friend of my friend is also my friend*. Zhou et al. (2019) confirmed the extended contact phenomenon with a wide-ranging meta-analysis. There is also *depersonalized* extended contact. Repeated experiments demonstrate that positive effects can occur even if the outgroup friends involved are unknown to the person. But, in yet another contextual effect, this depersonalized effect requires ingroup normative support (Gómez et al., 2018). Extended contact can also improve intergroup attitudes over and above the positive influence of direct, face-to-face intergroup contact (Vezzali et al., 2014).

Third, even *imagined intergroup contact* tends to have positive effects (Turner et al., 2007, Experiments 2 and 3). Miles and Crisp (2014) meta-analyzed studies of imagined intergroup contact. They uncovered in these studies a significant reduction in both implicit (IAT) and explicit intergroup prejudice. Consider two such studies. In Italy, fourth graders revealed increased outgroup trust and future contact intentions 1 week after imagined contact with an unknown immigrant child (Vezzali et al., 2012). And just thinking about contact can attenuate anticipatory physiological responses during real interaction with a member of an outgroup (West et al., 2015). This phenomenon even extends to animals. Imagined contact with farm animals and pets improves some attitudes toward them moderated by SDO and prior contact (Auger & Amiot, 2019).

Some psychologists remain "deeply skeptical" about such simulated social contact, but they do not cite specific, testable reasons for their skepticism (Bigler & Hughes, 2010, p. 132). One replication study did not find the imagined contact effect (R. A. Klein et al., 2014); and we do not as yet know how long the effects remain for adults. In addition, data from Slovenia suggest that the effect operates less strongly when working memory capacity is minimal (Marić et al., 2019).

Fourth, *impersonal media contact*, such as watching African Americans play such high-status roles as judges on television, can also erode prejudice. It can also ease the anxiety that often accompanies initial direct intergroup contact, as shown by West et al. (2015; see also Fujioka, 1999; Graves, 1999; Herek & Capitanio, 1997; Schiappa et al., 2005, 2006). An Italian study of 185 high school students revealed that even videos of cross-group friendship reduced negative stereotypes and increased willingness to engage in intergroup contact (Vezzali et al., 2019). Page-Gould and Zhou (in press), employing another meta-analysis, found positive effects for such impersonal media contact.

The most fascinating of these media investigations is Paluck's (2009) test of a radio soap opera featuring messages about reducing prejudice, violence, and trauma in the embattled African nation of Rwanda. She found that the program was quite successful in changing the listeners' perceptions of the social norms and their behaviors regarding a range of topics from intertribal marriage and trust to empathy and trauma healing. But the effort did not significantly alter the listeners' personal beliefs. Yet, changing norms is in itself crucially important for changing behavior which in time—given cognitive dissonance processes (Stone & Fernandez, 2008)—may well ultimately lead to attitude change.

Finally, there is *virtual contact* made possible by computer communication. This type of indirect contact is less threatening than direct contact, and it enables many more people to experience interacting with members of groups different from their own. This process can reduce prejudice over 12 months (White et al., 2014), but its effects are generally smaller than either direct contact or extended contact (Lemmer & Wagner, 2015).

Part of the processes underlying these vicarious contact phenomena involve the perception of normative changes, and part is mediated by a positive change in metastereotypes—what you believe the outgroup thinks of your ingroup (Gómez & Huici, 2008; Vorauer et al., 1998). These indirect contact effects are especially important for those who live in segregated areas without outgroup neighbors (Christ et al., 2010; Turner & West, 2012; Wölfer et al., 2019). Indirect contact prepares them for later direct contact.

These five indirect contact processes clarify that intergroup contact effects spread broadly—a vital point for social policy.

INTERGROUP TRUST AS A DEPENDENT VARIABLE

The bulk of intergroup contact research uses prejudice as the central dependent variable. But there is also a sizable research literature on contact that features intergroup trust as the central dependent variable—a factor of particular concern to political science. This area has witnessed contradictory results caused by a regrettably flawed and highly publicized article.

Robert Putnam (2007) published a paper in which he claimed that diverse communities in the United States had significantly less trust of their neighbors and other forms of depleted social capital.[6] Diverse areas, he maintained, suffer from a reduction in both ingroup and outgroup solidarity. Along with low trust, he held that such areas also endure lower confidence in local government, leaders, and news media; reduced political efficacy; less voting; fewer contributions to charity; less reported happiness; more television viewing; and fewer friends. He broached these sweeping

[6] Although largely ignoring the many hundreds of studies that show the prejudice-reducing power of intergroup contact, the mass media immediately leaped on this study with such headlines as "Harvard Study Says Diversity Is Bad for You" and "Diversity Harms Human Relations." A *Wall Street Journal* columnist pronounced "the death of diversity" (Henninger, 2007). And segregationists misappropriated it to argue against affirmative action in college admissions cases in federal courts.

conclusions on the basis of his analysis of a one-level, cross-sectional American survey together with community surveys from 41 nonrandom American areas of varying sizes.

Intergroup contact research does not support Putnam's highly publicized conclusions. Take, for instance, a 1991 probability survey conducted in embattled Northern Ireland at the height of the Troubles. Among both Roman Catholics and Protestants, cross-denominational contact related positively and significantly to trust as well as outgroup attitudes, forgiveness, and perspective taking. The solid correlation between cross-group friendship and trust was +.41. Indeed, contact related to greater trust even among those of both religions who had the very worst experiences from the region's bloody sectarian conflict (Hewstone et al., 2006). Similar findings for trust and other positive reactions from intergroup contact have been found in both Northern Ireland and South Africa by Tropp and her colleagues (Tropp et al., 2017) and in Germany by Gundelach and Freitag (2014).

One study set out to test Putnam's claims across 28 European countries (Gesthuizen et al., 2008). It failed to confirm his contentions. Instead, it found that economic inequality and a national history of continuous democracy were the key predictors of the wide differences in social capital between European nations.

Why the discrepancies between Putnam's analysis and most of the entire intergroup contact research literature? One set of problems involves his gross aggregation across ethnic groups and imprecise measurement of "diversity." Various minorities in the United States have substantial differences in social capital with typically larger levels of distrust among minority groups (Tropp, 2008), nor does Putnam distinguish between "diversity" at the broad community level and the neighborhood level where the opportunities for intergroup contact are maximized. We also do not know if these areas are stable or in the midst of rapid transition—"gentrification" with Whites rapidly replacing Blacks or Blacks leaving segregated neighborhoods and rapidly replacing Whites. Both of these hectic situations can obviously diminish intergroup trust.

Another reason for the discrepancies involves indirect effects. These need to be detected by multilevel models more powerful than the simple regressions used by Putnam. Schmid et al. (2014) demonstrated the point by using a multilevel path analysis with data from a large English probability survey sample. They found negative direct effects for the majority British respondents, but they also found that diversity was linked indirectly with increased trust via positive contact and lower threat. And these positive indirect effects canceled out most of the negative direct effects.

But the major reason for Putnam's divergent results is that he simply omits both *intergroup contact* and *segregation* in his published analyses. This was a serious mistake leading directly to his unsubstantiated conclusions. When other investigators insert these key variables into their analyses, the results are dramatically altered. For instance, Stolle et al. (2008) used Canadian and American data and replicated Putnam's results when they did not consider intergroup contact. But when they examined responses from those individuals who regularly talked to their neighbors, they found that these individuals were far less influenced by the racial and ethnic character of their neighborhood. Thus, social ties moderate negative effects of diversity just as contact theory would predict.

Similarly, Rothwell (2010) studied how residential segregation of minorities can severely restrict intergroup contact and alter trust in American cities. He analyzed the same data and employed the same methods as an earlier investigation by Alesina and La Ferrara (2002) that had results that mirrored those of Putnam. But Rothwell made one crucial change: He added a comprehensive measure of *neighborhood segregation*. This single change sharply reversed the findings. Rothwell concluded that residential "integration increases trust, and if anything, diversity fosters trust for any given level of segregation" (p. 1). He then replicated this finding using voting behavior, instead of trust, as the dependent variable. Rothwell concluded that earlier analyses that had excluded measures of neighborhood segregation all suffered from an omitted variable bias.

Yet the issue was not finally settled at this point, because Rothwell had used different data sets from Putnam. It remained for Uslaner (2011a, 2011b, 2012) to resolve the debate. He used the same data set as Putnam had used and found the same results as Rothwell. In repeated analyses, Uslaner showed that *residential segregation*, not diversity per se, is highly associated with reduced trust. This is the case because segregation severely limits intergroup contact. Next, with two surveys—one of which Putnam had used—Uslaner demonstrates that American residents of integrated neighborhoods who have diverse social networks evince substantially greater trust.

There is also a microlevel process involved. Van Assche et al. (2018) replicated Putnam's results with data from the Netherlands, when they did not control for segregation and other means of limiting intergroup contact. But the authors found that the diminished trust and greater political cynicism in more diverse settings was actually limited to those who were high on both authoritarianism and SDO. Recall from Chapter 5 of this volume that authoritarians tend to avoid contact with outgroups. Once again, we see that Putnam's distrust conclusions operate when opportunities for intergroup contact are limited either structurally or personally.

Putnam's mistake was not new; earlier, the same mistake was routinely made. A half-century ago, many investigators repeatedly found that racial prejudice and discrimination were greatest in those areas of the racially segregated South that had the highest proportion of Black citizens. This effect, first highlighted by Key (1949) and later confirmed in multiple publications (e.g., Blalock, 1957; Oliver & Wong, 2003; Pettigrew, 1957; Pettigrew & Campbell, 1960; Pettigrew & Cramer, 1959), appears to be due to the perceived physical threat of a greater number of outgroup members living in one's area. But these studies all took place in areas with strict racial segregation.

The early investigators (including me) failed to see that these negative effects of diversity could be offset by the greater intergroup contact that could ensue if there were no structural barriers to the contact. These dual, albeit opposing, effects of diversity—greater threat and greater contact—have now often been demonstrated (e.g., Pettigrew et al., 2010; Wagner et al., 2003, 2006). Hence, by concentrating exclusively on White threat from the proportional size of the Black population, researchers committed the single-factor fallacy by ignoring the role of racial segregation limiting positive interracial contact effects (Pettigrew & Hewstone, 2017). Unfortunately, Putnam (2007), in his much-publicized article, repeated this same mistake 6 decades later.

Regrettably, the Putnam publication established a model that has since been followed by many researchers in political science. Not surprisingly, when a meta-analysis of such studies was conducted, it concluded that diversity leads to reduced trust (Dinesen et al., 2020; Dinesen & Sønderskov, in press). They found that out of 87 study-pooled correlations based on 1,001 estimates, only 11 showed diversity increasing trust, 16 more essentially had no effects, 15 uncovered tiny effects of diversity decreasing trust, 18 revealed modest effects of declining trust, and the remaining 27 had more substantial effects of reduced trust. A few of the studies included in this meta-analysis did check on contact effects, but these analyses are ignored in the overall meta-analytic conclusion.

Two pertinent examples illustrate the problem. Recall earlier the Alesina and La Ferrara (2002) study that replicated Putnam's results but had its results reversed by Rothwell (2010) by simply adding a control for neighborhood segregation. But in the Danish meta-analysis, only the original results without the segregated control are cited. Consider also a well-executed study conducted in the German city of Konstanz by Gundelach and Freitag (2014). Dinesen and his colleagues (2020) recorded the results of this study as showing one of the three strongest findings indicating that diversity reduces trust (p. 8).[7] But the Konstanz authors themselves reached a sharply different conclusion from these same data: "Referring to intergroup contact theory and group specific effects of diversity, [this] paper challenges the notion that ethnic diversity has overwhelmingly negative effects on social trust" (Gundelach & Freitag, 2014, p. 1236). Why the difference in interpretations? The usual reason: The first ignores contact effects, the second includes them.

In sum, contact theory cannot be effectively critiqued when measures of contact and group segregation are omitted from the analysis. The Rothwell and Uslaner findings are consistent with the basic contentions of intergroup contact theory. Diversity involves both intergroup threat *and* greater contact; the problem lies in understanding how they both function within the same model rather than selecting one or the other as the key process.

Bringing together the results of multiple studies, a contextual model emerges that combines both the intergroup contact and the threat factors. There is a delicate balance between contact and threat effects. A two-wave longitudinal study of White English respondents found that anti-outgroup prejudice increased only in those communities that were becoming more ethnically mixed *and* segregated (Laurence et al., 2018). The existing level of prejudice in an area prior to the entry of the newcomers (Kotzur et al., 2018) is also important. In addition, as previously observed, threat is aroused when the outgroup comes suddenly in large numbers and during a short time period. This happened, for instance, when large numbers of Albanian refugees suddenly fled to Italy following the 1990 breakdown of the Albanian Communist government. Anti-Albanian prejudice in Italy rose sharply in this period.

If there are relatively few newcomers spread over time, contact effects will generally be dominant if there is negligible segregation. Given enough time, positive contact effects will emerge even if the incoming group is rather large—again, if there is little or no segregation preventing intergroup contact. In Chapter 8 of this volume, I find that areas with *small* numbers of the outgroup actually tended to vote in far more prejudiced ways than

[7] The Danish authors of the meta-analysis considered contact effects in separate analyses. They ignored relevant social psychological studies and concluded that while the role of contact is "very complicated," it "changes the effect of ethnic diversity on social trust very little" (Dinesen et al., 2020, p. 13; Dinesen & Sønderskov, in press, p. 16). Their measures of interethnic contact that support this conclusion are highly questionable. Indeed, Uslaner (personal communication, October 22, 2019) shows that their measure of diversity is actually a measure of segregation!

areas with large numbers of the outgroup—usually large cities where the outgroup's presence had taken firm roots over a lengthy period. The key to this formulation is to check on any barriers to intergroup contact that exist. Housing segregation is obviously one such barrier. But there are more subtle obstacles as well. There is a classic context effect involving the local economy (Knowles & Tropp, 2018). A healthy, robust local economy mutes threat effects in mixed areas, thus allowing contact processes to operate more fully.

BUT WHAT ABOUT NEGATIVE INTERGROUP CONTACT?

Of course, not all intergroup contact reduces prejudice and improves intergroup relations. Some adverse contact can enhance prejudice, reinforce negative stereotypes, and harm intergroup relations generally.

Imagine a tense checkpoint on the Palestinian West Bank (Conover, 2006; Pettigrew, 2003). Neither the Israeli soldiers nor the Palestinian civilians passing through had chosen to be in this fearful situation. Both parties are understandably threatened. The soldiers fear the possibility of a suicide bomber or other attacks upon them. The Palestinians fear humiliation and violence from the gun-toting soldiers. Contrary to the assertions of some critics, no intergroup contact theorist has ever held that such a stressful situation would cause anything other than to exacerbate intergroup conflict. Note the crucial elements in the situation. Both groups are understandably highly threatened, and the checkpoint situation starkly violates major characteristics of effective intergroup contact—involuntary contact that is at best superficial between tense, fearful interactants of unequal status in the situation.

Early research on intergroup contact focused on positive contact situations. Into the 21st century, however, social psychologists began to pay special attention to situations involving negative contact. One might initially think that negative contact effects would simply be the mirror image of positive contact effects, that negative contact would produce heightened intergroup prejudice. But the relevant findings from throughout the world turn out to be more complex. For example, both positive and negative contact influence affective dimensions of prejudice, but negative contact has especially strong effects on such cognitive dimensions of prejudice as stereotypes (Aberson, 2015).

Negative intergroup contact is not as common as positive contact, but its effects can be more forceful. Research repeatedly finds that respondents report considerably more positive than negative encounters with outgroup members.[8] This reflects in large part that we are likely to repeat pleasant experiences and avoid unpleasant ones. But some studies hold that negative contact has a larger impact than positive contact. Using Australian and American samples, Barlow and colleagues (2012) noted that the quantity of negative contact related more closely to increased prejudice than the quantity of positive contact related to reduced prejudice. They incorrectly regarded their results as universally reflecting greater category salience of negative contact. However, in an apparent exception to the "bad is stronger than good" principle (Baumeister et al., 2001; Kahneman & Tversky, 1979; Rozin & Royzman, 2001; Tierney & Baumeister, 2020), other research typically fails to replicate this result (Arnadóttir et al., 2018; Bagci & Turnuklu, 2019; Christ et al., 2008; Pettigrew & Tropp, 2011, Chapter 12). This discrepancy in findings may be caused in part by contrasting empirical measures.

In addition, negative contact tends to make group memberships more salient (Graf et al., 2014), as well as often having an adverse effect on intergroup attitudes (Hayward et al., 2017). Indeed, a U.K. study on negative contact with immigrants showed that it not only related to more negative attitudes toward immigrants but also reduced intentions to engage in further contact (Meleady & Forder, 2019). Moreover, there was a negative spillover to other outgroups. With a reverse version of the STE with positive contact, this study noted a reduction in intention to have contact with other outgroups following negative contact with immigrants. Not surprisingly, different emotions are also evoked—anger and fear compared with negative contact and happiness with positive contact (Kauff et al., 2017).

The most important results are obtained when both positive and negative intergroup contacts are considered simultaneously. An Icelandic analysis found little evidence of positive–negative asymmetry with either direct or extended contact (Arnadóttir et al., 2018). Instead, evidence emerged that positive contact *buffers* the negative effects of negative contact and that negative contact *enhances* the benefits of positive contact. These effects held only for direct contact and were strongest for the majority group. No such interaction was found for extended intergroup contact.

This buffering finding is important and had been found earlier in a more extensive study conducted in three conflict areas—Northern Ireland, Cyprus,

[8] There is a problem with the reporting of negative contact. Those respondents who are already prejudiced against other outgroups often quickly report negative experiences with a new outgroup. This leaves open whether they really had a negative experience or are just reporting negative expectations (Kotzur et al., 2018).

and the southern border of Arizona (Paolini et al., 2014). These investigators checked on television-mediated and imagined intergroup contact as well as direct, face-to-face intergroup contact. They found that positive contact in the past significantly reduced the adverse effects of negative intergroup contact in the present. Similarly, positive direct intergroup contact can lessen the adverse attitudinal effects of negative mass media news (Fuochi et al., 2020).[9]

Buffering has also been found in yet another conflict area—Turkey. Bagci and colleagues (2020) in five separate studies involving Kurds, Syrians, and lesbian, gay, bisexual, and transgender target groups found that prior positive intergroup contact significantly reduced the likelihood that prejudiced Turks would avoid later contact with the outgroup.

Two large probability surveys conducted in Germany provide the most extensive data sets testing both positive and negative contact (Christ et al., 2008; Heitmeyer, 2005, 2007; Pettigrew & Tropp, 2011). These German data paint a complex picture. First, like other studies, the German surveys find that there is far more positive than negative contact except in special situations of open conflict. This fact helps to explain why the direct contact meta-analysis could locate only 21 (4%) studies reporting negative contact (Pettigrew & Tropp, 2006, 2011).

Second, although the German data show that positive contact's correlation with reduced prejudice (−.47) is larger than that of negative prejudice enhancing prejudice (+.28), the strongest link (−.49) is achieved by considering both types simultaneously—positive contact minus negative contact. Indeed, those German respondents who report *both* positive and negative contact with foreign residents demonstrate almost as much acceptance of immigrants as those reporting only positive contact. Again, we see how positive contact can act as a critical buffer against the adverse effects of negative contact. The demographic analysis of these data shows that those Germans reporting both positive and negative intergroup contact tend to be young and have far more intergroup contact of all types than other respondents—a hopeful sign for the future (Pettigrew & Tropp, 2011, pp. 191–192). More research attention to negative contact is needed, but it must be considered together with positive contact.

[9] Other contextual effects have been found that buffer the negative effects of prejudice and discrimination. For example, Arab Americans who are Muslim buffer with salient religious practices the discrimination they face (Shah, 2019).

How Does Intergroup Contact Improve Outgroup Attitudes?

A sufficient number of studies of three likely microlevel mediators of contact effects had been conducted by 2007 to allow tests with small meta-analyses (Pettigrew & Tropp, 2008). Using a novel application of meta-analysis developed by Shadish (1996), these analyses tested for (a) new knowledge of the outgroup gained by the contact, (b) lessened anxiety, and (c) increased empathy and perspective taking.

These more focused meta-analyses revealed that two mediators in particular mediate the contact's reduction in prejudice: Optimal contact reduces anxiety about intergroup interaction while it increases empathy and perspective taking (Pettigrew & Tropp, 2008). New knowledge was the least powerful of the three tested. A later longitudinal study confirmed this result (Swart et al., 2011; see also Aberson & Haag, 2007).

Anxiety has often been found to be crucially involved in contact effects across diverse cultures. In one study of White Americans, Hong Kong Chinese, and Buddhist Thais, positive contact predicted reduced intergroup anxiety, and negative contact predicted increased anxiety in all three cultures (Techakesari et al., 2015).

Empathy has proven to be a key factor also. A U.K. analysis found empathy mediated the association between secure attachment and reduced prejudice (Boag & Carnelley, 2016). And a Swedish study of 456 high school students found empathy, together with authoritarianism and SDO, to be a direct predictor of generalized prejudice consisting of eight prejudice scales (Bäckström & Björklund, 2007). Empathy correlated highly and negatively with SDO (–.49)—consistent with the description of high SDOs as dominant, tough-minded, self-interested, and relatively uncaring seekers of power.

These results are also consistent with the finding that liberals tend to be more empathetic than conservatives. In research that included samples from Germany, Israel, and the United States, liberals wanted to feel more empathy and did experience more empathy than conservatives in all three samples. They were also more willing to help others in the United States and Germany. But ingroup ties remain strong; in all samples, both liberals and conservatives wanted to feel less empathy for outgroup members than ingroup members (Hasson et al., 2018).

The two strongest mediators of contact's effects—decreased anxiety and increased empathy—are both emotional. And it was generally thought that contact effects are largely emotional in character. But Hodson et al. (2018) persuasively maintained that cognitive factors are also importantly involved. They showed how effective intergroup contact can shape ideology, enhance cognitive flexibility, and foster creativity.

Deprovincialization

Broadening the role of empathy in mediating contact effects, repeated intergroup contact can, in time, cause people to reappraise their own group and culture. I named this process *deprovincialization* (Pettigrew, 2010a).[10] The term refers to diminished provincialism, to removing provincial blinders. It indicates a growing acceptance of other peoples and cultures. Deprovincialized individuals are more experienced in the wider world; they learn that their group's norms, customs, and lifestyles are not the only ways to manage the social world successfully. This new perspective individualizes and "humanizes" outgroup members. It also serves to provide a fresh perspective on your own group and culture.

Deprovincialization, then, leads one to reappraise not only outgroups but also your ingroup. This reappraisal can but does not necessarily mean that you now regard your own group and culture less positively—just differently. Deprovincialization allows one to respect, even admire, other peoples and cultures while looking at your own group in a new and more complex way. The late U.S. Supreme Court Associate Justice Ruth Bader Ginsberg provides a pertinent example. While a student at the law schools of Harvard and Columbia, she became especially interested in civil procedure—which, among other important functions, determines the cases that are heard. Then she had the opportunity to study in Sweden and learn about that country's civil procedure. "Reading and observing another system," she later commented, "made me understand my own system so much better" (Biskupic, 2020).

A primary, but not the only, means of becoming less provincial is through intergroup contact. And if one is spending more time with the outgroup, this obviously translates to spending less time with ingroup members. Notice, too, how it is consistent with the basic Big Five trait of Openness to Experience, which I showed previously is closely connected with intergroup threat, anxiety, prejudice, and contact (see Perry & Sibley, 2013).

Marilynn Brewer (2008) expanded the idea by pointing out the similarity of deprovincialization with her own concept of *social identity complexity*. Persons scoring high on her complexity measure report being involved with numerous cross-cutting groups that they perceive to have little overlap in memberships. Such persons, she posited, are in effect deprovincialized. Indeed, they have been found to be more tolerant of outgroups and more

---

[10] I thought of this term while spending extended time in Germany at the University of Muenster. It came to me easily, as at the time I was in the process of being deprovincialized myself.

in favor of affirmative action programs and multiculturalism.[11] Brewer further speculated that her cognitive mechanism may well be involved in such non-face-to-face contact effects as extended and imagined contact.

Research in South India with 351 participants from diverse caste backgrounds supports Brewer's speculation (Reimer et al., 2019). Those with cross-group friendships reported a wider range of people as "us" rather than "not us" in terms of caste, religion, and nationality.

Maykel Verkuyten and his Utrecht University colleagues (2010) directly tested the deprovincialization idea. They measured ingroup identification with two items: "How important is it to you that you are Dutch?" and "Are you proud to be Dutch?" They measured ingroup feelings with a feeling thermometer. These two measures—ingroup identification and ingroup feelings—were combined and used as the measure of ingroup distance. With three separate surveys of native Dutch participants, Verkuyten's multilevel analysis revealed that positive contact with ethnic outgroups related to a stronger endorsement of multiculturalism and a general distancing from the ingroup. Strong national identity, on the other hand, relates positively with anti-immigrant prejudice in both Germany and the Netherlands (Pettigrew & Tropp, 2011, p. 154).

These results supporting the deprovincialization thesis are consistent with earlier findings. Positive intergroup contact is negatively associated in multiple probability surveys with the strength of German identity (Pettigrew, 2009b). Intergroup contact and the support of multiculturalism have been found positively correlated in New Zealand (Ward & Masgoret, 2006). And the positive intergroup contact link with favorable attitudes toward multiculturalism was uncovered in another Netherlands study as well (Velasco González et al., 2008).

The most thorough of these confirming reports comes from Switzerland (Green et al., 2018). Eva Green and her University of Lausanne colleagues, using multilevel regression analyses with 136 Swiss districts, showed that at the personal level, encounters with immigrants related to a reappraisal of national ingroup boundaries by attenuating ethnic views of nationhood. And once again we encounter buffering effects. This Swiss study found that at the macrodistrict level, immigrant presence buffered the impact of conservative ideological opinion climates.

The consistency of these findings across four nations strongly suggests that deprovincialization is yet another positive consequence of direct, positive intergroup contacts.

---

[11] In order not to contaminate this test, Brewer was careful to omit racial and ethnic group memberships from her measure of social identity complexity.

A POTENTIALLY NEGATIVE EFFECT OF INTERGROUP CONTACT

One potentially negative result of positive intergroup contact concerns the ability of minorities to mobilize for change. Minority members typically reveal less prejudice against the majority after positive intergroup contact—although we have noted that this change is often less than the simultaneous prejudice reduction of majority members (Tropp & Pettigrew, 2005b). At first reading, this latter result seems beneficial for intergroup relations. But if the minority is still subject to continued discrimination, they need to protest their mistreatment. Yet, liking your oppressors deters protest. Numerous studies demonstrate that minority members who have experienced the most intergroup contact are in general more reluctant to protest for change (Becker et al., 2013; Dixon et al., 2010; Dovidio et al., 2016; Saguy et al., 2009; S. C. Wright & Lubensky, 2009).

Some writers have seized on this phenomenon alone to argue against the value of intergroup contact in general. But this one process is not the whole story of how intergroup contact affects minority protest. At least four other relevant processes at the individual level of analysis must be considered.

First, intergroup contact also improves the attitudes of members of the advantaged group toward both the disadvantaged group and intergroup policies. Mallett et al. (2008) reported that majority members who showed greater perspective taking of the minority were most likely to join in collective action to oppose hate crimes committed against African Americans as well as against gay men and lesbians. Çakal et al. (2011) showed that White South Africans' positive contact was associated with support for the Black South Africans' cause. Having positive contact with someone who has been arrested lessens support for publicizing arrest records and alters views of recidivism risk (Lageson et al., 2019). Likewise, Fingerhut (2011) found that positive contact often motivates heterosexual allies' involvement in the lesbian, gay, bisexual, transgender, queer and/or questioning movement. This effect weakens majority members' resolve to maintain the discriminatory status quo and encourages the minority to believe that protest can succeed (Pettigrew & Tropp, 2011).

The most extensive research on this point was conducted in Northern Cyprus, Romania, and Israel (Çakal et al., 2019). Advantaged group members in all three areas who had contact with the local minority expressed greater endorsement of social change and less discrimination. This persistent effect was variously mediated by greater trust and perspective taking as well as by reduced anxiety.

Second, intergroup contact allows the disadvantaged to ascertain to what extent majority members are aware of the moral inconsistency of their position, which can then be exploited in protests for change. In America's civil rights movement, Black Southerners who knew Whites best realized that many Whites did, in fact, sense Myrdal's (1944) "American dilemma"—that is, that White Americans worried that racial discrimination may somehow be "unAmerican" and "unChristian." Thus, the Movement ensured that protests made full use of national and religious symbols from American flags to the singing of the national anthem and church hymns.

Third, minority contact with sympathetic majority members can bolster and encourage protest. Droogendyk et al. (2016) showed, with data from both Australia and Canada, that majority members who provided "supportive contact" to international students and immigrants actually encouraged heightened collective action engagement by minorities. Moreover, increased perceptions of the existence of injustice against them proved to be a major mediator of the link between supportive contact and increased motivation for collective action. The authors' concept of supportive contact is useful in that it is more specific than the vague term of "positive contact," for it implies direct and empathic engagement (see also Becker et al., 2013).

Finally, intergroup contact can also heighten a disadvantaged group's sense of group relative deprivation (Pettigrew, 2015b, 2016; H. J. Smith et al., 2012; Walker & Smith, 2002). Contact provides the opportunity for minorities to learn what the majority possesses that is denied them. Thus, group discrimination ratings were markedly higher for those Inuits who had contact with mainstream Canadian culture (Poore et al., 2002).

Before concluding that intergroup contact undermines progress, the reader might also reflect on historical and contemporary examples. Recall the active engagement of Whites in both the American civil rights movement and the anti-apartheid struggle in South Africa.[12] In his autobiography *Long Walk to Freedom*, Nelson Mandela (1994) wrote of those who shared with him "the ups and downs of the liberation struggle" (p. 104), including Joe Slovo, Ruth First, and Bram Fischer—all of them White. Opposition to interracial cooperation was, in fact, a key policy difference that divided the Pan Africanist Congress from the African National Congress. A later example is found in the large numbers of young American Whites who support the Black Lives Matter movement (Holland & Swanson, 2016). Indeed, Sawyer and Gampa (2018) discovered that both explicit and implicit racial biases of White participants in the movement improved. For Black

[12] I am indebted to Miles Hewstone for this pertinent point.

participants, implicit views did not change, but explicit pro-Black views were modified.

Positive, but not negative, intergroup contact increased Whites' support for the Black Lives Matter movement (Meleady & Vermue, 2019). This enhanced support for a Black American cause was mediated by a reduction in SDO. Similarly, in the United Kingdom, positive intergroup contact correlated with more support for collective action to protect the rights of European immigrants in the Brexit negotiations. This, too, was mediated by a reduction in SDO. However, negative intergroup contact related to increased SDO and less support for collective action.

All of these complex processes must be considered when we extrapolate contact theory's effects to the macrolevel of societal protest. Unfortunately, I know of no study to date that investigates all of these individual-level processes simultaneously. But the initial studies revealing this possibly negative effect of contact were all *single-level* studies. Their critique of contact theory needed a multilevel test. And Kauff and his coresearchers (2017) soon published a more rigorous, multilevel assessment.

The critics' claim that contact holds back social change was examined in two cross-sectional general population surveys—one across 22 European nations (using the European Social Survey), and the other using national data in Switzerland. Both studies used multilevel techniques, which takes into account the fact that individuals are nested in higher order units, such as neighborhoods and regions—an approach that underlines once again that the effects of contact not merely are interpersonal but also occur in a broader, societal frame.

Employing multilevel analyses, these researchers found that majority members' positive contact *positively* influenced ethnic minority members' support for ingroup rights at the *societal level* (Kauff et al., 2016). Specifically, minority members were more likely to support antidiscrimination laws and immigrant rights when living in social contexts in which majority members have positive intergroup contact experiences. This finding underlines that, even if some studies measuring contact only at the one microlevel have found that contact can hold back minority members' pursuit of social change, contact at the societal level (living in an area where majority group members report positive intergroup contact) can help empower them to support policies on behalf of their ingroup. This latter finding could not have been detected without the use of multilevel modeling to measure contact at the meso- and macrolevels, rather than just at the microlevel.

Thus, this research provides evidence across two studies in support of a "mobilization" rather than a "demobilization" hypothesis: Majority members' favorable contact at the social context level was associated with *increased* willingness on the part of the minority to endorse their ingroup rights. In addition, both studies replicated the positive association between majority members' intergroup contact and their greater support of minority rights, in line with the first process considered above concerning contact's effects on the majority (see also Dixon et al., 2007).

A Note on the Policy Implications of Intergroup Contact Theory

The intensively researched contact theory has led to successful applications in multiple areas—especially in educational settings as well as in intergroup relations. Yet a few critics ignore this expanding literature and argue that the theory has not been tested thoroughly enough to warrant being applied as yet.

Paluck et al. (2019) set an unrealistically high bar for contact studies to warrant application. They considered only studies that feature random assignment of subjects and delayed outcome measures for application. Random assignment of subjects eliminates the vast majority of survey studies.[13] This argument is a renewal of the old clash between laboratory experiments and field research. The former allows more control but leaves open the practical question, "Does it work outside of the laboratory context and in the real world?" Field work, such as probability surveys, can answer the "real-world" question but at the expense of full control.

Both approaches together would seem to be the ideal situation, and that is what we have in the intergroup contact domain. The Paluck group (2019) disagreed. They mustered a small sample of 27 studies that meet their strict criteria. But, weakening their argument, their research with select studies once again reveals that intergroup contact significantly *diminishes* prejudice. And I noted earlier from meta-analytic findings that the more rigorous the research, the *stronger*—not weaker—the link between intergroup contact and diminished prejudice.

Their second requirement of delayed outcome measures is clearly justified and is in fact extensively employed in recent intergroup contact research. There is now widespread use in contact research of longitudinal cross-lagged and growth curve analyses. Often these analyses span months, up to 1 year or more; thus, they meet the delayed outcome criterion as well as provide

[13] Surveys can administer both full and quasi-experiments, and such survey experiments could usefully be employed in contact research. See both Schuman and Presser (1996) and Schlüter and Schmidt (2010).

guidance on causal direction. The critics seem unaware of this sizable body of international research.

Paluck and her colleagues (2019) also criticized the intergroup contact research literature for not having studies that address the four "scope" conditions of the Allport hypothesis. This observation is mistaken. Among other studies, Koschate and van Dick (2011) tested all four of the key conditions and found intergroup cooperation to mediate the other three—equal status, common goals, and authority sanction. The equal status condition was checked on by J. Kende et al. (2018). The authority sanction condition has been particularly investigated (e.g., Green et al., 2020; Pettigrew & Tropp, 2011).

We can all agree that rigorous experimental work on contact effects would be ideal to have in greater abundance. But for practical reasons of finances and opportunity, we know why such research is relatively rare in the discipline—especially in field research that is the mainstay of contact work. By the stringent standards put forth by Paluck et al. (2019), only limited areas in social psychology would deserve application. Indeed, it would eliminate practical application of much of Paluck's own important work on norms.

Critics of using social science to guide social policy typically favor a standard generally higher than that required for scientific audiences. Policy advocates, such as Phoebe Ellsworth (1991), counter that social psychology should "tell what we know" rather than "wait for Godot" (p. 77). Science is dynamic and open-ended; *final* conclusions are never reached; *all* the evidence is never in. Besides, the standard that will prevail for intergroup policy if no intergroup contact theory ideas are employed is hardly rigorous and exacting. In fact, it will typically consist of the highly questionable conventional wisdom of political decision makers (Langenberg, 1991).

CONTEXTUAL EFFECTS OF INTERGROUP CONTACT

Even more than most social psychological phenomena, intergroup contact has numerous contextual factors at all three basic levels of analysis.

Microlevel Contextual Effects

We have seen frequently that intergroup contact connects tightly with an array of different components of the broad prejudice syndrome at the microlevel of analysis—from authoritarianism and anxiety to SDO and the absence of empathy (Pettigrew & Tropp, 2011). These tight ties signal that there will be many contextual factors in intergroup contact phenomena at the microlevel of analysis. And emotion is typically involved. Miller et al. (2004) showed that both positive (e.g., proud, hopeful) and negative (e.g., irritation, disgust) emotions mediate the effects of both SDO and intergroup contact on prejudice.

In fact, this chapter earlier noted that intergroup attitudes, anxiety, and perspective taking all mediated the STE of intergroup contact (Vezzali & Giovannini, 2012). And SDOs also mediated STEs, with those low on SDO revealing the strongest STE (Schmid et al., 2012).

Contact researchers have particularly checked on personality variables as potentially important contextual variables at the microlevel. For example, two Big Five personality factors—Agreeableness and Openness to Experience—relate positively to experiencing intergroup contact. White American psychology majors who are high on these two factors are more likely to initiate intergroup contact with both African Americans and Asian Americans and interpret the contact favorably (Jackson & Poulsen, 2005). Similarly, Vezzali et al. (2018) longitudinally tested Italian and immigrant high schoolers. They uncovered among both groups a bidirectional relationship between intergroup contact quality and the same two Big Five dimensions—greater Agreeableness and Openness to Experience.

Other research has also noted this link in a reverse causal direction. Dhont et al. (2014) demonstrated in a study of Belgian high school students that an intergroup intervention lowered SDO levels, with higher quality contact especially reducing SDO. Their second study, with a cross-lagged longitudinal design, demonstrated further that SDO can be decreased overtime by positive intergroup contact. This is a critical finding. Recall in Chapter 5 of this volume how SDO is a basic personality component of prejudice representing the competitive worldview.

Attachment theory has also been assessed by contact researchers. As would be expected, Italian subjects with secure attachment bonds are more likely to participate in intergroup contact. Replicating the two studies just described, structural equation modeling uncovered an indirect effect of Openness to Experience, leading to heightened intergroup contact (Boccato et al., 2015).

Mesolevel Contextual Effects

Three of the scope conditions of intergroup contact theory take place largely at the mesolevel—equal status of the groups in the contact situation, common goals, and intergroup cooperation. As such, these situational variables operate as moderators at the mesolevel of analysis. They are facilitating but not essential conditions for positive contact effects (Pettigrew & Tropp, 2006, 2011).

One major type of contextual variable at the mesolevel for contact variables involves other contextual variables. For example, direct intergroup contact is made more likely by prior indirect contact. Five longitudinal studies involving subjects of different ages from Germany, the Netherlands, Sweden, and Northern Ireland and using cross-lagged models reveal this contextual effect (Wölfer et al., 2019). Furthermore, this investigation found this link to be mediated by a reduction in intergroup anxiety. In short, indirect contact lowers initial anxiety about cross-group interaction, and this in turn leads to more face-to-face contact.

Macrolevel Contextual Effects

Once again, cultural differences emerge as important contexts. J. Kende et al. (2018) meta-analytically tested intergroup contact theory across 36 cultures. Using the meta-analytic base of Pettigrew and Tropp (2006) and 477 separate studies with 187,025 participants, the authors found that such contact had larger effects in cultures characterized by egalitarian values. Consistent with contact theory's principal contention, each of the 36 cultures revealed a negative relationship between intergroup contact and prejudice. But although the effect still operated in cultures with hierarchical values, it was markedly reduced in these cultures. J. Kende et al. determined that the cultural context made a difference somewhat greater than the moderator of equal status in the contact situation measured at the individual level.

A major study of 20 European nations tested the importance of authority support for intergroup contact—the fourth of contact theory's facilitating factors. Green et al. (2020) investigated how official policies governing immigration shaped threat perception and everyday contact with immigrants. These Swiss researchers used multilevel regression with the European Social Survey Round 7's 32,000 citizens. They found at the mesolevel that intergroup contact was once again related to both less symbolic and realistic threat perceptions of immigration; at the macrolevel of countries, they found that tolerant policies related to enhanced everyday intergroup contact and reduced symbolic threat perceptions. Further evidence that institutional support enhances the positive effects of intergroup contact, a significant cross-level interaction emerged. The link between contact and reduced threat was stronger in nations with *more tolerant policies* regarding immigrants.

The definitive research that demonstrates how normative structures act as critical contextual variables for intergroup contact effects was conducted by Oliver Christ and his German colleagues (Christ et al., 2014). They analyzed with multilevel methods seven large-scale European surveys—five were cross-sectional and two longitudinal.

Contact studies typically look for positive contact effects at the level of individuals. But this research specifically tested for macrolevel effects of positive intergroup contact reducing prejudice with a variety of macrolevel entities—regions, districts, and neighborhoods—and found that these macro-effects were *larger* than the contact effects at the microindividual level. In four of the surveys, Christ and his coworkers demonstrated that this significant macroeffect was largely mediated by more *tolerant norms*. The authors stressed the importance of this macrolevel process, as it can simultaneously impact large numbers of people, many of whom have not themselves had the intergroup contact.

Later, a Swiss research group, using different data and methods, confirmed the finding that intergroup contact can moderate the effects of social norms involving prejudice (Visintin et al., 2019). They concluded that intergroup contact is "a potent tool for reducing conformity to intolerant and anti-egalitarian norms."

These findings add a critically significant component to both the theory of and empirical support for intergroup contact. Note once again that this significant advance could not have been found without multilevel statistical techniques.

Sound Familiar?

The alert reader will have undoubtedly noticed that there is something quite familiar about these contextual relationships with intergroup contact. Indeed, one after another, these correlations of moderators and mediators with contact are systematically the reverse of the correlates with prejudice specified in Chapter 5 of this volume. This trend is further evidence that we are dealing here with a *prejudice syndrome* consisting of a group of tightly interrelated variables, as I discuss in Chapter 9.

SOLVING A NORMATIVE-CHANGE PUZZLE WITH INTERGROUP CONTACT THEORY

Public opinion on major issues typically shifts slowly (Page & Shapiro, 1992). Likewise, attitudes and norms also generally shift slowly. For example, a majority of African American children still attend largely segregated public schools today, more than a half century after the U.S. Supreme Court's famous desegregation ruling in 1954. The slow public acceptance of abortion rights decades after the Supreme Court ruling in *Roe v. Wade* in 1973 offers another example.

Major studies with different methods have looked closely at this phenomenon. Charlesworth and Banaji (2019) examined long-term attitude trends for both explicit and implicit attitudes (IAT) between 2007 and 2016 using time-series models with an internet population of American respondents. They checked on six areas—sexual orientation, race, skin tone, age, disability, and body weight. All explicit attitudes in these areas moved toward attitude neutrality; in other words, they all improved to some degree. But for implicit attitudes, tapped by the IAT, they remained the same for views of older persons and people with disabilities while becoming actually worse for body weight. But implicit attitudes did improve during this brief period for sexual orientation, race, and skin tone.

Gallup polls replicate the change for racial and sexual issues (Newport, 2013). Although only 4% of White Americans approved of Black–White marriages in 1958, 87% did by 1987. Only older Whites in any number (30%) opposed it by 1987; but the increase had been slow and steady over the 30 years of change spurred on by the unanimous 1967 U.S. Supreme Court case *Loving v. Virginia*, which ruled that laws forbidding racial intermarriage were unconstitutional.

The most extensive research following the 2015 Supreme Court ruling supporting same-sex marriage, *Obergefell v. Hodges*, was carried out by Tankard and Paluck (2017). Using both experiments and a five-wave longitudinal time-series, they determined that many Americans perceived the Court ruling as a signal of the nation's increasing support of same-sex marriage—in other words, the relevant norms were perceived to have changed. But they did not find marked alterations in attitudes concerning same-sex marriage. Again, new norms alone can change behavior, and new behavior typically leads in time to new attitudes that more closely mirror the new norms.

Rosenfeld (2017) studied this issue with survey data from both the General Social Survey and the American National Election Studies. But in contradiction to the Tankard–Paluck result, he found large attitude changes in greater acceptance of same-sex marriage and gay rights in general. The difference in the two studies' attitude results may reflect a difference in timing of when the attitudes were tested after the 2015 decision. Indeed, Rosenfeld held that no measured American public opinion attitude had changed more and faster than these views of same-sex marriage.

Why? What explains this apparently swift change in attitudes toward same-sex marriage, and toward gay men and lesbians in general? Rosenfeld found that intergroup contact was a major factor. With survey data, he discovered that the critical group changing their views were those Americans who had friends or family they knew who were gay or lesbian. Contact with out-of-the-closet gays and lesbians offers a key explanation.

In Chapter 8, I turn to using contextual social psychology to understand the unexpected rise of extreme right-wing voting patterns throughout the Western world.

8 APPLYING CONTEXTUAL ANALYSES TO FAR-RIGHT VOTING PATTERNS

Imagine a middle-aged White man who has lived either on a farm or in a small town all his life. He graduated from the local high school and has a moderate but sufficient income. He is strongly prejudiced against outgroups, especially immigrants, and he scores highly on scales measuring authoritarianism and social dominance. Imagine further that he has rarely travelled beyond his home community. And, until recently, his community has traditionally had few minorities or immigrants in its population. So he has had sparse contact with people different from himself. Lately, however, immigrants have begun settling in his area in unprecedented numbers. He is threatened by this new development and is angry over his sense of relative deprivation. He feels that minorities and immigrants are being treated by the government much better than he is and that this is unfairly restricting his life and the lives of his children.

Some of the passages that appear in this chapter have been adapted from "Social Psychological Perspectives on Trump Supporters," by T. F. Pettigrew, 2017, *Journal of Social and Political Psychology*, *5*(1), pp. 107–116 (https://doi.org/10.5964/jspp.v5i1.750). CC BY 3.0.

https://doi.org/10.1037/0000210-009
Contextual Social Psychology: Reanalyzing Prejudice, Voting, and Intergroup Contact, by T. F. Pettigrew

As the reader has probably discerned, this description is a major prototype of voters for Donald Trump in the 2016 American presidential election. Of course, this is just one primary prototype; other types of people voted for Trump, such as elderly lifelong Republicans who faithfully vote for their party's candidates whoever they are.[1]

But it is truly remarkable that this capsule description is also a prime prototype for the pro-Brexit voters in the United Kingdom who wished to break ties with the European continent. More remarkable still is that it also describes the prototype voter for the extreme-right nationalist voters throughout continental Europe. From a social science perspective, the most significant aspect of these many similarities is that they have been, with minor discrepancies, repeatedly replicated across many countries by numerous studies conducted with a variety of measures by social scientists from different academic disciplines.

Consider in turn the microlevel voter patterns in the United States, Great Britain, and continental Europe to review the specific findings that compose this extraordinary phenomenon. Based on the earlier discussions on prejudice, authoritarianism, social dominance orientation, relative deprivation, and intergroup contact, the key predictor variables in these analyses will not surprise you.

THREE TYPES OF STUDIES

We are fortunate to have three types of research to draw on. Moreover, with small differences in emphases, these distinct research approaches basically agree on the fundamental social base of this eruption of far-right-wing voting throughout the Western world. Replication across contrasting methods is especially reassuring. And replication across academic disciplines is also reassuring when different theoretical and methodological approaches reach similar conclusions.

One methodological approach is the standard one of surveys of probability samples of potential voters conducted before and after the elections. These studies vary considerably in their complexity—from small Mechanical Turk

---

[1]Van Hiel and Brebels (2011) demonstrated with a retired Belgian sample why elderly conservative voters tend to stay so faithfully with their earlier political party. With 311 elderly subjects, they showed that political conservatism typically serves to protect their self-esteem by helping to place their personal history within a larger cultural context.

sample surveys[2] to elaborate longitudinal studies with large samples across multiple nations. Here I was exceedingly fortunate to be able to collaborate with two Belgian social psychologists who are experts on relevant surveys conducted throughout Europe—Jasper van Assche of Ghent University in Belgium and Kristof Dhont of the University of Kent in England.

A second approach combines the data from all the Gallup surveys conducted during the American presidential campaign with ecological data (Rothwell & Diego-Rosell, 2016). This unique effort analyzed the individual and geographic data from 125,000 Americans who had answered the Gallup surveys during the campaign. These first two methods used the Trump vote directly as their dependent variable.

A third approach, with American survey data analyzed by political scientist Diana Mutz (2018), used (instead of the Trump vote alone) the *difference* between the 2012 intention to vote for the Republican candidate for president, Mitt Romney, and the 2016 intention to vote for Trump as her key dependent variable. I call this the *Trump difference* dependent variable. Mutz analyzed large probability samples of Americans who were questioned in both October 2012 and October 2016. This survey measured social dominance orientation (SDO) but unfortunately did not tap the key predictors of authoritarianism and prejudice.

THE MICROLEVEL CONTEXT OF FAR-RIGHT VOTING

Before we consider the correlates of far-right voting at the mesosituational and macrosocietal levels, let us check on the corelates at the microindividual level of analysis.

Authoritarianism, SDO, and Prejudice

These three major social psychological predictors, discussed at length previously, provide the context for understanding right-wing voting in the United States, the United Kingdom, and continental Europe (Van Assche, Dhont, & Pettigrew, 2019). Table 8.1 provides an overview generated by 20 published studies. Using meta-analyses, Table 8.1 reveals the strong relationships between the three microlevel predictors and right-wing voting in all three areas. These effect sizes are unusually large for such survey-derived

[2] Mechanical Turk is an Amazon website for crowdsourcing remotely located subjects to participate in surveys and experiments for typically meager pay.

TABLE 8.1. Meta-Analytic Effect Size Estimates of Right-Wing Authoritarianism, Social Dominance Orientation, and Prejudice With Far-Right Support

	United States[a]	United Kingdom[b]	Europe[c]	Total
Authoritarianism	+.37	+.48	+.38	+.39
Social dominance orientation	+.40	+.35	+.37	+.38
Outgroup prejudice	+.44	+.48	+.53	+.48
N	7,798	2,892	4,562	15,252

Note. From "The Social-Psychological Bases of Far-Right Support in Europe and the United States," by J. Van Assche, K. Dhont, and T. F. Pettigrew, 2019, *Journal of Community and Applied Social Psychology, 29*(5), p. 390 (https://doi.org/10.1002/casp.2407). Copyright 2019 by Wiley. Adapted with permission.

[a]Data derived from Choma & Hanoch, 2017; Conway & McFarland, 2019; Crowson & Brandes, 2017; Ludeke, Klitgaard, & Vitriol, 2018; Martens et al., 2018; Federico & Golec de Zavala, 2018; Feldman, 2017; Van Assche, Dhont, & Pettigrew, 2019, Studies 2a and 2b; and J. D. Wright & Esses, 2019.
[b]Data derived from Golec de Zavala et al., 2017, Studies 1 and 2; Peitz et al., 2018, Study 2; Van Assche, Dhont, & Pettigrew, 2019, Study 3; Meleady et al., 2017; Zmigrod et al., 2018.
[c]Data derived from Leone et al., 2014, Studies 1a, 1b, 2; Meloen et al., 1996; Van Assche, Dhont, Van Hiel, & Roets, 2018; Van Assche, Van Hiel, Dhont, & Roets, 2019; Van Hiel, 2012; Van Hiel et al., 2007; Van Hiel & Mervielde, 2002. Further details are provided in Van Assche, Dhont, & Pettigrew, 2019.

variables. Using her Trump difference indicator, Mutz (2018) also found a significantly positive effect with SDO.

Consistent with the dual process model, Van Assche, Dhont, and Pettigrew (2019) demonstrated with longitudinal data that prejudice mediated the effects of both authoritarianism and SDO on right-wing voting. In other words, these two key personality variables had their effects on right-wing voting almost completely through their influence on heightened outgroup prejudice.

This finding is not new; it was uncovered well before Trump and Brexit arrived on the scene. Thus, Cohrs and Stelzl (2010) used meta-analysis to analyze ideological attitudes and anti-immigrant attitudes across 155 samples from 17 nations around the world. Their findings mirrored the contentions of the dual process model. Authoritarianism was especially important in such nations as Germany and Italy, where immigrants were often viewed as increasing the crime rate. SDO, on the other hand, was especially important in such nations as Spain with relatively high unemployment rates—thus, arousing fears of losing jobs and status.

Many American commentators first resisted the finding that prejudice is at the core of Trump's support. But 2019 events that shook the nation's democratic foundations altered this reluctance. Trump's unashamedly racist attack on four minority women in the U.S. House of Representatives; the Charlotte rally crowd's "Send her home!" chant; Trump's labeling of the pandemic Covid-19 virus as "the Chinese flu"; and the horrendous mass shootings by extremists in the Texas city of El Paso, the Ohio city of Dayton, and elsewhere were so blatant that this consistent research finding finally began to win wider popular acceptance. Later, Trump's dismissal of anti-racism efforts as "anti-American" sealed this understanding.

Trump Voters

Given the nature of these hotly contested elections with their racist and extreme rhetoric, we should not be surprised at the substantial size of these effects. Reflect first on the Trump campaign in 2016 (Pettigrew, 2017b). The Trump movement is not unique for the United States—to name four: the Andrew Jackson presidency in the 1830s, the anti-immigrant Know Nothing movement in the 1850s, the George Wallace racist movement in the 1960s,[3] and the now moribund reactionary Tea Party movement (2009–2017). All of these political movements were politically extreme, broke precedent, and involved strong outgroup prejudice. Still, the Trump movement has been even more overtly authoritarian, socially dominant, and bigoted than even these past movements.

A Second Andrew Jackson?

Trump has compared himself to Jackson, and this claim actually has some validity. Both were wealthy and claimed to represent the less fortunate. Both disregarded precedent and altered the way the federal government operated. Both had raging tempers, although Jackson did not have Twitter to vent his anger. Both were deeply racially prejudiced—especially against Black Americans. Trump was twice cited by the U.S. Justice Department for discriminating against Black renters and often disparages Black neighborhoods and nations. Jackson owned hundreds of slaves and opposed abolition. He also treated Native Americans atrociously—especially the Trail of Tears removal of Native American tribes in the Southeast following Jackson's Indian Removal Act of 1830. Trump, too, repeatedly disparages Native Americans. From pushing through the Dakota Access Pipeline across Native American land to calling Elizabeth Warren "Pocahontas," he apparently regards the original Americans much as he does immigrants.

[3] In many ways, the Wallace vote in 1968 was a sign of things to come. Reg Murphy (1972), the astute former editor of the *Atlanta Constitution*, wrote half-a-century ago, "The basic Wallace appeal is going to last through the 1970s. He may not be the man leading it. Another populist with a sectional following and a bigoted background might take over. But the feeling of class politics is a part of America now" (p. 4a).

There are, of course, differences between the two. They certainly differed in their views of military service. And Jackson is the only American president to pay off the nation's debt, whereas Trump has run up the national debt to never-before levels. Trump was impeached, and Jackson was not. Ironically, Jackson tried to eliminate the Electoral College; had he succeeded, Trump would not have become president.

The comparison between the two men is relevant because they drew on remarkably analogous areas to win 188 years apart! Darmofal and Strickler (2019) showed that the two men enjoyed surprisingly similar geographic bases of support. When counties are used as the unit of analysis, the voting in 2016 is predicted better by the voting patterns for Jackson in 1828 than the voting patterns of 1976! The authors focused on Pike County in Kentucky as a prototypical Jackson–Trump location and Hampshire County, Massachusetts, as its liberal polar opposite. Partisan polarization in American politics, they demonstrated, is not new in American politics.

Authoritarianism

Although found among left-wingers (e.g., Dusso, 2017; Sidanius & Pratto, 1999), authoritarianism is more numerous among right-wingers throughout the world (Meloen, 1993). In the United States, Republicans began averaging higher on authoritarianism than Democrats well before the rise of Trump (Hetherington & Weiler, 2009). One investigation found that societal threat was positively associated with the mean state percentage of the Republican vote in elections for the House of Representatives from 1946 to 1992—but *only in conservative states* (McCann, 2009b). So the party began to learn over the past half-century how to appeal to this segment of the American electorate in various ways.

Since Richard Nixon's "Southern strategy," the Republican Party has employed strategies that appeal to bigotry with "dog whistles"—slightly subtle code words for race and other minorities designed to be heard by racists but not by nonracists. Nixon opposed racial school desegregation by claiming it was not for racist reasons but only because he opposed the "dangerous busing" needed to achieve interracial schools. Ronald Reagan began his campaign in 1980 by giving a states' rights speech in Philadelphia, Mississippi, quite near where three civil rights workers had been brutally and famously lynched earlier. George H. W. Bush in 1988 ran a campaign ad featuring Willie Horton, a fearsome-looking African American murderer whom his opponent, Michael Dukakis, had temporarily released from jail—

a television ad for which Bush's campaign manager, Lee Atwater, apologized years later ("Gravely Ill," 1991). Implausibly, Bush himself claimed that he had not realized Horton was an African American.

Trump was even less subtle. It remained for him to break the unwritten rules of American politics and appeal directly and openly to authoritarians and those who score high on SDO. He accomplished this largely by an engaging style developed earlier as a television celebrity that his followers found entertaining even if they sometimes partly disagreed with him (Reicher & Haslam, 2016). "Collective narcissism" (Federico & Golec de Zavala, 2018)—the belief in the unique greatness of America—also played a part: "Make America great again," "Take back your country" and "Put America first" proved to be effective slogans (Calamur, 2017). Collective narcissism is not unique to the United States. It was also a foremost factor in the United Kingdom's Brexit vote and in Poland's vote for its far-right Law and Justice Party (Marchlewska et al., 2018).

Knuckey and Hassan (2020) looked more closely at the role of authoritarianism among Trump's 2016 voters. They found the predictor had a greater effect on his support than in any prior presidential election studied. It proved to be important for both supporters with and without a college education. And authoritarianism was especially involved with Trump's voters, for it played a less significant role in the 2016 House of Representatives election.[4]

Trump has repeatedly made unconcealed use of prejudice against outgroups ranging from "dangerous" Muslims to Mexican "rapists." Telling American-born minority citizens "to go back where you came from" reached a new level of overt racism. His dedicated followers loved it—as was apparent when the Charlotte rally audience began loudly to chant "Send her back!" in reference to Somali-born representative Ilhan Omar of Minnesota. Breaking with so-called political correctness (McCarthy, 2019), Trump blared openly what many of his followers had been thinking and saying privately. Numerous outgroup prejudices characterize his dedicated followers, not just anti-immigrants but antioutgroups in general.

These racist tactics helped to increase 2016 voter turnout in lower status areas—not unlike George Wallace's campaign years before. In addition, preelection publicity that minorities were planning to vote in large numbers

[4] But authoritarianism did also play a role for the Republican candidates down ticket (Algara & Hale, 2019).

for Clinton undoubtedly stirred many White Republicans to turn out too. Actually, the African American turnout fell below that of 2008 and 2012.[5] Differential turnout was a key factor in Clinton's narrow losses in North Carolina, Michigan, and Pennsylvania that determined the final result.

The Role of Education

Virtually all studies of the Trump electorate found those individuals to be somewhat less educated on average than Clinton voters (e.g., Abramowitz, 2019). Trump was well aware of this, and he even declared during the primaries in 2016, "I love the poorly educated!" (Hafner, 2016). This phenomenon of the poorly educated voting Republican marks a massive social class voting shift since the days of Franklin Roosevelt in the 1930s. Kitschelt and Rehm (2019) traced this remarkable change in detail. They showed that the college-educated, financially comfortable segment of the American voting public has moved strongly from the Republican to the Democratic party, whereas the noncollege, largely financially comfortable segment has moved in the opposite direction—from Democratic to Republican. Worrisome for the Republicans is the fact that the first of these groups moving to the Democrats is an expanding portion of the electorate (from 2% to 14% over the past 60 years), whereas the second group is declining in significance (from 42% to 22% during these same years).

Typically, however, this research has used a simple bifurcation—college versus noncollege. However, this crude measure undoubtedly missed the full importance of education in the election results. One analysis of the American National Election Studies of the 2012 and 2016 elections found that verbal ability was a highly significant *negative* predictor of Trump's vote but not for Romney's vote (Ganzach et al., 2019). By contrast, verbal ability was a positive correlate of both the Obama and Hillary Clinton votes. Indeed, lower verbal ability proved to be a more important correlate of Trump's vote than education per se. This revealing finding links with research on Ireland's 2018 abortion referendum (G. Murphy et al., 2019). Those Irish voters with low cognitive ability were especially susceptible to forming false memories for fake news that aligned with their beliefs.

---

[5] This turnout reduction was a result of three factors: (a) Like many others, African Americans thought Clinton was going to win easily; (b) Russian "fake news" especially concentrated on them in these states; and (c) some African Americans undoubtedly bitterly remembered racist aspects of Hillary Clinton's primary campaign against Obama in 2008.

The "Authentic" Theory

Three management specialists offer a highly speculative theory that attempts to explain "the authentic appeal of the lying demagogue" (Hahl et al., 2018). They claimed that this occurs when the political system suffers from a "crisis of legitimacy," and they provided several one-level surveys using Mechanical Turk samples that they believe support their theory. Their postelection survey showed that Trump voters typically did not see him as warm and sincere but rather justified their support in terms of his being "authentic."

The chief problem with this theory is that it commits the one-factor fallacy. The authors write as if they believe that their theory explains the complete Trump phenomenon while overlooking the vast research literature throughout the social sciences on both it and the comparable elections in Europe. The authors made the erroneous argument that authoritarianism has no causal relationship with the Trump vote. They contended that the causal relation goes in reverse—they are more authoritarian because they are in the "socio-political space" reacting to the crisis of legitimacy. Given the genetic and developmental background of authoritarianism over time and the recency of the so-called crisis of legitimacy, this argument is clearly groundless. Furthermore, this claim ignores the many longitudinal studies that firmly document the causal link between authoritarianism and Trump voters (e.g., Van Assche, Dhont & Pettigrew, 2019).

The point that this "authenticity" article is trying to make is captured far better by a study of "fusion with political leaders" (Kunst et al., 2019). A literal "visceral feeling of oneness" with Trump predicts Republicans' willingness to persecute Muslims, Iranians, and immigrants beyond that predicted by other variables (Kunst et al., 2019). Relative deprivation increased this "fusion" with Trump. And this phenomenon was well illustrated at a New Hampshire rally when Trump mistook a follower for a protester and mocked a him for being overweight: "That guy has got a serious weight problem—go home, start exercising!" The victim of this public shaming did not take offense. In fusion with Trump, he later exclaimed he "loved the guy!" (Haberman & Sullivan, 2019).

William James (1896) touched on this issue years ago with his famous speech on the "will to believe." His remarks centered on religious beliefs. But James's contentions apply to this current concept of fusion when it comes to explaining why pro-Trump voters continued to support him even as increasing evidence against him mounted during his 2020 impeachment trial.

The Role of Religion

Similar reactions of Trump voters can occur from the growing number of one- or two-issue American voters. For instance, four fifths of Evangelicals and "born-agains" voted for Trump largely on the basis of abortion and racial issues, though some of them disapproved of his behavior to some degree (Martinez & Smith, 2016). And they continued later to give him far higher approval ratings than other Americans gave him (G. A. Smith, 2017). In fact, in 2018, regular churchgoers reported almost no regret whatsoever in having voted for Trump. Almost all of the few Trump voters who did express regrets were overwhelmingly people who never attended church (Edsall, 2019). When in 2019 Mark Galli, the retiring editor of the conservative publication *Christianity Today*, directly attacked Trump, many Evangelistic leaders came forward to defend the president and strongly attack Galli and the editorial.

Underlying this phenomenon is a general finding concerning religion and racial views. A meta-analysis of 55 studies revealed strong positive links among White Americans between religious ingroup identity and prejudice against racial outgroups. Only religious agnostics proved racially tolerant as a group (Hall et al., 2010).

Allport, a religious Episcopalian, wrestled uncomfortably with this phenomenon for years. Indeed, his last published paper was on the subject (Allport & Ross, 1967). He argued that those with an extrinsic religious orientation were prejudiced but those with an intrinsic orientation would be largely tolerant. Allport and Michael Ross produced a scale to measure the two types the data that supported his contention. For an update on this work together with a third proposed type—religion as quest—see Batson and Stocks (2005).

Recall, too, the Abelson et al. (1982) study described in Chapter 5 of this volume. These researchers analyzed American survey data and discovered that positive and negative feelings toward politicians are almost independent of each other. Moreover, they found these affect reports to be less semantically filtered and less subject to consistency pressures than trait judgments. So, Evangelicals can hold positive feelings of Trump and his right-wing policies while holding negative feelings about his irreligious tweets, narcissism, racism, and treatment of women.

Explaining in Part His Apparent Enduring Popularity

A common media error involves assuming that social categories do not change overtime. For example, surveys during Trump's presidential years kept showing that his support among Republicans remained fairly stable regardless of repeated serious problems for him personally and his administration. Media commentators found this amazing without realizing that those survey respondents who called themselves "Republicans" in surveys did not constitute an air-tight, stable category. Those who earlier had identified themselves as Republicans but who came to oppose Trump's leadership often no longer identified as Republicans. They typically did not favor Democrats either; rather, they tended to join the growing ranks of those respondents who identified themselves in surveys as "independents." Gallup calls them "Lean Republicans" (Laloggia, 2019). And their attitudes tended to track closely with those who remain in the Republican Party except for their views on Trump and his administration.

At the same time, some former Democrats and Independents who liked Trump began calling themselves Republicans. These two simultaneous trends explain in part why Trump's favorability ratings held reasonably steady among those who still identified with his party. Former Republicans who rejected Trumpism often no longer identified with the party when questioned by surveys, and some former Democrats and Independents who favored Trump began identifying as Republicans.

By 2019, Americans described themselves as "independents" (41%) more often than either Democrat (30%) or Republican (28%; J. M. Jones, 2020). These new independents are younger and more often male than partisans, and over time more of them lean Democratic than lean Republican (Laloggia, 2019). The key point here is that contextual factors themselves also change overtime.

The Trump–Prejudice Link Involves Two-Way Causation

Trump's tactics act to increase prejudice and embolden the already prejudiced to act out their beliefs. One study found that its subjects believed that prejudice norms and actual prejudiced attitudes had increased over the election period against groups that Trump had targeted (e.g., immigrants, Muslims) but not against untargeted groups (e.g., atheists, alcoholics; Crandall et al., 2018).

Hate crimes in the United States reached a 5-year high in 2016 during the presidential primary (Barrouquere, 2017). In 2017, hate crimes rose 17% over 2016—the third largest annual increase on record. School teachers reported that many of their students were emboldened to use slurs and other hostile comments against minorities, immigrants, and Muslims (Costello, 2016). Counties that hosted a 2016 Trump rally witnessed a 226% increase in reported hate crimes compared with similar counties without such a rally (Kunzelman & Galvan, 2019), and racist graffiti, harassment, threats, and still more hate crimes all rose sharply following Trump's election victory (Reilly, 2016; Southern Poverty Law Center, 2016). This phenomenon has occurred elsewhere; right-wing voting across German cities is highly related to hate crimes (Rees et al., 2019).

As Trump's rhetoric grew more extreme, this violence effect continued. His reference to the "good people" among the neo-Nazis protesting in Charlottesville, Virginia, and similar statements have consequences. There were 663 hate crimes in the very month of the Charlottesville encounter—the second-highest monthly tally in almost a decade (Kunzelman & Galvan, 2019). An innovative study employing Google searches to predict the 2016 presidential election found standard White supremacy terms (e.g., "Adolf Hitler") to be the single best predictor of Trump's following (Ma-Kellams et al., 2018).

Similarly, after the French election of 2012, the racist campaign of Marine Le Pen moved perception of social norms to the right (Portelinha & Elcheroth, 2016). *Modeling*—learning from and following the behavior of others—is a major mechanism of social learning and is a widely studied phenomenon in psychology (e.g., Bandura, 1986). An American survey experiment revealed how highly publicized modeling by powerful elite figures like Trump, especially if they are not effectively countered by other elite figures, can have substantial consequences (Newman et al., 2020).

During the presidential primaries in February 2016, Feldman (2017) found a significant positive relationship between authoritarianism and favorable evaluations of Trump emerged among Republicans (Feldman, 2017).[6] This early finding is important because none of the evaluations of the other Republican primary candidates revealed such a connection. In other words, Trump was selectively appealing to the most authoritarian Republicans and siphoning them off from the other primary candidates, some of whom had authoritarian tendencies of their own.

Remember that authoritarianism is especially invoked by threat. And authoritarian leaders have long understood that they can attract followers by enhancing the perception of dangerous threats to the society and offering simple solutions (Mols & Jetten, 2016). Sometimes the threats are real—as with Hitler and Weimar's hyperinflation. But Trump continually made patently false claims of massive voter fraud, sharp increases in crime,

[6] Another investigation found that blatant prejudice against Muslims was also a major correlate of Trump's primary support in 2016 (Tucker et al., 2019).

unvetted immigration, and other fictitious phenomena. Voter fraud has not been uncovered, and crime rates have been declining. Both violent and property crime rates have been falling for decades (Statista, 2017) with immigrant rates considerably less than that of native counterparts (Adelman et al., 2017; Sampson, 2008). America has long routinely employed some of the most intensive vetting of immigrants of any nation.

This "fake news" may even have particularly influenced former Obama voters and won Trump the 2016 election, as three political scientists speculated (Gunther et al., 2019).[7] Trump successfully counted unfavorable news by claiming that it—not his erroneous claims—was fake news.

Trump also countered the mounting evidence that he was a racist by claiming that "there wasn't a racist bone in his body"—a hoary claim that many of his followers have undoubtedly made themselves (Kristof, 2019). What lies behind such a statement is the belief that their negative views of African Americans are valid, and therefore to hold such views is hardly prejudice. Yet those making such a defensive claim are reflecting their awareness of America's antiracism norm, and their possible violation of the norm.

Most American politicians have traditionally sought to provide optimistic messages. Even at the depth of the Great Depression, Franklin Roosevelt held in his 1933 inaugural address that "we have nothing to fear but fear itself." By contrast, Trump emphasizes what White Americans have supposedly lost and need to regain. It is as if he intuitively understands the *negativity bias*—that the pain of losses is greater than the pleasure of gains by roughly a factor of four—a phenomenon found in many areas of psychology (e.g., Baumeister et al., 2001; Kahneman & Tversky, 1979; Rozin & Royzman, 2001; Tierney & Baumeister, 2020).

Virtually all of Trump's public speeches, when compared with those of previous U.S. presidents, typically involve extreme language—both positive ("tremendous," "the greatest," "beautiful") and negative ("ridiculous," "nasty," "scum," "scam"; Milbank, 2019). Such hyperbole adds to the "crisis" atmosphere purveyed to his followers. And it was successful: Security concerns regarding immigrants proved to be another major predictor of Trump's 2016 voters (J. D. Wright & Esses, 2019).

[7] Later analysis cast doubt on this possibility (Abramowitz, 2019). My own analysis makes me less certain than Abramowitz—largely because of the very narrow margins Trump won by in such key electoral states as Michigan, North Carolina, and Pennsylvania in 2016. Lower-than-expected turnout characterized each of these states—especially by minorities.

With a background of genuine terrorist threats, Middle East conflict, and a recent "great recession," even imagined threats seemed plausible—especially to citizens who are already easily threatened and who have witnessed rapid change in their localities. Trump's speeches, studded with such absolutist terms as "losers" and "complete disasters," are classic authoritarian statements.

Remember, too, that threat from new competition also operates for those who score high on the SDO measure. We have noted that high SDO individuals are typically dominant, driven, tough-minded, disagreeable, and relatively uncaring seekers of power. They believe in a "dog-eat-dog" world, and they report being motivated by self-interest and self-indulgence (Dovidio et al., 2017; Levin et al., 2002). Does that description remind you of anyone? Trump's clear hierarchical distinctions between groups at the top of society (Whites) and those "bad hombres" and "sh—hole countries" on the bottom (immigrants, Blacks, Latinx, and Africans) are classic social dominance statements.

As specified by the dual motivation process model, both authoritarianism and SDO involve a deep sense of threat. Unwittingly feeding this threat, the U.S. Census announced in 2015 that before 2050, "Whites," as defined by the Census, will likely comprise less than half of the American population. Furthermore, the Census projected that by 2060, 64% of children will belong to racial and ethnic minorities. This would make America a so-called majority–minority nation. Such a vision obviously strikes both high authoritarians and high SDOs as enormously intimidating. Indeed, the far-right in both America and France has seized on this fear in what it calls the great replacement theory—that Whites are being replaced by non-European immigrants.

Repeated experiments by Maureen Craig, Jennifer Richeson, and others have revealed just how intensely threatening this projected future is for many White Americans. Both survey and experimental research studies have found that when the demographic shifts now underway are made salient, many White American and White Canadian subjects react with more negative attitudes about other racial groups (e.g., Alba et al., 2005; Craig & Richeson, 2014a, 2014b; Craig et al., 2017, 2018; Major et al., 2018; Outten et al., 2012). Moreover, they also show increased support for politically conservative policies and candidates.

This threat effect is quite broad, encompassing even some relatively liberal subjects whose initial position left further room to move to the right (Craig & Richeson, 2014b, footnotes 1, 2, and 7). But, as you would anticipate, the negative effect is especially strong for people who are easily threatened—such as those with high levels of White ethnic identification and those who support Trump (Major et al., 2018). The phenomenon is not limited to Whites. Craig and Richeson (2018) also found the effect among African Americans and Asian Americans when they were informed about the rapid growth of Hispanic Americans. The phenomenon is also not limited to North America; it has also been demonstrated with British and Italian samples (Shepherd et al., 2018).

That "status threat" is involved is clearly revealed by another study that eliminated the effect when the demographic information was accompanied by "assuaging" information. Thus, those subjects who were assured that *the social status of groups was unlikely to change* did not show the threatened effect (Craig & Richeson, 2014b).

Craig et al. (2018) offered suggestions on how to restrain the impact of this demographic threat. For instance, do not use "us versus them" framing when presenting the demographic projections. Include in the "White" group those with one White parent who identify White—a rapidly growing subgroup.

In addition, much greater public emphasis on key points that are often ignored can soften the perceived threat. For example, Whites will remain a strong *plurality* of the American population. Moreover, the so-called majority minority is hardly a unified block of like-minded citizens. As there are great cultural differences and diverse experiences in the United States between the major ethnic groups, there are also great differences within these broad categories—from Chinese Americans to Pakistani Americans among "Asians" to Puerto Rican Americans to Chilean Americans among "Latinx." Even among African Americans, there are Caribbean-born, African-born, and native-born subgroups. These many versions of so-called non-Whites vary greatly. Indeed, they often have much more in common with White Americans than they do with other minorities.

Finally, fearful White Americans underestimate their nation's extraordinary ability to assimilate peoples from around the globe. Indeed, most of these threatened "Whites" are themselves products of not-so-long-ago immigrants to America when many of the same fears a century ago were directed toward their group—as in such claims as Roman Catholics are taking over the country; if Al Smith were to be elected president in 1928, the Pope will come over and rule the nation![8] Without realizing it, most

[8] Scottish Americans, my own ethnicity, were viewed 2 centuries ago to be potentially unpatriotic and dangerous because of earlier Scottish participation with the British Army in the Revolutionary War. Some Scots were literally forced across the New York and Vermont borders into Canada after the war (Allison, 2015, p. 158).

threatened White Americans represent living testimony to this often-ignored but impressive feature of (largely White) inclusiveness of the United States. I hope that one distant positive outcome of this demographic threat phenomenon could be a more inclusive, multiracial conception of just who are prototypical Americans. And social psychological research has shown that such a more complex prototype in itself would reduce intergroup prejudice and increase openness to the world (Waldzus et al., 2003).

America's rich diversity is on full display at the winter and summer Olympics and should be emphasized on the sports pages. From Greco-Roman wrestling and Alpine skiing to curling and fencing, the nation has the distinct advantage of sending contestants from a wide range of backgrounds and cultural traditions to the Games. But to the easily and highly threatened, these considerations have been often disregarded as irrelevant to their deep sense of status loss and reduced group dominance.

The Brexit Vote in the United Kingdom

The United Kingdom had its own equivalent of Trump in Nigel Farage[9]—a former commodities trader and a founder of the United Kingdom Independence Party (UKIP) who successfully led the fight for the U.K. Brexit vote to leave the European Union (EU). He then moved on to form another pro-leave party simply called the Brexit Party. He even came to Jackson, Mississippi, in 2016 to deliver a speech for Trump. Farage copied many of Trump's techniques and, like Trump, successfully split his country into bitter divisions and won a slim pro-Brexit victory. With his new Brexit Party, he next won numerous seats for the EU parliament in a 2019 election and helped Johnson's Tories win in 2019 by not running candidates in key districts. Appeals to authoritarianism, social dominance, and prejudice were at the core of Farage's successful message. So, again, it is not surprising that the three variables in Table 8.1 predict the Brexit vote well.[10]

---

[9] By 2019, American-born Boris Johnson, head of the Conservative Party and prime minister, also resembled Trump in style. His all-out, unprecedented efforts ramming through Brexit created a national political crisis.

[10] The United Kingdom witnessed a heated public debate over whether prejudice was involved in the pro-Brexit vote in spite of the overwhelming evidence that it was at the very core of the Brexit movement (e.g., Hutchings & Sullivan, 2019; Meleady et al., 2017; Van Assche, Dhont, & Pettigrew, 2019). American conservatives followed suit. In an extended discussion of Brexit and the United Kingdom's "populist revolution," *The Wall Street Journal* never once mentioned the words *prejudice* or *racism*—the major correlates of the phenomena (G. Baker, 2019).

Right-Wing Voters in Continental Europe

Like the UKIP and Brexit parties, other European democracies have witnessed similar movements in recent years—for example, Austria's Freedom Party, Belgium's Vlaams Blok, France's National Rally (formerly the National Front), Germany's Alternative for Germany Party, Italy's Five-Star and League Parties, and Poland's Law and Justice Party.

Even the Netherlands, with its long history of intergroup tolerance (De Vries & Pettigrew, 1994; Pettigrew & Meertens, 1996), succumbed to this trend.[11] Geert Wilders's Party for Freedom espouses intense hatred of Islam, immigrants, and the EU. Often called "the Dutch Trump," Wilders admires Trump and even gave a speech for him at the 2016 Republican convention. Years earlier, he came to New York City after the 9/11 tragedy to preach against Islam. All these movements particularly galvanized male nationalists who were less educated than the general population and more prejudiced, authoritarian, and socially dominant—hence the results in Table 8.1.

Relative Deprivation

The principal media interpretation for explaining Trump's 2016 followers involves economics. Trump loyalists were assumed to have often lost their jobs to Mexico and China and to be understandably angry. Little mention was made of the principal reason for massive job losses: the accelerating pace of automation.

Some mass media writers, reading one another's work and nonrandomly interviewing a few unemployed workers, latched on to this too-simple theory as *the* primary explanation for Trump's 2016 victory. Mutz (2018) called this the "left behind" theory and joins with other social scientists in disproving it. With her "Trump difference" dependent variable, she found that anxiety among high-status groups was more prognostic of the vote than the grievances about past treatment among low-status groups. Her finding

[11] I lived in the Netherlands for 4 enjoyable years during the late 1980s and early 1990s while doing research at the Netherlands Institute for Advanced Study in the Humanities and Social Sciences and teaching at the University of Amsterdam. This experience led me to greatly admire the nation, its people, and its culture. I would emphasize that Wilders has faced strong opposition, often been charged with incitement to violence, and has had other Dutch parties vow not to join in coalition with his party. The Netherlands' old intergroup norms of tolerance have definitely weakened, but they still operate (De Vries & Pettigrew, 1994; Pettigrew & Meertens, 1996).

coincides with the "relative gratification" findings previously reported that show how some of the wealthy join with the relatively deprived in evincing greater anti-immigrant antagonism (Jetten et al., 2015, 2017).

From her perspective as a political scientist, Mutz found that two issues in particular were especially predictive of voting shifts between 2012 and 2016: declining American dominance in the world and the declining dominance of Whites in America. The latter point coincides with the majority–minority demographic threat just discussed.

The Initial Theory

Single-factor theories are always dubious (Pettigrew & Hewstone, 2017). The claim was that economically deprived and often unemployed, angry working-class voters in basic manufacturing areas switched political parties and voted for "change." This argument ignores the fact of the greatly depleted power of labor unions. By 2019, union membership had dipped to only 10.3% of wage and salary workers—the lowest in decades (K. Gibson, 2020). The unions could no longer turn out the Democratic vote as they had for previous decades—a significant factor in key industrial states.

This media caricature may fit some followers, especially in the swing states of Michigan, Ohio, Pennsylvania, and Wisconsin. But this contention does not provide a major explanation for Trump's 2016 support generally. The argument first lost much of its credence when Silver (2016) estimated that the median annual income of Trump supporters was a solid $72,000. The most extensive study of voting intentions later provided an estimate of $81,898 for Trump backers' mean household income. Instead of being far poorer than Clinton voters, this figure was slightly above the $77,046 for those who had an unfavorable view of Trump (Rothwell & Diego-Rosell, 2016).

Actually, a strong contextual effect is involved in the link between income and the 2016 Trump presidential vote. Annual median incomes across counties in the United States can vary by as much as 10 times or more. Thus, it makes sense to view a voter's income within the local context of individual income. When Ogorzalek et al. (in press) did precisely this, they found that Trump's supporters tended to be relatively poor by national standards of White American income but relatively well-off among local Whites. Their sense of relative deprivation, then, was a sense of national deprivation—not a comparison with their local contexts.

Rothwell and Diego-Rosell (2016), with their combined Gallup survey data of 125,000 American adults, also challenged the widespread view of Trump's 2016 supporters in various ways. Trump followers were *less* likely than others to be looking for work, unemployed, or part-time employed. And those voters living in districts with more manufacturing were actually *less* favorable to Trump. Nor were his followers largely living and working in postal areas where employment in manufacturing had declined since 1990. Underlying these results in part is the fact that blue-collar Trump supporters tend to work in occupations that are largely shielded from Chinese and Mexican competition—transportation, repair, and construction (Rothwell & Diego-Rosell, 2016).

Later, D. N. Smith and Hanley (2018), analyzing the 2016 American National Election Study, concluded that "Trump's supporters voted for him mainly because they share his prejudices, not because they're financially stressed" (p. 195).

To be sure, social mobility has been declining in the United States. Contrary to the popular theory, however, people who live in areas with *greater* mobility voted *more* Republican (Campante & Yanagizawa-Drott, 2016). This was even true in the crucial "swing states," and it is a trend that has been detected in other relevant elections.

But these findings do not mean that social class and economics played no role whatsoever in this tight election. As we know from Chapter 6 in this volume, instead of absolute deprivation, social psychologists stress the importance of *relative deprivation.* Disappointing comparisons to relevant referents are often more significant than factual changes (Pettigrew, 2015b, 2016; H. J. Smith et al., 2012). What voters *think* is true is more important in elections than the actual truth.

Trump adherents in 2016 felt deprived relative to what they expected to possess at that point in their lives and relative to what they erroneously perceived other "less deserving" groups have acquired. When asked about Black income, many Whites tend to think of high-status Black exemplars (e.g., highly paid professional athletes and entertainers) they have heard about. This tendency unrealistically reduces their estimates of the vast Black–White income and wealth gap in the United States (Kraus et al., 2019).

Rapidly rising costs of housing and prescription drugs have aggravated their financial concerns. Their savings may not allow the type of ideal retirements they had long envisioned. And hopes for their children advancing beyond their status and going to college are being dashed by rising tuitions. Remember that in their youth these older voters experienced some relatively good times for workers, and they expected these improving opportunities to continue.

Working-class families had previously depended on low-tuition state institutions of higher learning for educational and employment mobility.

In the 1950s, I attended the University of Virginia for $250 a semester. But state legislatures throughout the country have sharply reduced funding to these schools, forcing rising tuitions. Thus, Trump adherents are typically not personally economically destitute, but they are often feeling deprived *relative* to their hopes and expectations.

Trump exploited this sense of relative deprivation brilliantly in 2016. He articulated issues snugly within the authoritarian worldview of his admirers. His words, claims, and lies appalled many Americans, but he knew his target audience well. In their analysis, Reicher and Haslam (2016) described Trump's carefully staged 2016 rallies in detail. Calling them "identity festivals" that embodied a politics of hope, they noted how they were choreographed to bind the attendees into a nationalist movement with immigrants, the so-called elite and the media (whose members were forced to sit in a cordoned-off back section) as the enemies. Criticism of Trump by the media and other sources (such as Hillary Clinton calling some of his followers "deplorables") only enhanced the movement and served to confirm Trump's assertions against their common "enemies."

Trump's oft-repeated slogan, "Make America great *again*," augmented the movement's thrust. It represented a brash reactionary call to return to an earlier time when America's position in the world was unchallenged; when American presidents, vice-presidents and Supreme Court judges were all White men; when immigration was restricted and widespread racial segregation persisted; when American workers saw their real wages rising; and when the government's affirmative action programs largely helped White men (e.g., the G.I. Bill of Rights, federal housing loans). Trump's popular slogan was an effective bid to invoke what Robert Jones (2016) pointedly labeled "nostalgia politics." This nostalgic form of deprivation can be found in the United Kingdom as well as in the United States (Gest et al., 2018).

Relative deprivation is also a major factor in the United Kingdom and in continental Europe. Recall the study described in Chapter 6 of this volume that examined the association between group relative deprivation (GRD) and ethnic threat across 20 European countries controlling for intergroup contact and value priorities (Meuleman et al., 2020). These probability surveys assessed 32,813 respondents' feelings of group deprivation compared with immigrants. A multilevel structural equation model demonstrated a close association between the GRD and both symbolic and economic threat from immigrants.

GRD proved to be a vital mediating factor on both the micro- and macrolevels across the 20 nations. At the individual level, GRD mediated the impact of one's socioeconomic position on the perceptions of threat.

At the societal level, GRD mediated the relationship between the society's economic context and perceived ethnic threat. We noted previously that for the 20-nation sample, the aggregated GRD and perceived ethnic threat correlates +.79—accounting for 62% of the variance among the nations' citizens' sense of threat. And we know from Chapter 6 in this volume that GRD and perceived threat are important correlates of both prejudice and far-right-wing voting. So, nations high on both GRD and perceived ethnic threat tend to evince strong far-right voting: the United Kingdom, France, Belgium, Hungary, and the Czech Republic.[12] Nations low on both variables include Sweden, Denmark, Germany, Finland, and Norway; these are nations, with the lone exception of Germany, without substantial extreme right-wing voting.[13] Recall, also, that GRD *fully* mediates the relation between contextual economic factors and ethnic threat. Thus, the sense of GRD at both the individual and national levels enhances the perceived ethnic threat posed by Europe's massive immigration.

The importance of GRD in European voting is not a new phenomenon; it had emerged as a critical factor in the 2012 French presidential election involving Marine Le Pen running as the National Front candidate. Urbanska and Guimond (2018) showed that GRD was a significant correlate of National Front voting even with SDO controlled. They argued that her rhetoric of being mistreated by the government compared with the new immigrants allowed her to gain votes even beyond the most prejudiced segment of the French electorate. This same theme later became central in the protests of the "yellow jackets" (*gilets jaunes*)—economic protests throughout France. This, too, was a populist movement but not a straight follow-on from the Le Pen movement, for it attracted participants of many political persuasions from the far left to the far right (Rose & Baker, 2018).

[12] Hungary, in particular, led by its far-right-wing prime minister, Victor Orban, has been especially hostile to Europe's new migration wave and was censured by the EU's parliament in 2018. Two Czech sociologists found Hungarians, together with Greeks, to be the most anti-immigrant in Europe (Chaloupkova & Salamounova, 2006). Another study found attitudes toward Muslim immigrants to be especially intense in Hungary and the Czech Republic (Bruneau et al., 2018). A third study, conducted by the Pew Research Center of just Western European nations, found Italy, Portugal, Austria, and Switzerland to be highest on a general prejudice measure that involved Jews, Muslims, immigrants, and nativism (Diamant, 2018). As usual, personal familiarity with Jews or Muslims related to lowered prejudice.

[13] Nevertheless, these nations still witness at the microlevel many of the same prejudice and authoritarianism relationships with far-right-wing voting as in other European nations. For Sweden, see Jylhä et al. (2019).

As in previous analyses, personality traits also relate to far-right-wing voting. In Italy, such voting correlated with both low Openness to Experience and high need for closure (Chirumbolo et al., 2003).

THE MESOLEVEL AND MACROLEVEL CONTEXTS OF FAR-RIGHT VOTING

The extraordinary parallels between the extreme right-wing movements throughout the West are not confined to the microlevel of individuals. The similarities extend as well to the meso- and macrolevels of analysis.

Intergroup Contact

We saw in Chapter 7 of this volume that a major means of reducing intergroup prejudice is through optimal intergroup contact (Pettigrew, 1998; Pettigrew & Tropp, 2006, 2011). So it is noteworthy that growing evidence shows that Trump's White supporters had experienced far less contact with minorities than other White Americans. For instance, Rothwell and Diego-Rosell (2016) discovered that "the racial and ethnic isolation of Whites at the zip-code level is one of the strongest predictors of Trump's 2016 support" (p, 14). This finding remains true for both non-Hispanic Whites in general and for the smaller subset of White Republicans, and this lack of intergroup contact relationship with Trump voting emerges while controlling for dozens of other variables.

Consistent with this finding, these researchers also found that Trump's 2016 support *increased* as an area's distance from the Mexican border increased. In other words, the less the opportunity to meet Mexicans, the *greater* the Trump support. If you have Mexican American friends, you are unlikely to believe Trump when he accuses them of being "rapists." We have noted that throughout the world, intergroup contact has been shown typically to diminish prejudice by reducing intergroup fear and inducing empathy (Pettigrew & Tropp, 2006, 2008, 2011). Its extreme absence for most Trump fans is a major factor that has been virtually ignored in the postelection analyses. Such limited intergroup experience left Trump's 2016 backers more vulnerable to his slashing outgroup attacks.

Similar findings emerged in research on the U.K. Brexit vote. The limited extent of voters' social networks and their propensity not to travel beyond their hometown had stronger effects than income in shaping their nationalistic, anti-immigrant support for leaving the EU. If they had no intergroup friends and rarely traveled, British voters were far more likely to vote for Brexit. But those who had spent time with a foreigner were 15% less likely to have voted to leave (Maguire, 2016).

Intergroup contact, once again, proved significant. Positive intergroup contact predicted voting against leaving the EU, and negative intergroup contact predicted voting for leaving the EU (Meleady, Seger, & Vermue, 2017).

Timing Is Crucial

Major urban areas, such as London and Liverpool, with large, established immigrant populations voted strongly to remain in the EU, whereas English and Welsh areas with relatively few immigrants voted heavily to leave the EU.[14] But when a longitudinal analysis is applied, the key variable emerges: the *speed of change* in the immigrant population.

Areas with modest immigrant populations in 2000 that had witnessed more than a 200% rise in immigrants by 2015 voted an astounding 94% to leave the EU ("Explaining the Brexit Vote," 2016). This striking result is yet another example of the delicate balance between threat and contact—the dual effects of diversity (Green et al., 2016; Knowles & Tropp, 2018; Pettigrew & Hewstone, 2017; Wagner et al., 2006). London and other major British cities had long experience with immigrants and had increased their diversity somewhat gradually. Time had reduced the sense of threat and enhanced positive intergroup contact. But for small towns and rural districts with a sudden and rapid entry of immigrants, perceived threat prevailed and optimal contact was as yet minimal.

A quite similar process occurred in small Midwestern towns in the United States with rapid increases in Latinx immigration. According to Adamy and Overberg (2016b), areas in which the diversity index rose by 150% witnessed a 67% vote for Trump in 2016. Think of Arcadia, Wisconsin, which had job growth—not restricted jobs (Adamy & Overberg, 2016a). Arcadia's plentiful jobs attracted rapid in-migration from below the Mexican border—roughly 1,500 miles away. The resulting perceived threat, unalleviated by a period of intergroup contact, made many rural and small-town White Midwesterners respond positively to Trump's harsh anti-immigrant

[14] Every voting district in Scotland voted to remain in the EU. The powerful Scottish National Party worked hard to remain in the EU and emphasized Scotland's dependence on trade with Europe—especially Scotch whiskey. Being overruled once again by English voting, Scotland's independence movement gained further support—including from my close relatives in Glasgow.

rhetoric in 2016. This interpretation is supported by the macrofindings of Rothwell and Diego-Rosell (2016) discussed earlier.

But in many key electoral states, small towns such as Dravosburg, Pennsylvania, with few additions to their tiny minority populations, still witnessed huge margins for Trump in 2016 (Edsall, 2017). Here we see how the lack of intergroup contact made White voters vulnerable to the openly racist and anti-immigrant appeals of the Trump campaign without the existence of a direct minority threat in their immediate locality.

Taking a longer perspective, however, time is on the side of acceptance of social diversity. Although humans often react negatively to threats of change in social diversity in the short term, the initial negative effects are compensated in the long term by the beneficial effects of intergroup contact (Ramos et al., 2019; see also Tropp, 2019). The timing involved, as we have seen, can be lengthened by any impediments to intergroup contact, such as intergroup segregation.

Another Parallel

At the macroeconomic level, the far-right-wing voting throughout continental Europe has yet another parallel with the 2016 American election. Save for a few regional exceptions in France and Greece, the largest electoral gains for rightist support were in regions and nations that were relatively *spared* the worse of the 2009 to 2013 economic crisis (Stockemer, 2017). As in the United States, those areas hit hardest by the earlier economic turndown tended to vote *against* the far right. Consistent with this finding, surveys throughout five Western European nations found that far-right party supporters were not very different from others in views of their national economy, but they were more nativist and more likely to believe that "life is worse than it was 50 years ago" (Stokes, 2018). Another macropredictor of far-right-wing voting in continental Europe involved crime, which the right-wing parties made a major issue, as did the Trump and Brexit campaigns. A meta-analysis of 48 research papers on far-right voting in Western Europe found that it correlated significantly with high crime rates (Amengay & Stockemer, 2019).

A FINAL WORD

No one factor describes far-right supporters. But an array of factors, stretching across the three major levels of analysis and reflecting five key social psychological phenomena previously discussed in detail, can help to account for this extraordinary political trend throughout much of the Western world. And we should remember that just as in Obama's victory in 2008 (Pettigrew, 2009a), the Trump victory in 2016 required a "perfect storm" of simultaneous factors to overcome a 3 million vote deficit—reduced Democratic voter turnout in part because surveys had shown Hillary Clinton winning, Russian interference, and the peculiarities of America's strange Electoral College system.

The social psychological contextual factors are not unique to the United States. We have reviewed the many studies of the United Kingdom's and continental Europe's far-right-wing voters that show results strikingly similar to the data on the 2016 American election. Authoritarianism and social dominance attitudes have been routinely found to correlate significantly with far-right voting in nations throughout Europe. These voters share with Trump's 2016 supporters similar views of women, minorities, immigrants, and free-market economics. Three major nationalist grievances of Europe's far-right arise from economic changes, political elitism and immigration—with immigration the most intense issue (Ivarsflaten, 2008). American research suggests that much the same can be said about the 2016 Trump movement.

The implications of this analysis for scholars who study these political phenomena in democracies are threefold. First, despite vast differences in political structures and economic circumstances between Western nations, there are a surprising number of similarities of contextual factors across these various right-wing political movements. Second, these similarities suggest that those conducting research on one such movement might well look to research in other countries for additional ideas and variables.

Finally, the actual operation of the social psychological variables and theories detailed here need to be integrated within a broad political context. Political and social psychological approaches are mutually supportive—not antithetical. Future research must bring them together in multilevel models. Thus, Norpoth (2016) predicted months in advance that Trump would win in 2016 based only on primary results. Abramowitz (2019), a political scientist, developed a nine-variable regression that predicts 98% of the 2016 Trump vote across states. His chief predictors are (a) the state's percentage of Whites without college training, (b) the Trump margin in comparison with Romney's 2012 vote, (c) the state's general conservatism, and (d) the state's turnout. The first three of these factors are positive predictors, and the fourth is a negative predictor. Note that all four are macrolevel variables that provide indications of each state's political norms.

The high prediction percentage reflects in part the fact that Abramowitz is dealing with a relatively small number of macrounits—namely, states. This chapter's social psychological analysis supplies the micro- and mesolevel variables that underlie the operation of his macrovariables.

On occasion, we have already witnessed some important examples of their dual effects. For example, prejudice as a microlevel predictor of the Trump vote in the data from the 2016 American National Election Survey actually causes such standard demographic factors as age and education to lose their explanatory power (D. N. Smith & Hanley, 2018). Similarly, lower cognitive ability proved to be a more important predictor than income (Ganzach et al., 2019).

The full and definitive accounts of the momentous 2016 and 2020 presidential votes await the combining of these different approaches across disciplines into multilevel models.

9 LOOKING AHEAD

Ask yourself: What differentiates *social* psychology from general psychology? Surely, the very title of the field implies that social psychologists specialize in placing psychological phenomena in their *social* contexts. As such, the discipline could become a vital mesolevel link between the microlevel of psychology and the largely macrolevel of the other social sciences—especially sociology, political science, cultural anthropology, and economics.

Psychology's "cognitive revolution" of the 1960s and 1970s that exclusively concentrated on cognitive factors not only shortchanged the importance of emotion but often ignored social context (Pettigrew, 2018a). Slowly, however, more focus on social context has characterized research in social psychology. This volume has presented the case for the field to pay still greater attention to the context of psychological phenomena.

https://doi.org/10.1037/0000210-010
Contextual Social Psychology: Reanalyzing Prejudice, Voting, and Intergroup Contact, by T. F. Pettigrew

CULTURAL CONTEXTS FOR BASIC SOCIAL PSYCHOLOGICAL PHENOMENA

Many prominent social psychologists—such as Triandis (1994), Shinobu Kitayama, Hazel Markus, and Richard Nisbett (A. P. Fiske et al., 1998)—have long focused on cultural effects, and the International Academy for Intercultural Research includes many social psychologists who specialize in cultural research. But social psychologists generally have not been active in this domain using the latest multilevel statistical tools. *Cross-Cultural Analysis* (Davidov et al., 2011), a leading volume for this area, has 51 contributors, only one of whom is a self-identified social psychologist.

This situation is starting to change. The new methodological tools have encouraged social psychologists to begin to consider how history and culture influence basic social psychological phenomena at multiple levels. This volume has attempted to record some of this work, much of it done in Europe.

HISTORY AND TIME AS CONTEXT

Culture and norms, of course, shift over time. So many contextual analyses must consider time as context. We have previously noted a number of such studies. In fact, some of the most informative studies in social psychology have involved over-time data. Remember the previously mentioned Sherif (1935, 1937, 1966; see also Pettigrew, 1991a) studies on the autokinetic effect and Robbers' Cave. Their important findings emerged only because Sherif persisted in testing his subjects over many trials.

In 2003, Dean Simonton wrote a concise chapter in the *Annual Review of Psychology* advocating the importance for social psychologists of both quantitative and qualitative analyses of historical data. Simonton demonstrated his point with a variety of historical analyses of high achievers and their social contexts (e.g., Simonton, 1977). Such studies are necessarily contextual. And throughout this book I have cited significant research using historical data.

Recall the studies of the lasting effects of slavery in the southern United States. Slavery relates today to the region's far-right voting (Acharya et al., 2018) and greater acceptance of violence as reflected in its laws (D. Cohen, 1996). Recall, too, the studies that showed threatening periods in a nation's history tended to evince greater authoritarianism, greater distrust of government, enhanced desire for an authoritarian leader, and increased prejudice and discrimination against minorities (Bianchi et al., 2018; Doty et al., 1991; Sales, 1973; Sprong et al., 2019). The most remarkable of these historical studies reached back centuries and found that anti-Jewish discrimination from 1100 to 1800 in urban Europe flared up in cold winters where food shortages were most intense (R. W. Anderson et al., 2017). The best known of these social psychological analyses of historical trends is the claim by Steven Pinker (2011) that violence trends have actually been declining over recent centuries.

ARE SOCIAL PSYCHOLOGICAL THEORY AND FINDINGS UNIVERSAL?

Back in the 1950s, America's social sciences, including social psychology, were greatly concerned about the universality of social processes across cultures. Are findings in one cultural context likely to be found in another cultural context? Or is cross-cultural generalization unlikely, even ethnocentric? In social psychology, critics wondered if the discipline's results were not confined to America's college students who participated as experimental subjects.

Such harsh critiques were partly a product of a misinterpretation of the cultural relativism movement in cultural anthropology advanced by Franz Boas (1887) and his famous Columbia University students. Boas held that a people's beliefs and practices should be understood in terms of *their* culture. It was an attack on the provincialism that pervaded early social science when Western social scientists used their own cultural understandings to judge and misinterpret non-Western cultures (Geertz, 1984). But this sound doctrine became twisted into a contention that all comparisons across cultures were necessarily in themselves questionable and even potentially racist.

The contextual research detailed in this book is relevant to this history. This work largely involved adult subjects—answering the old attack that social psychological research is restricted to student subjects (Sears, 1986). Moreover, I investigated the research literatures on five topics that are at the core of social psychology: prejudice, authoritarianism, group attribution, relative deprivation, and intergroup contact. And in each I have drawn on studies throughout the world that repeatedly replicate the basic phenomena—even such complex processes as the secondary contact effect and a wide variety of moderating and mediating processes.

Recall, too, the broad range of nations cited throughout this book. The research came from more than 50 nations, including all of Europe and North America and parts of Asia (China, Hong Kong, India, Japan, Mongolia, Pakistan, Singapore, Thailand) and South America (Argentina, Brazil, Chile), as well as Australia, Cyprus, Iceland, Israel, New Zealand, Palestine, Turkey and South Africa. This great variety of countries offered many different cultural and normative contexts for the social psychological processes under study. Yet the same basic trends emerged across this extensive sampling of the world.

Consider two further examples of universalism. The stereotype content model with its focus on competence and warmth also meets the valuable property of operating similarly across vastly different cultures and groups (S. T. Fiske et al., 2002). Similarly, Schwartz (1992) has shown universals for his values scale across 20 nations. It can now be stated with confidence that social psychological findings and theory are *not* limited to America or to experiments with college students.

TEACHING IMPLICATIONS OF A CONTEXTUAL EMPHASIS

The examples of strong contextual effects described throughout this volume are necessarily drawn from social psychological phenomena with which I am most familiar. Readers will undoubtedly be able to think of other contextual examples in many other areas of the discipline. By 2019, PsycINFO explicitly listed the term *contextual social psychology* as a main subject in 97 references. Thus, the trend toward contextual social psychology is underway and, I hope, will continue to expand.

There are significant teaching implications of this growing emphasis on contextual effects. First, joint undergraduate and graduate courses with other social sciences—particularly sociology and political science—become not only possible but highly desirable. In the successful spirit of the International Society of Political Psychology, for example, such joint courses could give students a broader picture of how social science operates at multiple levels.

Second, it would also further the development of contextual and cross-disciplinary work if there were more research conferences on such specific topics as voting, criminality, and intergroup discrimination that are focused upon by numerous social science disciplines. For instance, psychology's Society for the Psychological Study of Social Issues and sociology's Society for the Study of Social Problems have never had a joint meeting even though their interests overlap considerably.

Third, the contextual approach calls for sharply expanded statistics courses for undergraduates as well as graduate students. For undergraduates, perhaps, it would suffice to let them know about the existence, uses, and importance of latent variables, structural equation models, mixed models, and multilevel models without their actually learning how to conduct such analyses. For graduate students, the full complement of methods is necessary now and certainly in the future—not just the limited statistics sufficient for restricted laboratory studies. It is my conjecture that such graduate statistics courses are already in place in major departments throughout much of the world, although not necessarily required in graduate programs. But even to be able to read the research journals of the future, such courses will need to exist throughout social psychology programs of all sizes.

THEORETICAL IMPLICATIONS OF A CONTEXTUAL EMPHASIS

The Prejudice Syndrome

Throughout this volume, I have noted the same positive and negative predictors emerging in discussions of prejudice, the attributional bias, relative deprivation, intergroup contact, and right-wing voting. Think of all the variables that closely relate, positively or negatively, to prejudice and to one another: authoritarianism, anxiety, biased group attributions, intergroup contact, individual threat, collective threat, meta-stereotypes, social dominance orientation, stereotype threat, trust, forgiveness, empathy, perspective taking, group and individual relative deprivation, values of security, power, universalism and benevolence values, need for closure, Openness to Experience, deprovincialization, agreeableness, knowledge of the outgroup, ingroup identification, political tolerance, and perceptions of outgroup variability.

Recall also how these many correlates of prejudice are themselves intercorrelated. If a variable—say, openness to experience—is a positive predictor of intergroup contact, then it is highly likely to be a negative predictor of prejudice. In Chapter 5 of this volume, I noted that this snug network of prejudice predictors strongly suggests that we should consider prejudice as a syndrome of variables operating at all three levels of analysis rather than as simply a characteristic of individuals.

In addition, it is notable that the mediational processes of these predictors tend to reoccur across domains. Thus, the effects of personal values and basic traits on prejudice are largely mediated by authoritarianism and social dominance measures. In turn, the effects of authoritarianism and social dominance orientation on such variables as intergroup contact and right-wing voting are largely mediated by prejudice. Group relative deprivation mediates the effects of a nation's economic effects on individual threat that, in turn, predicts prejudice. This consistency of causal sequencing throughout the many studies cited in this book is surprising and impressive and offers another reason for thinking about prejudice and other important dependent variables in multilevel terms.

One reservation is important. To maintain that there is a prejudice syndrome operating at all three major levels of analysis is not to claim that there are no significant differences between various types of prejudices. A Belgium research group looked at this in detail (Meuleman et al., 2019). They found that gender traditionalism reinforced antihomosexuality but tempered Islamophobia. Anti-immigration attitudes were especially related to social class, whereas anti-Semitism and antihomosexuality related strongest to religious involvement. Yet I still found a basic commonality running through all the various types of outgroup prejudice.

German survey data also yield a common factor across multiple types of prejudices. Using structural equation modeling, Andreas Zick and his colleagues (2008) found a common prejudice factor across multiple cross-sectional and panel studies that they termed "group-focused enmity," and it was strongly predicted by a generalized ideology of inequality.

Three-Level Concepts

These consistencies strongly suggest that it would be useful to think of such key constructs as prejudice as a three-level entity. Indeed, one of the most desirable outcomes of greater attention to context would be the development of three-level concepts. Chapter 5 of this volume makes the case for viewing prejudice not simply as an individual characteristic but as a syndrome involving all three major levels of analysis that both broadens and deepens our understanding of intergroup prejudice. Chapters 6, 7, and 8 did the same for relative deprivation, intergroup contact, and right-wing voting.

Prejudice can also be advantageously thought of as a characteristic of situations and even geographic regions. This approach would consider the importance of mesolevel *prejudice places* and macrolevel *prejudice regions* as well as prejudiced individuals. A pointed example of prejudice places are Civil War statues.[1] By glorifying a war to maintain slavery, the statues induce racially prejudiced responses from many White Americans. One need only note that the neo-Nazis and Ku Klux Klan members chose quiet Charlottesville, Virginia, for their "unite the right" mass racist rally in 2017 precisely because Mr. Jefferson's university town was about to take down a stature of Confederate General Robert E. Lee. Just as important, these monuments to the past signal to Black Americans that they are not valued as full-fledged American citizens.

My native South serves as a prime instance of a prejudice region. This does not mean that all Whites residing in the nation's 13 southeastern states are racially prejudiced. But it does hold that living in these states, where racist norms still persist, induces racial prejudice. Those White Americans reared in the North and West who move south later in life tend to become more racially prejudiced. And White Americans reared in the South who move north or west later tend to become less racially prejudiced. Thus, both groups modify their racial stance as a function of living in the midst of or out of the South's racial norms (e.g., Middleton, 1976).

I hope that more such three-level syndromes will emerge from contextual analyses.

Finally, the contextual approach would further three great strengths of social psychology as a discipline.[2] First, social psychology is a *relevant discipline*; it speaks to important human values. Second, social psychology is *useful*; it offers creative solutions to critical social problems. Third, social psychology is *cumulative*; it offers replicable, reliable results of social value. I believe this tri-level approach would enhance all three of the discipline's strengths—relevance, usefulness, and cumulativeness.

This volume has *not* argued that all social psychological work in the future should be contextually orientated, but it has maintained that far more attention should be paid to the social context of the discipline's various phenomena. Although not a new idea, it has been too often ignored. For further support, I close with pertinent quotations from two major figures of 20th-century social psychology.

[1] I passed these statues every day on my way to high school in Richmond, Virginia.

[2] I am indebted to Chris Crandall for this point.

SUPPORT FROM THE PAST

At various times in its century-long history, social psychology's leaders have called for contextual analyses. But their calls have typically gone unanswered. This book is yet another effort to encourage contextual scholarship comparable to the appeals from two major figures of the past.

Mort Deutsch Has the Next-to-Last Word

Deutsch's social context orientation is sharply demonstrated in his concise critiques of equity theory (Deutsch, 1975), dissonance (Deutsch, 1962), and other basic social psychological phenomena. A first-generation Lewinian student who was skilled at both laboratory and large-scale field research, Deutsch put the matter succinctly in a candid autobiographical chapter. He called for a *social* social psychology to supplement the existing largely *individual* social psychology (Deutsch, 1999): "American social psychology . . . has been too focused on what goes on in the isolated head of the subject, with a corresponding neglect of the social reality in which the subject is participating" (pp. 25, 29).

And Kurt Lewin Has the Last Word

Although not the "founder of American social psychology," as some erroneously claim ("Kurt Lewin," 2020), Lewin has had great influence on the discipline. Despite his brief time in America (1933–1947), Kurt Lewin managed to shape much of early social psychological theory. And he advanced the key point of this book forcefully:

> Every action one performs has some specific "background," and is determined by that background. A statement or gesture which may be quite appropriate between companions in a swimming pool may be out of place, even insulting, at a dinner party. Judgment, understanding, perception are impossible without a related background, and the meaning of every event depends directly upon the nature of its background. (Lewin, 1948, p. 145)

References

Abelson, R. P., Kinder, D. R., Peters, M. D., & Fiske, S. T. (1982). Affective and semantic components in political person perception. *Journal of Personality and Social Psychology*, *42*(4), 619–630. https://doi.org/10.1037/0022-3514.42.4.619

Aberson, C. L. (2015). Positive intergroup contact, negative intergroup contact, and threat as predictors of cognitive and affective dimensions of prejudice. *Group Processes & Intergroup Relations*, *18*(6), 743–760. https://doi.org/10.1177/1368430214556699

Aberson, C. L., & Haag, S. C. (2007). Contact, perspective taking, and anxiety as predictors of stereotype endorsement, explicit attitudes, and implicit attitudes. *Group Processes & Intergroup Relations*, *10*(2), 179–201. https://doi.org/10.1177/1368430207074726

Abrahamson, D. (1970). *Our violent society*. Funk & Wagnalls.

Abramowitz, A. I. (2019, August 8). Did Russian interference affect the 2016 election results? *Sabato's Crystal Ball*. http://centerforpolitics.org/crystalball/articles/did-russian-interference-affect-the-2016-election-results/

Abrams, D., Travaglino, G. A., Grant, P. R., Templeton, A., Bennett, M., & Lalot, F. (2019). Mobilizing IDEAS in the Scottish Referendum: Predicting voting intention and well-being with the Identity-Deprivation-Efficacy-Action-Subjective well-being model. *British Journal of Social Psychology*, *59*(2), 425–446. https://doi.org/10.1111/bjso.12355

Acharya, A., Blackwell, M., & Sen, M. (2018). *Deep roots: How slavery still shapes Southern politics*. Princeton University Press.

Ackerman, N. W., & Jahoda, M. (1950). *Anti-semitism and emotional disorder*. Harpers.

Ackermann, K., & Ackermann, M. (2015). The Big Five in context: Personality, diversity and attitudes toward equal opportunities for immigrants in Switzerland. *Swiss Political Science Review*, *21*(3), 396–408. https://doi.org/10.1111/spsr.12170

Adamy, J., & Overberg, P. (2016a, November 9). Counties that experienced rapid diversification voted heavily for Donald Trump. *The Wall Street Journal*. https://www.wsj.com/articles/counties-that-experienced-rapid-diversification-voted-heavily-for-donald-trump-1478741076

Adamy, J., & Overberg, P. (2016b, November 1). Places most unsettled by rapid demographic change are drawn to Donald Trump. *The Wall Street Journal*. https://www.wsj.com/articles/places-most-unsettled-by-rapid-demographic-change-go-for-donald-trump-1478010940

Adelman, R., Reed, L. W., Markle, G., Weiss, S., & Jaret, C. (2017). Urban crime rates and the changing face of immigration: Evidence across four decades. *Journal of Ethnicity in Criminal Justice*, *15*, 52–77. https://doi.org/10.1080/15377938.2016.1261057

Adler, N. E., Epel, E. S., Castellazzo, G., & Ickovics, J. R. (2000). Relationship of subjective and objective social status with psychological and physiological functioning: Preliminary data in healthy white women. *Health Psychology*, *19*(6), 586–592. https://doi.org/10.1037/0278-6133.19.6.586

Adler, N. E., & Stewart, J. (2010). Health disparities across the lifespan: Meaning, methods, and mechanisms. *Annals of the New York Academy of Sciences*, *1186*(1), 5–23. https://doi.org/10.1111/j.1749-6632.2009.05337.x

Adorno, T. W., Frenkel-Brunswik, E., Levinson, D. J., & Sanford, R. N. (1950). *The authoritarian personality*. Harper & Row.

Ainsworth, M. D. S., Blehar, M. C., Waters, E., & Wall, S. (1978). *Patterns of attachment*. Erlbaum.

Alba, R., Rumbant, R. G., & Marotz, K. (2005). A distorted nation: Perceptions of racial/ethnic group sizes and attitudes toward immigrants and other minorities. *Social Forces*, *84*(2), 901–919. https://doi.org/10.1353/sof.2006.0002

Alesina, M., & La Ferrara, E. (2002). Who trusts others? *Journal of Public Economics*, *85*(2), 207–234. https://doi.org/10.1016/S0047-2727(01)00084-6

Alford, J. R., Funk, C. L., & Hibbing, J. R. (2005). Are political orientations genetically transmitted? *The American Political Science Review*, *99*(2), 153–167. https://doi.org/10.1017/S0003055405051579

Algara, C., & Hale, I. (2019). The distorting effects of racial animus on proximity voting in the 2016 elections. *Electoral Studies*, *58*, 58–69. https://doi.org/10.1016/j.electstud.2019.02.001

Alker, H. A., Jr. (1969). A typology of ecological fallacies. In M. Dugan & S. Rokkan (Eds.), *Quantitative ecological analysis* (pp. 69–86). Massachusetts Institute of Technology.

Allison, S. (2015). *Driv'n by fortune*. Dundurn.

Allport, G. W. (1937). *Personality: A psychological interpretation*. Holt.

Allport, G. W. (1954). *The nature of prejudice*. Addison-Wesley.

Allport, G. W. (1958). *The nature of prejudice* (abridged). Doubleday Anchor.

Allport, G. W., & Boring, E. G. (1946). Psychology and social relations at Harvard University. *American Psychologist*, *1*(4), 119–122. https://doi.org/10.1037/h0061868

Allport, G. W., & Kramer, B. M. (1946). Some roots of prejudice. *The Journal of Psychology, 22*(1), 9–39. https://doi.org/10.1080/00223980.1946.9917293

Allport, G. W., & Pettigrew, T. F. (1957). Cultural influence on the perception of movement: The trapezoidal illusion among Zulus. *Journal of Abnormal and Social Psychology, 55*(1), 104–113. https://doi.org/10.1037/h0049372

Allport, G. W., & Postman, L. (1947). *The psychology of rumor*. Holt.

Allport, G. W., & Ross, J. M. (1967). Personal religious orientation and prejudice. *Journal of Personality and Social Psychology, 5*(4), 432–443. https://doi.org/10.1037/h0021212

Almond, G., & Verba, S. (1963). *The civic culture*. Princeton University Press. https://doi.org/10.1515/9781400874569

Altemeyer, B. (1981). *Right-wing authoritarianism*. University of Manitoba Press.

Altemeyer, B. (1988). *Enemies of the people*. Jossey-Bass.

Altemeyer, B. (1996). *The authoritarian specter*. Harvard University Press.

Al-Zahrani, S. S., & Kaplowitz, S. A. (1993). Attributional biases in individualistic and collectivistic cultures: A comparison of Americans with Saudis. *Social Psychology Quarterly, 56*(3), 223–233. https://doi.org/10.2307/2786780

Amengay, A., & Stockemer, D. (2019). The radical right in Western Europe: A meta-analysis of structural factors. *Political Studies Review, 17*(1), 30–40. https://doi.org/10.1177/1478929918777975

Amrheim, V., & Greenland, S. (2017). Remove, rather than redefine, statistical significance. *Nature Human Behaviour, 1*(9), 1. https://doi.org/10.1038/s41562-017-0224-0

Anastasio, P., Bachman, B., Gaertner, S., & Dovidio, J. (1997). Categorization, recategorization and common ingroup identity. In R. Spears, P. J. Oakes, N. Ellemers, & S. A. Haslam (Eds.), *The social psychology of stereotypes and group life* (pp. 236–256). Blackwell.

Anderson, C. J., Bahnik, S., Barnett-Cowan, M., Bosco, F. A., Chandler, J., Chartier, C. R., Cheung, F., Christopherson, C. D., Cordes, A., Cremata, E. J., Della Penna, N., Estel, V., Fedor, A., Fitneva, S. A., Frank, M. C., Grange, J. A., Hartshorne, J. K., Hasselman, F., Henninger, F., . . . Zuni, K. (2016). Response to comment on "Estimating the Reproducibility of Psychological Science." *Science, 351*(6277), 1037-e. https://doi.org/10.1126/science.aad9163

Anderson, R. W., Johnson, N. D., & Koyama, M. (2017). Jewish persecutions and weather shocks: 1100–1800. *Economic Journal, 127*(602), 924–958. https://doi.org/10.1111/ecoj.12331

Arnadóttir, K., Lolliot, S., Brown, R., & Hewstone, M. (2018). Positive and negative intergroup contact: Interaction not symmetry. *European Journal of Social Psychology, 48*(6), 784–800. https://doi.org/10.1002/ejsp.2365

Asbrock, F., Sibley, C. G., & Duckitt, J. (2010). Right-wing authoritarianism and social dominance orientation and the dimensions of generalized prejudice: A longitudinal test. *European Journal of Personality, 24*, 324–340. https://doi.org/10.1002/per.746

Asch, S. E. (1955). Opinions and social pressure. *Scientific American, 193*, 31–35. https://doi.org/10.1038/scientificamerican1155-31

Asch, S. E. (1956). Studies of independence and conformity: I. A minority of one against a unanimous majority. *Psychological Monographs, 70*(9), 1–70. https://doi.org/10.1037/h0093718

Atkinson, J. W., & Hoselitz, B. F. (1958). Entrepreneurship and personality. *Explorations in Entrepreneurial History, 10*, 107–112.

Auger, B., & Amiot, C. E. (2019). The impact of imagined contact in the realm of human-animal relations: Investigating a superordinate generalization effect involving both valued and devalued animals. *Journal of Experimental Social Psychology, 85*, Article 103872. https://doi.org/10.1016/j.jesp.2019.103872

Ávila-Batista, A. C., Rueda, F. J. M., & Filho, N. H. (2019). Construcción y evidencias de una escala abreviada de autoinforme para evalual el autoitaraismo [Construction and validity evidence of a brief self-report scale to assess authoritarianism]. *Acta Colombiana de Psicologia, 22*(1), 31–51. https://doi.org/10.14718/ACP.2019.22.1.3

Bäckström, M., & Björklund, F. (2007). Structural modeling of generalized prejudice: The role of social dominance, authoritarianism, and empathy. *Journal of Individual Differences, 28*(1), 10–17. https://doi.org/10.1027/1614-0001.28.1.10

Bagci, S. C., & Gungor, H. (2019). Associations between perceived positive and negative parental contact and adolescents' intergroup contact experiences. *International Journal of Intercultural Relations, 69*, 76–86. https://doi.org/10.1016/j.ijintrel.2019.01.002

Bagci, S. C., & Turnuklu, A. (2019). Intended, unintended, and unknown consequences of contact. *Social Psychology, 50*(1), 7–23. https://doi.org/10.1027/1864-9335/a000355

Bagci, S. C., Turnuklu, A., & Tercan, M. (2020). Positive intergroup contact decreases the likelihood that prejudicial attitudes become behavioral tendencies. *European Journal of Social Psychology, 50*(3), 597–613. https://doi.org/10.1002/ejsp.2646

Baker, G. (2019, December 6). A British test for the populist revolution. *The Wall Street Journal*, C1–C2. https://www.wsj.com/articles/a-british-test-for-the-populist-revolution-11575647973

Baker, P. E. (1934). *Negro–White adjustment*. Association Press. https://doi.org/10.2307/2961780

Bales, R. F. (1950). *Interaction process analysis*. Addison-Wesley.

Bales, R. F. (1970). *Personality and interpersonal behavior*. Holt, Rinehart, & Winston.

Bales, R. F. (1999). *Social interaction systems: Theory and measurement*. Transition Publishers.

Bales, R. F., & Cohen, S. (1979). *SYMLOG*. Free Press.

Bandura, A. (1986). *Social foundations of thought and action: A social cognitive theory*. Prentice Hall.

Barker, M. (1984). *The new racism: Conservatives and the ideology of the tribe*. Aletheia Press.

Barlow, F. K., Paolini, S., Pedersen, A., Hornsey, M. J., Radke, H. R. M., Harwood, J., Rubin, M., & Sibley, C. G. (2012). The contact caveat: Negative contact predicts increased prejudice more than positive contact predicts reduced prejudice. *Personality and Social Psychology Bulletin, 38*(12), 1629–1643. https://doi.org/10.1177/0146167212457953

Baron, R. M., & Kenny, D. A. (1986). The moderator–mediator variable distinction in social psychological research: Conceptual, strategic, and statistical considerations. *Journal of Personality and Social Psychology, 51*(6), 1173–1182. https://doi.org/10.1037/0022-3514.51.6.1173

Barrouquere, B. (2017, November 13). FBI: Hate crimes reach 5-year high in 2016, jumped as Trump rolled toward presidency. *Southern Poverty Law Center Hatewatch*. https://www.splcenter.org/hatewatch/2017/11/13/fbi-hate-crimes-reach-5-year-high-2016-jumped-trump-rolled-toward-presidency-0

Bartholomew, K. (1990). Avoidance of intimacy. *Journal of Social and Personal Relationships, 7*(2), 147–178. https://doi.org/10.1177/0265407590072001

Batson, C. D., & Ahmad, M. Y. (2009). Using empathy to improve intergroup attitudes and relations. *Social Issues and Policy Review, 3*(1), 141–177. https://doi.org/10.1111/j.1751-2409.2009.01013.x

Batson, C. D., & Stocks, E. L. (2005). Religion and prejudice. In J. F. Dovidio, P. Glick, & L. A. Rudman (Eds.), *On the nature of prejudice: Fifty years after Allport* (pp. 413–427). Blackwell. https://doi.org/10.1002/9780470773963.ch25

Baumeister, R. F., Bratslavsky, E., Finkenauer, C., & Vohs, D. K. (2001). Bad is stronger than good. *Review of General Psychology, 5*(4), 323–370. https://doi.org/10.1037/1089-2680.5.4.323

Becker, J. C., Wright, S. C., Lubensky, M. E., & Zhou, S. (2013). Friend or ally: Whether cross-group contact undermines collective action depends on what advantaged group members say (or don't say). *Personality and Social Psychology Bulletin, 39*(4), 442–455. https://doi.org/10.1177/0146167213477155

Beelmann, A., & Heinemann, K. S. (2014). Preventing prejudice and improving intergroup attitudes: A meta-analysis of child and adolescent training programs. *Journal of Applied Developmental Psychology, 35*(1), 10–24. https://doi.org/10.1016/j.appdev.2013.11.002

Beierlein, C., Asbrock, F., Kauff, M., & Schmidt, P. (2015). Short scale authoritarianism. *Gesis*, 1–27.

Benjamin, D. J., Berger, J. O., Johanneson, M., Nosek, B. A., Wagenmakers, E.-J., Berk, R., Bollen, K. A., Brembs, B., Brown, L., Camerer, C., Cesarini, D., Chambers, C. D., Clyde, M., Cook, T. D., De Boeck, P., Dienes, Z., Dreber, A., Easwaran, K., Efferson, C., . . . Johnson, V. E. (2018). Redefine statistical significance. *Nature Human Behavior, 2*, 6–10. https://doi.org/10.1038/s41562-017-0189-z

Benjamin, L. T., & Crouse, E. M. (2002). The American Psychological Association's response to *Brown v. Board*: The case of Kenneth B. Clark. *American Psychologist, 57*(1), 38–50. https://doi.org/10.1037/0003-066X.57.1.38

Bentler, P. M. (1985). *Theory and implementation of EQS: A structural equations program*. BMDP Statistical Software.

Bergmann, W., & Erb, R. (1986). Kommunikationslatenz, moral, und offentliche meining [Latent communication, moral, and public meaning]. *Kölner Zeitschrift für Soziologie und Sozialpsychologie, 38*, 223–246.

Bergsieker, H. B., Leslie, L. M., Constantine, V. S., & Fiske, S. T. (2012). Stereotyping by omission: Eliminate the negative, accentuate the positive. *Journal of Personality and Social Psychology, 102*(6), 1214–1228.

Bianchi, E. C., Hall, E. V., & Lee, S. (2018). Reexamining the link between economic downturns and racial antipathy: Evidence that prejudice against Blacks rises during recessions. *Psychological Science, 29*(10), 1584–1597. https://doi.org/10.1177/0956797618777214

Bigler, R. S., & Hughes, J. M. (2010). Reasons for skepticism about the efficacy of simulated social contact interventions. *American Psychologist, 65*(2), 132–133. https://doi.org/10.1037/a0018097

Binder, J., Zagefka, H., Brown, R., Funke, F., Kessler, T., Mummendey, A., Maquil, A., Demoulin, S., & Leyens, J.-P. (2009). Does contact reduce prejudice or does prejudice reduce contact? A longitudinal test of thee contact hypothesis among majority and minority groups in three different European countries. *Journal of Personality and Social Psychology, 96*(4), 843–856. https://doi.org/10.1037/a0013470

Biskupic, J. (2020, January 8). *How Ruth Bader Ginsburg is trying to check the conservative majority*. Microsoft News. https://www.msn.com/en-us/news/us/how-ruth-bader-ginsburg-is-trying-to-check-the-conservative-majority/ar-BBYKDxJ

Bizumic, B., & Duckitt, J. (2018). Investigating right wing authoritarianism with a very short authoritarianism scale. *Journal of Social and Political Psychology, 6*(1), 129–150. https://doi.org/10.5964/jspp.v6i1.835

Blalock, H. M. (1957). Per cent non-white and discrimination in the South. *American Sociological Review, 22*(6), 677–682. https://doi.org/10.2307/2089197

Blalock, H. M. (1984). Contextual-effects models: Theoretical and methodological issues. *Annual Review of Sociology, 10*, 353–372. https://doi.org/10.1146/annurev.so.10.080184.002033

Blumer, H. (1958). Race prejudice as a sense of group position. *Pacific Sociological Review, 1*(1), 3–7. https://doi.org/10.2307/1388607

Boag, E. M., & Carnelley, K. B. (2016). Attachment and prejudice: The mediating role of empathy. *British Journal of Social Psychology, 55*(2), 337–356. https://doi.org/10.1111/bjso.12132

Boas, F. (1887). Museums of ethnology and their classification. *Science, 9*(228), 587–589. https://doi.org/10.1126/science.ns-9.228.587-a

Bobo, L. D. (1999). Prejudice as group position: Microfoundations of a sociological approach to racism and race relations. *Journal of Social Issues, 55*(3), 445–472. https://doi.org/10.1111/0022-4537.00127

Boccato, G., Capozza, D., Trifiletti, E., & Di Bernardo, G. A. (2015). Attachment security and intergroup contact. *Journal of Applied Social Psychology, 45*(11), 629–647. https://doi.org/10.1111/jasp.12325

Borenstein, M., Hedges, L. V., Higgins, J. P. T., & Rothstein, H. R. (2009). *Introduction to meta-analysis*. Wiley. https://doi.org/10.1002/9780470743386

Borgatta, E. F., Bales, R. F., & Couch, A. S. (1954). Some findings relevant to the great man theory of leadership. *American Sociological Review, 19*(6), 755–759. https://doi.org/10.2307/2087923

Boyack, K. W., Klavans, R., & Börner, K. (2005). Mapping the backbone of science. *Scientometrics, 64*(3), 351–374. https://doi.org/10.1007/s11192-005-0255-5

Boyle, S. P. (1962). *The desegregated heart: A Virginian's stand in time of transition*. Morrow.

Brameld, T. (1946). *Minority problems in the public schools*. Harper.

Brandt, M. J., & Henry, P. J. (2012). Inequality and gender differences in authoritarianism. *Personality and Social Psychology Bulletin, 38*(10), 1301–1315. https://doi.org/10.1177/0146167212449871

Brauer, M., & Curtin, J. J. (2018). Linear mixed-effects models and the analysis of nonindependent data. *Current Directions in Psychological Science, 28*(2), 164–169. https://doi.org/10.1037/met0000159

Brewer, M. B. (2008). Deprovincialization: Social identity complexity and outgroup acceptance. In U. Wagner, L. Tropp, G. Finchilescu, & C. Tredoux (Eds.), *Improving intergroup relations—Building on the legacy of Thomas F. Pettigrew* (pp. 160–176). Blackwell. https://doi.org/10.1002/9781444303117.ch11

Brewer, M. B., & Miller, N. (1984). Beyond the contact hypothesis: Theoretical perspectives on desegregation. In N. Miller & M. B. Brewer (Eds.), *Groups in contact: The psychology of desegregation* (pp. 281–302). Academic Press. https://doi.org/10.1016/B978-0-12-497780-8.50019-X

Brophy, I. N. (1945). The luxury of anti-Negro prejudice. *Public Opinion Quarterly, 9*(4), 456–466. https://doi.org/10.1086/265762

Brown, R., Eller, A., Leeds, S., & Stace, K. (2007). Intergroup contact and intergroup attitudes: A longitudinal study. *European Journal of Social Psychology, 37*(4), 692–703. https://doi.org/10.1002/ejsp.384

Brown, R., & Hewstone, M. (2005). An integrative theory of intergroup contact. *Advances in Experimental Social Psychology, 37*, 255–343. https://doi.org/10.1016/S0065-2601(05)37005-5

Bruneau, E., Ktelly, N., & Laustsen, L. (2018). The unique effects of blatant dehumanization on attitudes towards Muslim refugees during the European "refugee crisis" across four countries. *European Journal of Social Psychology, 48*(5), 645–662. https://doi.org/10.1002/ejsp.2357

Bulmer, M. (1984). *The Chicago School of Sociology: Institutionalization, diversity, and the rise of sociological research*. University of Chicago Press.

Butler, J. C. (2000). Personality and emotional correlates of right-wing authoritarianism. *Social Behavior and Personality, 28*(1), 1–14. https://doi.org/10.2224/sbp.2000.28.1.1

Cacioppo, J. T., Berntson, G. G., Sheridan, J. F., & McClintock, M. (2000). Multilevel integrative analyses of human behavior: Social neuroscience and the complementing nature of social and biological approaches. *Psychological Bulletin, 126*(6), 829–843. https://doi.org/10.1037/0033-2909.126.6.829

Çakal, H., Halabi, S., Cazan, A.-M., & Eller, A. (2019). Intergroup contact and endorsement of social change motivations: The mediating role of intergroup trust, perspective-taking, and intergroup anxiety among three advantaged groups in Northern Cyprus, Romania and Israel. *Group Processes & Intergroup Relations*. Advance online publication. https://doi.org/10.1177/1368430219885163

Çakal, H., Hewstone, M., Schwär, G., & Heath, A. (2011). An investigation of the social identity model of collective action and the "sedative" effect of intergroup contact among Black and White students in South Africa. *British Journal of Social Psychology, 50*(4), 606–627. https://doi.org/10.1111/j.2044-8309.2011.02075.x

Calamur, K. (2017, January). A short history of "America first." *The Atlantic*. https://www.theatlantic.com/politics/archive/2017/01/trump-america-first/514037

Campante, F., & Yanagizawa-Drott, D. (2016, December 9). Did declining social mobility cause Trump's rise? In a word, no. *The Big Idea*. http://www.vox.com/the-big-idea/2016/12/9/13895184/social-mobility-economic-anxiety-trump-chetty

Campbell, D. (1959). *Systematic errors to be expected of the social scientist on the basis of a general psychology of cognitive bias* [Paper presentation]. American Psychological Association Annual Meeting, Cincinnati, OH, United States.

Campbell, E. Q., & Pettigrew, T. F. (1959a). *Christians in racial crisis: A study of the Little Rock Ministry*. Public Affairs Press.

Campbell, E. Q., & Pettigrew, T. F. (1959b). Racial and moral crisis: The role of Little Rock ministers. *American Journal of Sociology, 64*(5), 509–516. https://doi.org/10.1086/222547

Campbell, W. (1986). *Forty acres and a goat*. Peachtree Publishers.

Capozza, D., & Rattazzi, A. M. M. (1999). Stereotypes and attribution processes in a multi-ethnic Italian province. *Journal of Community & Applied Social Psychology, 9*(3), 231–235. https://doi.org/10.1002/(SICI)1099-1298(199905/06)9:3<231::AID-CASP508>3.0.CO;2-8

Capshew, J. H. (1992). Psychologists on site: A reconnaissance of the historiography of the laboratory. *American Psychologist, 47*(2), 132–142. https://doi.org/10.1037/0003-066X.47.2.132

Carroll, J. (2001). *Public overestimates U.S. Black and Hispanic populations*. Gallup. https://news.gallup.com/poll/4435/public-overestimats-us-black-hispanic-population.aspx

Cartwright, D. (1979). Contemporary social psychology in historical perspective. *Social Psychology Quarterly, 42*(1), 82–93. https://doi.org/10.2307/3033880

Chaloupkova, J., & Salamounova, P. (2006). Attitudes towards immigrants and the impact of migration in European countries [Czech]. *Czech Sociological Review*, *42*(1), 57–80.

Charlesworth, T. E. S., & Banaji, M. R. (2019). Patterns of implicit and explicit attitudes: I. Long-term change and stability from 2007 to 2016. *Psychological Science*, *30*(2), 174–192. https://doi.org/10.1177/0956797618813087

Chirumbolo, A., Sensales, G., & Kosic, A. (2003). Ideologia, personalità e bisogno di chiusura cognitiva [Ideology, personality, and need for cognitive closure]. *Giornale Italiano di Psicologia*, *30*(1), 69–93.

Choma, B. L., & Hanoch, Y. (2017). Cognitive ability and authoritarianism: Understanding support for Trump and Clinton. *Personality and Individual Differences*, *106*(1), 287–291. https://doi.org/10.1016/j.paid.2016.10.054

Christ, O., Asbrock, F., Dhont, K., Pettigrew, T. F., & Wagner, U. (2013). The effects of intergroup climate on immigrants' acculturation preferences. *Zeitschrift fur Psychologie mit Zeitschrift fur Angewandte Psychologie*, *221*(4), 252–257. https://doi.org/10.1027/2151-2604/a000155

Christ, O., Hewstone, M., Tausch, N., Wagner, U., Voci, A., Hughes, J., & Cairns, E. (2010). Direct contact as a moderator of extended contact effects: Cross-sectional and longitudinal impact on outgroup attitudes, behavioral intentions, and attitude certainty. *Personality and Social Psychology Bulletin*, *36*(12), 1662–1674.

Christ, O., Schmid, K., Lolliot, S., Swart, H., Stolle, D., Tausch, N., Ramiah, A. A., Wagner, U., Vertovec, S., & Hewstone, M. (2014). Contextual effect of positive intergroup contact on outgroup prejudice. *Proceedings of the National Academy of Sciences*, *111*(11), 3996–4000. https://doi.org/10.1073/pnas.1320901111

Christ, O., Sibley, C. G., & Wagner, U. (2012). Multilevel modeling in personality and social psychology. In K. Deaux & M. Snyder (Eds.), *The Oxford handbook of personality and social psychology* (pp. 239–260). Oxford University Press.

Christ, O., Ullrich, J., & Wagner, U. (2008, July). *The joint effects of positive and negative intergroup contact on attitudes and attitude strength* [Paper presentation]. European Association of Experimental Social Psychology 15th General Meeting, Opatija, Croatia.

Christie, R., & Jahoda, M. (1954). *Studies in the scope and method of "the authoritarian personality."* The Free Press.

Cialdini, R. B., & Trost, M. R. (1998). Social influence: Social norms, conformity and compliance. In D. T. Gilbert, S. T. Fiske, & G. Lindzey (Eds.), *The handbook of social psychology* (4th ed., Vol. 2, pp. 151–192). McGraw-Hill.

Cohen, D. (1996). Law, social policy, and violence: The impact of regional cultures. *Journal of Personality and Social Psychology*, *70*(5), 961–978. https://doi.org/10.1037/0022-3514.70.5.961

Cohen, J. (1990). Things I have learned (so far). *American Psychologist*, *45*(12), 1304–1312. https://doi.org/10.1037/0003-066X.45.12.1304

Cohrs, J. C., Moschner, B., Maes, J., & Kiekmann, S. (2005). The motivational bases of right-wing authoritarianism and social dominance orientation: Relations to values and attitudes in the aftermath of September 11, 2001. *Personality and Social Psychology Bulletin, 31*(10), 1425–1434. https://doi.org/10.1177/0146167205275614

Cohrs, J. C., & Stelzl, M. (2010). Ideological attitudes predict host society members' attitudes toward immigrants: Exploring cross-national differences. *Journal of Social Issues, 66*(4), 673–694. https://doi.org/10.1111/j.1540-4560.2010.01670.x

Coleman, J. S. (1966). *Equality of educational opportunity*. U.S. Office of Education.

Coleman, M. D. (2013). Emotion and the ultimate attribution error. *Current Psychology, 32*(1), 71–81. https://doi.org/10.1007/s12144-013-9164-7

Conover, T. (2006, March). The checkpoint. *The Atlantic*. http://www.theatlantic.com/magazine/archive/2006/03/the-checkpoint/304604/

Conway, L. G., III, & McFarland, J. D. (2019). Do right-wing and left-wing authoritarianism predict election outcomes? Support for Obama and Trump across two United States presidential elections. *Personality and Individual Differences, 138*, 84–87. https://doi.org/10.1016/j.paid.2018.09.033

Cook, S. W. (1984). Cooperative interaction in multiethnic contexts. In N. Miller & M. B. Brewer (Eds.), *Groups in contact* (pp. 155–185). Academic Press. https://doi.org/10.1016/B978-0-12-497780-8.50014-0

Costa, P. T., & McCrae, R. R. (1992a). Normal personality assessment in clinical practice: The NEO Personality inventory. *Psychological Assessment, 4*(1), 5–13. https://doi.org/10.1037/1040-3590.4.1.5

Costa, P. T., & McCrae, R. R. (1992b). *Revised NEO Personality Inventory (NEO-Pi-R) and NEO Five-Factor Inventory (NEO-FFI) manual*. Psychological Assessment Resources.

Costello, M. B. (2016). *The Trump effect: The impact of the presidential campaign on our nation's schools*. Southern Poverty Law Center. https://www.splcenter.org/sites/Default/files/splc_the_trump_effect.pdf

Craig, M. A., & Richeson, J. A. (2014a). More diverse yet less tolerant? How the increasingly diverse racial landscape affects White Americans' racial attitudes. *Personality and Social Psychology Bulletin, 40*(6), 750–761. https://doi.org/10.1177/0146167214524993

Craig, M. A., & Richeson, J. A. (2014b). On the precipice of a "majority-minority" America: Perceived status threat from the racial demographic shift affects white Americans' political ideology. *Psychological Science, 25*(6), 1189–1197. https://doi.org/10.1177/0956797614527113

Craig, M. A., & Richeson, J. A. (2018). Hispanic population growth engenders conservative shift among non-Hispanic racial minorities. *Social Psychological & Personality Science, 9*(4), 383–392. https://doi.org/10.1177/1948550617712029

Craig, M. A., Rucker, J. M., & Richeson, J. A. (2017). The pitfalls and promise of increasing racial diversity: Threat, contact, and race relations in the 21st century. *Current Directions in Psychological Science, 27*(3), 188–193. https://doi.org/10.1177/0963721417727860

Craig, M. A., Rucker, J. M., & Richeson, J. A. (2018). Racial and political dynamics of an approaching "majority-minority" United States. *The Annals of the American Academy of Political and Social Science, 677*(1), 204–214. https://doi.org/10.1177/0002716218766269

Crandall, C. S., Eshleman, A., & O'Brien, L. (2002). Social norms and the expression and suppression of prejudice: The struggle for internalization. *Journal of Personality and Social Psychology, 82*(3), 359–378. https://doi.org/10.1037/0022-3514.82.3.359

Crandall, C. S., Ferguson, M. A., & Bahns, A. J. (2000). When we see prejudice: The normative window and social change. In C. Stanger & C. S. Crandall (Eds.), *Frontiers of social psychology: Stereotypes and prejudice* (pp. 53–69). Psychology Press.

Crandall, C. S., Miller, J. M., Roman, Z., & Ferguson, M. (2020). *Disagreement about groups predicts reductions in prejudice* [Manuscript in preparation]. Department of Psychology, University of Kansas.

Crandall, C. S., Miller, J. M., & White, J. M., II. (2018). Changing norms following the 2016 U.S. presidential election: The Trump effect on prejudice. *Social Psychological & Personality Science, 9*(2), 186–192. https://doi.org/10.1177/1948550617750735

Crosby, F. J. (1976). A model for egoistical relative deprivation. *Psychological Review, 83*(2), 85–113. https://doi.org/10.1037/0033-295X.83.2.85

Crowell, J. A., Fraley, R. C., & Shaver, P. R. (1999). Measurement of individual differences in adolescent and adult attachment. In J. Cassidy & P. R. Shaver (Eds.), *Handbook of attachment: Theory, research, and clinical applications* (pp. 434–465). Guilford Press.

Crowson, H. M., & Brandes, J. A. (2017). Differentiating between Donald Trump and Hillary Clinton voters using facets of right-wing authoritarianism and social dominance orientation: A brief report. *Psychological Reports, 120*(3), 364–373. https://doi.org/10.1177/0033294117697089

Cunningham, W. A., Nezlek, J. B., & Banaji, M. R. (2004). Implicit and explicit ethnocentrism: Revisiting the ideologies of prejudice. *Personality and Social Psychology Bulletin, 30*(10), 1332–1346. https://doi.org/10.1177/0146167204264654

Dallago, F., & Roccato, M. (2008). Right-wing authoritarianism, Big Five and perceived threat to safety. *European Journal of Personality, 24*(2), 106–122.

Daniel Kahneman. (2018, December 29). In *Wikipedia*. https://en.wikipedia.org/wiki/Daniel_Kahneman

Darby, J. (1986). *Intimidation and the control of conflict in Northern Ireland*. Gill & Macmillan.

Darmofal, D., & Strickler, R. (2019). *Demography, politics, and partisan polarization in the United States, 1828–2016* (J. R. Porter & S. A. Matthews, Series Eds.; pp. 123–141). Springer-Verlag. https://doi.org/10.1007/978-3-030-04001-7

Davidov, E., Schmidt, P., & Billiet, J. (2011). *Cross-cultural analysis: Methods and applications*. Routledge.

Davies, K., Tropp, L., Aron, A., Pettigrew, T. F., & Wright, S. C. (2011). Cross-group friendships and intergroup attitudes: A meta-analytic review. *Personality and Social Psychology Review, 15*(4), 332–351. https://doi.org/10.1177/1088868311411103

De la Sablonnière, R., Tougas, F., Taylor, D. M., Crush, J., McDonald, D., & Perenlei, O. R. (2015). Social change in Mongolia and South Africa: The impact of relative deprivation trajectory and group status on well-being and adjustment to change. *Social Justice Research, 28*(1), 102–122. https://doi.org/10.1007/s11211-015-0236-8

De Tezanos-Pinto, P., Bratt, C., & Brown, R. (2010). What will the others think? In-group norms as a mediator of the effects of intergroup contact. *British Journal of Social Psychology, 49*(3), 507–523. https://doi.org/10.1348/014466609X471020

de Tocqueville, A. (1945). *Democracy in America* (Vols. 1 & 2). Vintage. (Original works published 1835 & 1840)

Deutsch, M. (1962). Dissonance or defensiveness? *Journal of Personality, 30*, 16–28.

Deutsch, M. (1975). Equity, equality, and need: What determines which value will be used as the basis for distributive justice? *Journal of Social Issues, 31*(3), 137–149. https://doi.org/10.1111/j.1540-4560.1975.tb01000.x

Deutsch, M. (1999). A personal perspective on the development of social psychology in the 20th century. In A. Rodrigues & R. V. Levine (Eds.), *Reflections on 100 years of experimental social psychology* (pp. 1–34). Basic Books.

Deutsch, M., & Collins, M. (1951). *Interracial housing: A psychological evaluation of a social experiment*. University of Minnesota Press.

De Vries, S., & Pettigrew, T. F. (1994). A comparative perspective on affirmative action: *Positieve aktie* in the Netherlands. *Basic and Applied Social Psychology, 15*(1–2), 179–199. https://doi.org/10.1207/s15324834basp1501&2_8

Dew, C. B. (2016). *The making of a racist*. University of Virginia Press.

Dhont, K., Roets, A., & Van Hiel, A. (2011). Opening closed minds: The combined effects of intergroup contact and need for closure on prejudice. *Personality and Social Psychology Bulletin, 37*(4), 514–528. https://doi.org/10.1177/0146167211399101

Dhont, K., Roets, A., & Van Hiel, A. (2013). The intergenerational transmission of need for closure underlies the transmission of authoritarianism and anti-immigrant prejudice. *Personality and Individual Differences, 54*(6), 779–784. https://doi.org/10.1016/j.paid.2012.12.016

Dhont, K., & Van Hiel, A. (2009). We must not be enemies: Interracial contact and reduction of prejudice among authoritarians. *Personality and Individual Differences*, *46*(2), 172–177. https://doi.org/10.1016/j.paid.2008.09.022

Dhont, K., Van Hiel, A., & Hewstone, M. (2014). Changing the ideological roots of prejudice: Longitudinal effects of ethnic intergroup contact on social dominance orientation. *Group Processes & Intergroup Relations*, *17*(1), 27–44. https://doi.org/10.1177/1368430213497064

Diamant, J. (2018, June 19). *Western Europeans vary in their nationalist, anti-immigrant and anti-religious minority attitudes*. Pew Research Center. https://www.pewresearch.org/fact-tank/2018/06/19/western-europeans-vary-in-their-nationalist-anti-immigrant-and-anti-religious-minority-attitudes

Dickersin, K., Lheritier, V., & Chapuis, F. (2005). NIH clinical trials and publication bias. *Online Journal of Current Clinical Trials*. Document No. 50.

Dickersin, K., & Min, Y. (1993). Publication bias: The problem that won't go away. *Annals of the New York Academy of Sciences*, *703*(1), 135–148. https://doi.org/10.1111/j.1749-6632.1993.tb26343.x

Diederik Stapel. (2020, March 17). In *Wikipedia*. https://en.wikipedia.org/wiki/Diederik_Stapel

Digman, J. M. (1990). Personality structure: Emergence of the five-factor model. *Annual Review of Psychology*, *41*, 417–440. https://doi.org/10.1146/annurev.ps.41.020190.002221

Digman, J. M. (1997). Higher-order factors of the Big Five. *Journal of Personality and Social Psychology*, *73*(6), 1246–1256. https://doi.org/10.1037/0022-3514.73.6.1246

Dinesen, P. T., Klemmensen, R., & Norgaard, A. S. (2016). Attitudes toward immigration: The role of personal predispositions. *Political Psychology*, *37*(1), 55–72. https://doi.org/10.1111/pops.12220

Dinesen, P. T., Schaeffer, M., & Sønderskov, K. M. (2020). Ethnic diversity and social trust: Narrative and meta-analytic review. *Annual Review of Political Science*, *23*. Advance online publication.

Dinesen, P. T., & Sønderskov, K. M. (in press). Ethnic diversity and social trust. A critical review of the literature and suggestions for a research agenda. In E. Uslaner (Ed.), *The Oxford handbook on social and political trust*. Oxford University Press.

Dixon, J., Durrheim, K., & Tredoux, C. (2007). Intergroup contact and attitudes toward the principle and practice of racial equality. *Psychological Science*, *18*(10), 867–872. https://doi.org/10.1111/j.1467-9280.2007.01993.x

Dixon, J., Durrheim, K., Tredoux, C., Tropp, L., Clack, B., & Eaton, L. (2010). A paradox of integration? Interracial contact, prejudice reduction and perceptions of racial discrimination. *Journal of Social Issues*, *66*(2), 401–416. https://doi.org/10.1111/j.1540-4560.2010.01652.x

Dominus, S. (2017, October 18). When the revolution came for Amy Cuddy. *The New York Times Magazine*. https://www.nytimes.com/2017/10/18/magazine/when-the-revolution-came-for-amy-cuddy.html

Doob, L. (1957). An introduction to the psychology of acculturation. *The Journal of Social Psychology, 45*(2), 143–160. https://doi.org/10.1080/00224545.1957.9714298

Doosje, B., & Branscombe, N. R. (2003). Attributions for the negative historical actions of a group. *European Journal of Social Psychology, 33*(2), 235–248. https://doi.org/10.1002/ejsp.142

Doty, R., Peterson, B., & Winter, D. (1991). Threat and authoritarianism in the United States, 1978–1987. *Journal of Personality and Social Psychology, 61*(4), 629–640. https://doi.org/10.1037/0022-3514.61.4.629

Dovidio, J. F., & Gaertner, S. L. (Eds.). (1986). The aversive form of racism. In J. F. Dovidio & S. L. Gaertner (Eds.), *Prejudice, discrimination and racism* (pp. 61–89). Academic Press.

Dovidio, J. F., Gaertner, S. L., Ufkes, E. G., Saguy, T., & Pearson, A. R. (2016). Included but invisible? Subtle bias, common identity, and the darker side of "we." *Social Issues and Policy Review, 10*(1), 6–46. https://doi.org/10.1111/sipr.12017

Dovidio, J. F., Glick, P., & Rudman, L. A. (Eds.). (2005). *On the nature of prejudice: Fifty years after Allport*. Blackwell. https://doi.org/10.1002/9780470773963

Dovidio, J. F., Love, A., Schellhaas, F. M. H., & Hewstone, M. (2017). Reducing intergroup bias through intergroup contact: Twenty years of progress and future directions. *Group Processes & Intergroup Relations, 20*(5), 606–620. https://doi.org/10.1177/1368430217712052

Dovidio, J. F., Mann, J., & Gaertner, S. I. (1989). Resistance to affirmative action: The implications of aversive racism. In F. Blanchard & F. Crosby (Eds.), *Affirmative action in perspective* (pp. 83–102). Springer-Verlag. https://doi.org/10.1007/978-1-4613-9639-0_7

Drake, S. C., & Cayton, H. R. (1962). *Black metropolis*. Harper & Row.

Dreeben, R. (2019). Samuel Stouffer. *Harvard Magazine, 121*(5), 86.

Droogendyk, L., Louis, W. R., & Wright, S. C. (2016). Empowering group members to engage in collective action: The role of supportive contact and shared supportive emotions. *Canadian Journal of Behavioural Science, 48*(4), 317–327. https://doi.org/10.1037/cbs0000058

Drury, D., Hutchison, P., & Abrams, D. (2016). Direct and extended intergenerational contact and young people's attitudes towards older adults. *British Journal of Social Psychology, 55*(3), 522–543. https://doi.org/10.1111/bjso.12146

Du Bois, W. E. B. (1994). *The souls of Black folk*. Gramercy Books. (Original work published 1903)

Duckitt, J. (1989). Authoritarianism and group identification. *Political Psychology, 10*(1), 63–84. https://doi.org/10.2307/3791588

Duckitt, J. (2006). Differential effects of right-wing authoritarianism and social dominance orientation on outgroup attitudes and their mediation by threat from and competitiveness to outgroups. *Personality and Social Psychology Bulletin, 32*(5), 684–696. https://doi.org/10.1177/0146167205284282

Duckitt, J., & Fisher, K. (2003). The impact of social threat on worldview and ideological attitudes. *Political Psychology*, *24*(1), 199–222. https://doi.org/10.1111/0162-895X.00322

Duckitt, J., & Sibley, C. G. (2007). Right wing authoritarianism, social dominance orientation and the dimensions of generalized prejudice. *European Journal of Personality*, *21*(2), 113–130. https://doi.org/10.1002/per.614

Duckitt, J., & Sibley, C. G. (2010). Personality, ideology, prejudice, and politics: A dual-process motivational model. *Journal of Personality*, *78*(6), 1861–1894. https://doi.org/10.1111/j.1467-6494.2010.00672.x

Duncan, O. D. (1966). Path analysis: Sociological examples. *American Journal of Sociology*, *72*(1), 1–16. https://doi.org/10.1086/224256

Duncan, O. D. (1975). *Introduction to structural equation models*. Academic Press.

Dunwoody, P. T., & Funke, F. (2016). The aggression-submission-conventionalism scale: Testing a new three factor measure of authoritarianism. *Journal of Social and Political Psychology*, *4*(2), 571–600. https://doi.org/10.5964/jspp.v4i2.168

Dunwoody, P. T., & Plane, D. L. (2019). The influence of authoritarianism and outgroup threat on political affiliations and support for antidemocratic policies. *Peace and Conflict*, *25*(3), 198–210. https://doi.org/10.1037/pac0000397

Durkheim, E. (1951). *Suicide*. Free Press. (Original work published 1897)

Dusso, A. (2017). Race and right-wing authoritarianism: How scoring high on authoritarianism does not necessarily lead to support for right-wing candidates. *Social Science Quarterly*, *98*(1), 244–260. https://doi.org/10.1111/ssqu.12302

DuVernay, A. (Director). (2014). *Selma* [Film]. Pathé.

Eadeh, F. R., & Chang, K. K. (2020). Can threat increase support for liberalism? New insights into the relationship between threat and political attitudes. *Social Psychological & Personality Science*, *11*(1), 88–96.

Edsall, T. B. (2017, November 16). White-on-White voting. *The New York Times*. https://www.nytimes.com/2017/11/16/opinion/trump-white-voting.html

Edsall, T. B. (2019, August 28). We aren't seeing White support for Trump for what it is. *The New York Times*. https://www.nytimes.com/2019/08/28/opinion/trump-white-voters.html

Ekehammar, B., Akrami, N., & Zakrisson, I. (2004). What matters most to prejudice: Big five personality, social dominance orientation, or right-wing authoritarianism? *European Journal of Personality*, *18*(6), 463–482. https://doi.org/10.1002/per.526

Eller, A., & Abrams, D. (2004). Come together: Longitudinal comparisons of Pettigrew's reformulated intergroup contact model and the common ingroup identity model in Anglo-French and Mexican-American contexts. *European Journal of Social Psychology*, *34*, 229–256.

Ellsworth, P. C. (1991). To tell what we know or wait for Godot? *Law and Human Behavior, 15*(1), 77–90. https://doi.org/10.1007/BF01044831

Elms, A. C. (1975). The crisis of confidence in social psychology. *American Psychologist, 30*(1), 967–976. https://doi.org/10.1037/0003-066X.30.10.967

Epskamp, S. (2019). Reproducibility and replicability in a fast-paced methodological world. *Advances in Methods and Practices in Psychological Science, 2*(2), 145–155. https://doi.org/10.1177/2515245919847421

Erikson, E. H. (1958). *Young man Luther*. Norton.

Erikson, E. H. (1969). *Gandhi's truth*. Norton.

Essed, P. (1984). *Alledaags racisme* [Everyday racism]. Sara.

Explaining the Brexit vote. (2016, July 16). *The Economist*, 48.

Farmer, H., & Maister, L. (2017). Putting ourselves in another's skin: Using the plasticity of self-perception to enhance empathy and decrease prejudice. *Social Justice Research, 30*(4), 323–354. https://doi.org/10.1007/s11211-017-0294-1

Feather, N. T. (2015). Analyzing relative deprivation in relation to deservingness, entitlement and resentment. *Social Justice Research, 28*(1), 7–26. https://doi.org/10.1007/s11211-015-0235-9

Feather, N. T., & McKee, I. R. (2008). Values and prejudice: Predictors of attitudes toward Australian Aborigines. *Australian Journal of Psychology, 60*(2), 80–90. https://doi.org/10.1080/00049530701449513

Federico, C. M., & Golec de Zavala, A. (2018). Collective narcissism and the 2016 U.S. presidential vote. *Public Opinion Quarterly, 82*(1), 110–121. https://doi.org/10.1093/poq/nfx048

Fein, S., Goethels, G. R., & Kugler, M. (2007). Social influence of political judgments: The case of presidential debates. *Political Psychology, 28*(2), 165–192. https://doi.org/10.1111/j.1467-9221.2007.00561.x

Feldman, S. (2017). Authoritarianism, threat, and intolerance. In E. Borgida, C. Federico, & J. Miller (Eds.), *At the forefront of political psychology: Essays in honor of John L. Sullivan*. Routledge.

Feldman, S., & Stenner, K. (1997). Perceived threat and authoritarianism. *Political Psychology, 18*(4), 741–770. https://doi.org/10.1111/0162-895X.00077

Felson, J. (2014). What can we learn from twin studies? A comprehensive evaluation of the equal environments assumption. *Social Science Research, 43*, 184–199. https://doi.org/10.1016/j.ssresearch.2013.10.004

Feskens, R., & Hox, J. J. (2011). Multilevel structural equation modeling for cross-cultural research: Exploring resampling methods to overcome small sample size problems. In E. Davidov, P. Schmidt, & J. Billiet (Eds.), *Cross-cultural analysis: Methods and applications* (pp. 341–356). Routledge.

Fiedler, K., Kutzner, F., & Krueger, J. I. (2012). The long way from *a*-error control to validity proper: Problems with a short-sighted false-positive debate. *Perspectives on Psychological Science, 7*(6), 661–669. https://doi.org/10.1177/1745691612462587

Fingerhut, A. W. (2011). Straight allies: What predicts heterosexuals' alliance with the LGBT community? *Journal of Applied Social Psychology, 41*(9), 2230–2248. https://doi.org/10.1111/j.1559-1816.2011.00807.x

Fiske, A. P., Kitayama, S., Markus, H. R., & Nisbett, R. E. (1998). The cultural matrix of social psychology. In D. T. Gilbert, S. T. Fiske, & G. Lindzey (Eds.), *The handbook of social psychology* (4th ed., Vol. 2, pp. 915–981). McGraw-Hill.

Fiske, D. W. (1949). Consistency of the factorial structures of personality ratings from different sources. *Journal of Abnormal and Social Psychology, 44*(3), 329–344.

Fiske, S. T. (2000). Stereotyping, prejudice, and discrimination at the seam between the centuries: Evolution, culture, mind and brain. *European Journal of Social Psychology, 30*(3), 299–322. https://doi.org/10.1002/(SICI)1099-0992(200005/06)30:3<299::AID-EJSP2>3.0.CO;2-F

Fiske, S. T., Bersoff, D. N., Borgida, E., Deaux, K., & Heilman, M. E. (1991). Social science research on trial: The use of sex stereotyping research in Price Waterhouse v. Hopkins. *American Psychologist, 46*(10), 1049–1060. https://doi.org/10.1037/0003-066X.46.10.1049

Fiske, S. T., Cuddy, A. J., Glick, P., & Xu, J. (2002). A model of (often mixed) stereotype content: Competence and warmth respectively follow from perceived status and competition. *Journal of Personality and Social Psychology, 82*(6), 878–902. https://doi.org/10.1037/0022-3514.82.6.878

Fleeson, W. (2012). Perspectives on the person: Rapid growth and opportunities for integration. In K. Deaux & M. Snyder (Eds.), *Oxford handbook of personality and social psychology* (pp. 33–63). Oxford University Press.

Fraley, R. C., Griffin, B. N., Belsky, J., & Rolsman, G. I. (2012). Developmental antecedents of political ideology: A longitudinal investigation from birth to age 18 years. *Psychological Science, 23*(11), 1425–1431. https://doi.org/10.1177/0956797612440102

Fraley, R. C., & Waller, N. G. (1998). Adult attachment patterns: A test of the typological model. In J. A. Simpson & W. S. Rholes (Eds.), *Attachment theory and close relationships* (pp. 77–114). Guilford Press.

Freitag, M., & Rapp, C. (2015). The personal foundations of political tolerance towards immigrants. *Journal of Ethnic and Migration Studies, 41*(3), 351–373. https://doi.org/10.1080/1369183X.2014.924847

Freriks, P. (1990, May 1). Franse anti-racisten willen handen vuil maken [French anti-racists want to get their hands dirty–that is, take action]. *De Volkskrant*, p. 2.

Freud, S. (1930). *Civilization and its discontents*. Macmillan.

Fritz, M. S., & MacKinnon, D. P. (2007). Required sample size to detect the mediated effect. *Psychological Science, 18*(3), 233–239. https://doi.org/10.1111/j.1467-9280.2007.01882.x

Fromm, E. (1941). *Escape from freedom*. Farrar & Rinehart.

Fujioka, Y. (1999). Television portrayals and African-American stereotypes: Examination of television effects when direct contact is lacking. *Journalism & Mass Communication Quarterly*, *76*(1), 52–75. https://doi.org/10.1177/107769909907600105

Fuochi, G., Voci, A., Veneziani, C. A., Boin, J., Fell, B., & Hewstone, M. (2020). Is negative mass media news always associated with outgroup prejudice? The buffering role of direct contact. *Group Processes & Intergroup Relations*, *23*(2), 195–213.

Gaertner, S. L., & Dovidio, J. F. (1986). Aversive racism. In M. P. Zanna (Ed.), *Advances in experimental social psychology* (Vol. 36, pp. 1–51). Academic Press.

Gaertner, S. L., Dovidio, J. F., Anatasio, P. A., Bachman, B. A., & Rust, M. C. (1993). The common ingroup identity model: Recategorization and the reduction of intergroup bias. *European Review of Social Psychology*, *4*(1), 1–26. https://doi.org/10.1080/14792779343000004

Gaertner, S. L., & McLaughlin, J. P. (1983). Racial stereotypes: Associations and ascriptions of positive and negative characteristics. *Social Psychology Quarterly*, *46*(1), 23–30. https://doi.org/10.2307/3033657

Gaertner, S. L., Rust, M. C., Dovidio, J. F., Bachman, B. A., & Anastasio, P. A. (1994). The contact hypothesis: The role of a common ingroup identity on reducing intergroup bias. *Small Group Research*, *25*(2), 224–249. https://doi.org/10.1177/1046496494252005

Ganzach, Y., Hanoch, B. L., & Choma, B. L. (2019). Attitudes toward presidential candidates in the 2012 and 2016 American elections: Cognitive ability and support for Trump. *Social Psychological & Personality Science*, *10*(7), 924–934. https://doi.org/10.1177/1948550618800494

Gardner, S., & Evans, J. (2018). *In Western Europe, familiarity with Muslims is linked to positive views of Muslims and Islam*. Pew Research Center. https://www.Pewresearch.org/fact-tank/2018/07/24/in-western-Europe

Gartrell, C. D. (1987). Network approaches to social evaluation. *Annual Review of Sociology*, *13*, 49–66. https://doi.org/10.1146/annurev.so.13.080187.000405

Gawronski, B. (2019). Six lessons for a cogent science of implicit bias and its criticism. *Perspectives on Psychological Science*, *14*(4), 574–595. https://doi.org/10.1177/1745691619826015

Geertz, C. (1984). Anti-anti-relativism. *American Anthropologist*, *86*(2), 263–278. https://doi.org/10.1525/aa.1984.86.2.02a00030

Gelfand, M. J., Harrington, J. R., & Jackson, J. C. (2017). The strength of social norms across human groups. *Perspectives on Psychological Science*, *12*(5), 800–809. https://doi.org/10.1177/1745691617708631

Gergen, K. J. (1973). Social psychology as history. *Journal of Personality and Social Psychology*, *26*(2), 309–320. https://doi.org/10.1037/h0034436

Gerlach, M., Farb, B., Revelle, W., & Amaral, L. A. N. (2018). A robust data-driven approach identifies four personality types across four large data sets. *Nature Human Behaviour*, *2*, 735–742. https://doi.org/10.1038/s41562-018-0419-z

Gest, J., Reny, T., & Mayer, J. (2018). Roots of the radical right: Nostalgic deprivation in the United States and Britain. *Comparative Political Studies, 51*(13), 1694–1719. https://doi.org/10.1177/0010414017720705

Gesthuizen, N., Van der Meer, T., & Scheepers, P. (2008). Ethnic diversity and social capital in Europe: Tests of Putnam's thesis in European countries. *Scandinavian Political Studies, 32,* 121–142.

Gibson, J. L., & Claassen, C. (2010). Racial reconciliation in South Africa: Interracial reconciliation: Interracial contact and changes over time. *Journal of Social Issues, 66*(2), 255–272. https://doi.org/10.1111/j.1540-4560.2010.01644.x

Gibson, K. (2020, January 22). *Union membership in the U.S. slid to record low in 2019.* https://www.cbsnews.com/news/union-membership-slid-to-record-low-in-2019/

Gilbert, D. T., King, G., Pettigrew, S., & Wilson, T. D. (2016). Comment on "Estimating the Reproducibility of Psychological Science." *Science, 351*(6277), 1037. http://doi.org/10.1126/science.aad7243

Gilbert, D. T., King, G., Pettigrew, S., & Wilson, T. D. (2017). *A response to the reply to our technical comment on "estimating the reproducibility of psychological science"* [Unpublished manuscript]. https://gking.harvard.edu/files/gking/files/gkpw_response_to_osc_rebutal.pdf

Gilbert, G. M. (1951). Stereotype persistence and change among college students. *Journal of Abnormal and Social Psychology, 46,* 245–254. https://doi.org/10.1037/h0053696

Glaeser, E. L. (2017). Sciences still young. *Harvard Magazine, 114*(1), 78–79.

Glass, G. V. (1976). Primary, secondary, and meta-analyses of research. *The Journal of Educational Research, 5*(10), 3–8.

Glass, G. V. (1978). Integrating findings: The meta-analysis of research. *Review of Research in Education, 5,* 351–379.

Glass, G. V. (2000, January). *Meta-analysis at 25* [Unpublished manuscript]. https://www.gvglass.info/papers/meta25.html

Glass, G. V., McGaw, B., & Smith, M. L. (1981). *Meta-analysis in social research.* Sage Publications.

Gluckstern, N. B., & Packard, R. W. (1977). The internal-external change agent team: Bringing change to a "closed institution." *The Journal of Applied Behavioral Science, 13*(1), 41–52. https://doi.org/10.1177/002188637701300104

Goldberg, L. R. (1993). The structure of phenotypic personality traits. *American Psychologist, 48*(1), 26–34. https://doi.org/10.1037/0003-066X.48.1.26

Goldberger, A. S. (1972). Structural equation models in the social sciences. *Econometrica, 40*(6), 979–1001. https://doi.org/10.2307/1913851

Golec de Zavala, A., Guerra, R., & Simão, C. (2017). The relationship between the Brexit vote and individual predictors of prejudice: Collective narcissism, right wing authoritarianism, social dominance orientation. *Frontiers in Psychology, 8,* Article 2023. https://doi.org/10.3389/fpsyg.2017.02023

Gómez, A., & Huici, C. (2008). Vicarious intergroup contact and role of authorities in prejudice reduction. *The Spanish Journal of Psychology, 11*(1), 103–114. https://doi.org/10.1017/S1138741600004169

Gómez, A., Tropp, L. R., Vázquez, A., Voci, A., & Hewstone, M. (2018). Depersonalized extended contact and injunctive norms about cross-group friendship impact intergroup orientations. *Journal of Experimental Social Psychology, 76*, 356–370. https://doi.org/10.1016/j.jesp.2018.02.010

Gorer, G. (1943). Themes in Japanese culture. *New York Academy of Sciences, 5*, 106–124.

Graf, S., Paolini, S., & Rubin, M. (2014). Negative intergroup contact is more influential, but positive intergroup contact is more common: Assessing contact prominence and contact prevalence in five Central European countries. *European Journal of Social Psychology, 44*(6), 536–547. https://doi.org/10.1002/ejsp.2052

Graf, S., & Sczesny, S. (2019). Intergroup contact with migrants is linked to support for migrants through attitudes, especially in people who are politically right wing. *International Journal of Intercultural Relations, 73*, 102–106. https://doi.org/10.1016/j.ijintrel.2019.09.001

Grant, P. R., Abrams, D., Robertson, D. W., & Garay, J. (2015). Predicting protest by disadvantaged skilled immigrants: A test of an integrated social identity, relative deprivation, collective efficacy (SIRDE) model. *Social Justice Research, 28*(1), 76–101. https://doi.org/10.1007/s11211-014-0229-z

Gravely ill, Atwater offers apology. (1991, January 13). *The New York Times*, A16.

Graves, S. B. (1999). Television and prejudice reduction: When does television as a vicarious experience make a difference? *Journal of Social Issues, 55*(4), 707–727. https://doi.org/10.1111/0022-4537.00143

Green, E. G. T., Sarrasin, O., Baur, R., & Fasel, N. (2016). From stigmatized immigrants to radical right voting: A multivariate study of the role of threat and contact. *Political Psychology, 37*(4), 465–480. https://doi.org/10.1111/pops.12290

Green, E. G. T., Visintin, E. P., & Sarrasin, O. (2018). From ethnic boundary demarcation to deprovincialization: The interplay of immigrant presence to ideological climate. *International Journal of Comparative Sociology, 59*(5–6), 383–402. https://doi.org/10.1177/0020715218801422

Green, E. G. T., Visintin, E. P., Sarrasin, O., & Hewstone, M. (2020). When integration policies shape the impact of intergroup contact on threat perceptions: A multilevel study across 20 European countries. *Journal of Ethnic and Migration Studies, 46*(3), 631–648. https://doi.org/10.1080/1369183X.2018.1550159

Greenfield, P. M. (2017). Culture change over time: Why replicability should not be the gold standard in psychological science. *Perspectives on Psychological Science, 12*(5), 762–771. https://doi.org/10.1177/1745691617707314

Greenwald, A. G., & Banaji, M. R. (1995). Implicit social cognition: Attitudes, self-esteem, and stereotypes. *Psychological Review, 102*(1), 4–27. https://doi.org/10.1037/0033-295X.102.1.4

Greenwald, A. G., & Lai, C. K. (2020). Implicit social cognition. *Annual Review of Psychology, 71*, 25-1 to 25-27.

Greenwald, A. G., McGhee, D. E., & Schwartz, J. L. K. (1998). Measuring individual differences in implicit cognition: The Implicit Association Test. *Journal of Personality and Social Psychology, 74*(6), 1464–1480. https://doi.org/10.1037/0022-3514.74.6.1464

Greenwald, A. G., Poehlman, T. A., Uhlmann, E., & Banaji, M. R. (2009). Understanding and using the Implicit Association Test III: Meta-analysis of predictive value. *Journal of Personality and Social Psychology, 97*(1), 17–41. https://doi.org/10.1037/a0015575

Greenwood, J. D. (2004). *The disappearance of the social in American social psychology*. Cambridge University Press.

Greitemeyer, T., & Sagioglou, C. (2016). Subjective socioeconomic status causes aggression: A test of the theory of relative deprivation. *Journal of Personality and Social Psychology, 111*(2), 178–194. https://doi.org/10.1037/pspi0000058

Grimm, K. J., Ram, N., & Estabrook, R. (2017). *Growth modeling: Structural equation and multilevel approaches*. Guilford.

Gundelach, B., & Freitag, M. (2014). Neighborhood diversity and social trust: An empirical analysis of interethnic contact and group-specific effects. *Urban Studies, 51*(6), 1236–1256. https://doi.org/10.1177/0042098013495578

Gunther, R., Beck, P. A., & Nisbet, E. C. (2019). "Fake news" and the defection of 2012 Obama voters in the 2016 presidential election. *Electoral Studies, 61*, Article 102030. https://doi.org/10.1016/j.electstud.2019.03.006

Gurr, T. R. (1970). *Why men rebel*. Princeton University Press.

Haberman, M., & Sullivan, E. (2019, August 16). After Trump body slams him, supporter says "I love the guy." *The New York Times*. https://www.nytimes.com/2019/08/16/us/politics/trump-fat-shames-frank-dawson.html

Hafner, J. (2016, February 24). Donald Trump loves the "poorly educated"—and they love him. *USA Today*. https://www.usatoday.com/story/news/politics/onpolitics/2016/02/24/donald-trump-nevada-poorly-educated/80860078/

Hahl, O., Kim, M., & Zuckerman Sivan, E. W. (2018). The authentic appeal of the lying demagogue: Proclaiming the deeper truth about political illegitimacy. *American Sociological Review, 83*(1), 1–33. https://doi.org/10.1177/0003122417749632

Hall, D. L., Matz, D. C., & Wood, W. (2010). Why don't we practice what we preach? A meta-analytic review or religious racism. *Personality and Social Psychology Review, 14*(1), 126–139. https://doi.org/10.1177/1088868309352179

Harris, L. T., & Fiske, S. T. (2006). Dehumanizing the lowest of the low: Neuroimaging responses to extreme out-groups. *Psychological Science, 17*(10), 847–853. https://doi.org/10.1111/j.1467-9280.2006.01793.x

Haslam, N. (2006). Dehumanization: An integrative review. *Personality and Social Psychology Review, 10*(3), 252–264. https://doi.org/10.1207/s15327957pspr1003_4

Hassan, M. K. (1987). Parental behaviour, authoritarianism and prejudice. *Manas, 34*(1–2), 41–50.

Hasson, Y., Tamir, M., Brahms, K. S., Cohrs, J. C., & Halperin, E. (2018). Are liberals and conservatives equally motivated to feel empathy toward others? *Personality and Social Psychology Bulletin, 44*(10), 1449–1459. https://doi.org/10.1177/0146167218769867

Hastorf, A. H., & Cantril, H. (1954). They saw a game: A case study. *Journal of Abnormal and Social Psychology, 49*(1), 129–134. https://doi.org/10.1037/h0057880

Hayes, A. F. (2013). *Introduction to mediation, moderation and conditional process analysis: A regression-based approach*. Guilford Press.

Hayward, L. E., Tropp, L. R., Hornsey, M. J., & Barlow, F. K. (2017). Toward a comprehensive understanding of intergroup contact: Descriptions and mediators of positive and negative contact among majority and minority groups. *Personality and Social Psychology Bulletin, 43*(3), 347–364. https://doi.org/10.1177/0146167216685291

Heider, F. (1958). *The psychology of interpersonal relations*. Wiley. https://doi.org/10.1037/10628-000

Heitmeyer, W. (Ed.). (2002). *Deutsche Zustände, Folge 1* [The German situation, Vol. 1]. Suhrkamp Verlag.

Heitmeyer, W. (Ed.). (2005). *Deutsche Zustände, Folge 4* [The German situation, Vol. 4]. Suhrkamp Verlag.

Heitmeyer, W. (Ed.). (2007). *Deutsche Zustände, Folge 6* [The German situation, Vol. 6]. Suhrkamp Verlag.

Helmreich, R. (1975). Applied social psychology: The unfulfilled promise. *Personality and Social Psychology Bulletin, 1*(4), 548–560. https://doi.org/10.1177/014616727500100402

Henninger, D. (2007, August 16). The death of diversity. *The Wall Street Journal*, A10.

Hepworth, J. T., & West, S. (1988). Lynchings and the economy: A time-series reanalysis of Hovland and Sears (1940). *Journal of Personality and Social Psychology, 55*(2), 239–247. https://doi.org/10.1037/0022-3514.55.2.239

Herek, G. M., & Capitanio, J. P. (1997). AIDS stigma and contact with persons with AIDS: Effects of direct and vicarious contact. *Journal of Applied Social Psychology, 27*(1), 1–36. https://doi.org/10.1111/j.1559-1816.1997.tb00621.x

Hetherington, M. J., & Weiler, J. D. (2009). *Authoritarianism and polarization in American politics*. Cambridge University Press. https://doi.org/10.1017/CBO9780511802331

Hewstone, M. (1989). *Causal attribution: From cognitive processes to cognitive beliefs*. Basil Blackwell.

Hewstone, M. (1990). The "ultimate attribution error": A review of the literature on intergroup causal attribution. *European Journal of Social Psychology, 20*(4), 311–335. https://doi.org/10.1002/ejsp.2420200404

Hewstone, M. (2003). Intergroup contact: Panacea for prejudice? *The Psychologist, 16*, 352–355.

Hewstone, M., Cairns, E., Voci, A., Hamberger, J., & Niens, U. (2006). Intergroup contact, forgiveness, and experience of "the troubles" in Northern Ireland. *Journal of Social Issues, 62*(1), 99–120. https://doi.org/10.1111/j.1540-4560.2006.00441.x

Hewstone, M., & Ward, C. (1985). Ethnocentrism and causal attribution in Southeast Asia. *Journal of Personality and Social Psychology, 48*(3), 614–623. https://doi.org/10.1037/0022-3514.48.3.614

Hirsh, J. B., DeYoung, C. G., & Peterson, J. B. (2009). Metatraits of the Big Five differentially predict engagement and restraints of behavior. *Journal of Personality, 77*(4), 1085–1102. https://doi.org/10.1111/j.1467-6494.2009.00575.x

Hodson, G. (2011). Do ideologically intolerant people benefit from intergroup contact? *Current Directions in Psychological Science, 20*(3), 154–159. https://doi.org/10.1177/0963721411409025

Hodson, G., Crisp, R. J., Meleady, R., & Earle, M. (2018). Intergroup contact as an agent of cognitive liberalization. *Perspectives on Psychological Science, 13*(5), 523–548. https://doi.org/10.1177/1745691617752324

Hodson, G., & Dhont, K. (2015). The person-based nature of prejudice: Individual difference predictors of intergroup negativity. *European Review of Social Psychology, 26*(1), 1–42. https://doi.org/10.1080/10463283.2015.1070018

Hodson, G., Harry, H., & Mitchell, A. (2009). Independent benefits of contact and friendship on attitudes toward homosexuals among authoritarians and highly identified heterosexuals. *European Journal of Social Psychology, 39*(4), 509–525. https://doi.org/10.1002/ejsp.558

Hodson, G., & Sorrentino, R. M. (1999). Uncertainty orientation and the Big Five personality structure. *Journal of Research in Personality, 33*(2), 253–261. https://doi.org/10.1006/jrpe.1999.2244

Hofstede, G. (2001). *Culture's consequence: Comparing values, behaviors, institutions and organizations across nations*. Sage.

Hofstede, G. (2017). *Compare countries*. Hofstede Insights. https://www.hofstede-insights.com/product/compare-countries/

Holland, J. J., & Swanson, E. (2016, September 5). *Poll: Support for Black Lives Matter grows among White youth*. PBS Newshour. http://www.pbs.org/newshour/rundown/poll-support-black-lives-matter-grows-among-white-youth

Holzkamp, K. (1971). *Kritische Psychologie* [Critical psychology]. Fischer.

Hopf, C. (1992). Authoritarians and their families: Qualitative studies on the origins of authoritarian dispositions. In W. F. Stone, G. Lederer, & R. Christie (Eds.), *Strength and weakness: The authoritarian personality today* (pp. 119–143). Springer-Verlag.

Hopf, C. (1993). Rechtsextremismus und Beziehungserfahrungen [Right-wing extremism and relational experiences]. *Zeitschrift für Soziologie*, *22*(6), 449–463. https://doi.org/10.1515/zfsoz-1993-0604

Houck, D. W., & Dixon, D. E. (Eds.). (2006). *Rhetoric, religion and the civil rights movement 1954–1965*. Baylor University Press.

House, J. (1981). Social structure and personality. In M. Rosenberg & R. Turner (Eds.), *Social psychology: Sociological perspectives* (pp. 525–561). Basic Books.

Hovland, C. L., & Sears, R. (1940). Minor studies of aggression: Correlation of lynchings with economic indices. *The Journal of Psychology*, *9*(2), 301–310. https://doi.org/10.1080/00223980.1940.9917696

Hox, J. J. (2010). *Multilevel analysis: Techniques and applications* (2nd ed.). Routledge. https://doi.org/10.4324/9780203852279

Hutchings, P. B., & Sullivan, K. E. (2019). Prejudice and the Brexit vote: A tangled web. *Palgrave Communications*, *5*, Article 5. https://doi.org/10.1057/s41599-018-0214-5

Inkeles, A., & Levinson, D. J. (1954). National character: The study of modal personality and socio-cultural systems. In G. Lindzey (Ed.), *Handbook of social psychology* (Vol. 2, pp. 977–1020). Addison-Wesley.

Inkeles, A., & Smith, D. (1974). *Becoming modern: Individual change in six developing countries*. Harvard University Press. https://doi.org/10.4159/harvard.9780674499348

Israel, J., & Tajfel, H. (Eds.). (1972). *The context of social psychology*. Academic Press.

Ivarsflaten, E. (2008). What unites right-wing populists in Western Europe? Re-examining grievance mobilization models in seven successful cases. *Comparative Political Studies*, *41*(1), 144–157.

Iversen, G. R. (1973). Recovering individual data in the presence of group and individual effects. *American Journal of Sociology*, *79*(2), 420–434. https://doi.org/10.1086/225554

Jackson, J. W. (1993). Contact theory of intergroup hostility: A review and evaluation of the theoretical and empirical literature. *International Journal of Group Tensions*, *23*, 43–65.

Jackson, J. W., & Poulsen, J. R. (2005). Contact experiences mediate the relationship between five-factor model personality traits and ethnic prejudice. *Journal of Applied Social Psychology*, *35*(4), 667–685. https://doi.org/10.1111/j.1559-1816.2005.tb02140.x

Jacoby-Senghor, D. S., Sinclair, S., Smith, C. T., & Skorinko, J. L. M. (2019). Implicit bias predicts liking of ingroup members who are comfortable with intergroup interaction. *Personality and Social Psychology Bulletin*, *45*(4), 603–615. https://doi.org/10.1177/0146167218793136

James, W. (1896). Will to believe. *New World, 5*, 327–347.

Jetten, J., Mols, F., Healy, N., & Spears, R. (2017). "Fear of falling": Economic instability enhances collective angst among societies' wealthy class. *Journal of Social Issues*, *73*(1), 61–79. https://doi.org/10.1111/josi.12204

Jetten, J., Mols, F., & Postmes, T. (2015). Relative deprivation and relative wealth enhance anti-immigrant sentiments: The V-curve re-examined. *PLOS ONE*, *10*(10), Article e0139156. https://doi.org/10.1371/journal.pone.0139156

John, L. K., Loewenstein, G., & Prelec, D. (2012). Measuring the prevalence of questionable research practices with incentives for truth-telling. *Psychological Science*, *23*(5), 524–532. https://doi.org/10.1177/0956797611430953

Jones, E. E. (1976). How do people perceive the causes of behavior? Experiments based on attribution theory offer some insights into how actors and observers differ in viewing the causal structure of their social world. *American Scientist*, *64*(3), 300–305.

Jones, E. E., & Nisbett, R. E. (1972). The actor and the observer: Divergent perceptions of the causes of behavior. In E. E. Jones, D. E. Kanouse, H. H. Kelley, R. E. Nisbett, S. Valins, & B. Weiner (Eds.), *Attribution: Perceiving the causes of behavior* (pp. 79–94). General Learning Press.

Jones, J. M. (2020, January 7). *U.S. party preferences steady during Trump era*. Gallup. https://news.gallup.com/poll/274694/party-preferences-steady-during-trump-era.aspx?utm_sources=alert&utm_medium=final&utm_co

Jones, J. M., & Pettigrew, T. F. (2005). Kenneth B. Jones Clark (1914–2005)—Obituary. *American Psychologist*, *60*, 649–651. https://doi.org/10.1037/0003-066X.60.6.649

Jones, R. P. (2016). *The end of White Christian America*. Simon & Schuster.

Jöreskog, K. G., & Van Thillo, M. (1972). *LISREL: A general computer program for estimating a linear structural equation system involving multiple indicators of unmeasured variables*. Educational Testing Service.

Joseph, J. (2013, March 13). The trouble with twin studies. *Mad in America*. https://www.madinamerica.com/2013/03/the-trouble-with-twin-studies/#

Jost, J. T. (2019a). Anger and authoritarianism mediate the effects of fear on support for the far right—What Vasilopoulos et al. (2019) really found. *Political Psychology*, *40*(4), 705–711. https://doi.org/10.1111/pops.12567

Jost, J. T. (2019b). The IAT is dead, long live the IAT: Context-sensitive measures of implicit attitudes are indispensable to social and political psychology. *Current Directions in Psychological Science*, *28*(1), 10–19. https://doi.org/10.1177/0963721418797309

Jost, J. T., Glaser, J., Kruglanski, A. W., & Sulloway, F. J. (2003). Political conservatism as motivated social cognition. *Psychological Bulletin*, *129*(3), 339–375. https://doi.org/10.1037/0033-2909.129.3.339

Judd, C. M., Westfall, J., & Kenny, D. A. (2012). Treating stimuli as a random factor in social psychology. *Journal of Personality and Social Psychology*, *103*(1), 54–69.

Jylhä, K. M., Rydgren, J., & Strimling, P. (2019). *Xenophobia among radical and mainstream rightwing party voters: Prevalence, correlates, and effects on voter mobility* (Working Paper 38). Department of Sociology, University of Stockholm. https://su.figshare.com/articles/Xenophobia_among_radical_and_mainstream_rightwing_party_voters_Prevalence_correlates_and_effects_on_voter_mobility/8282333

Kahneman, D., & Miller, D. T. (1986). Norm theory: Comparing reality to its alternatives. *Psychological Review, 93*(2), 136–153. https://doi.org/10.1037/0033-295X.93.2.136

Kahneman, D., & Tversky, A. (1979). Prospect theory: An analysis of decision under risk. *Econometrica, 47*(2), 263–291. https://doi.org/10.2307/1914185

Kanter, R. M. (1977). *Men and women of the corporation*. Basic Books.

Karlins, M., Coffman, T. L., & Walters, G. (1969). On the fading of social stereotypes: Studies in three generations of college students. *Journal of Personality and Social Psychology, 13*(1), 1–16. https://doi.org/10.1037/h0027994

Katz, D., & Braly, K. (1933). Racial stereotypes of 100 college students. *Journal of Abnormal and Social Psychology, 28*(3), 280–290. https://doi.org/10.1037/h0074049

Kauff, M., Asbrock, F., Wagner, U., Pettigrew, T. F., Hewstone, M., Schäfer, S. J., & Christ, O. (2017). (Bad) feelings about meeting them? Episodic and chronic intergroup emotions associated with positive and negative intergroup contact as predictors of intergroup behavior. *Frontiers in Psychology, 8*, Article 1449. https://doi.org/10.3389/fpsyg.2017.01449

Kauff, M., Green, E. G. T., Schmidt, K., Hewstone, M., & Christ, O. (2016). Effects of majority members' positive intergroup contact on minority members support for ingroup rights: Mobilizing or demobilizing effects? *European Journal of Social Psychology, 46*(7), 833–839. https://doi.org/10.1002/ejsp.2194

Kelman, H. C., & Fisher, R. J. (Eds.). (2016). *Herbert C. Kelman: A pioneer in the social psychology of conflict analysis and resolution*. Springer. https://doi.org/10.1007/978-3-319-39032-1

Kende, A., Tropp, L., & Lantos, N. A. (2017). Testing a contact intervention based on intergroup friendship between Roma and non-Roma Hungarians: Reducing bias through institutional support in a non-supportive societal context. *Journal of Applied Social Psychology, 47*(1), 47–55. https://doi.org/10.1111/jasp.12422

Kende, J., Phalet, K., Van Den Noortgate, W., & Fisher, R. (2018). Equality revisited: A cultural meta-analysis of the contact hypothesis. *Social and Psychological Sciences, 9*(8), 887–895.

Kenny, D. A., Kashy, D. A., & Bolger, N. (1998). Data analysis in social psychology. In D. Gilbert, S. T. Fiske, & G. Lindzey (Eds.), *The handbook of social psychology* (4th ed., Vol. 1, pp. 223–265). McGraw-Hill.

Kenny, D. A., Mannetti, L., Pierro, A., Livi, S., & Kashy, D. A. (2002). The statistical analysis of data from small groups. *Journal of Personality and Social Psychology, 83*(1), 126–137. https://doi.org/10.1037/0022-3514.83.1.126

Kephart, W. M. (1957). *Racial factors in urban law enforcement*. University of Pennsylvania Press. https://doi.org/10.9783/9781512817294

Key, V. O. (1949). *Southern politics in state and nation*. University of Tennessee Press.

Khan, S. S., & Liu, J. H. (2008). Intergroup attributions and ethnocentrism in the Indian subcontinent: The ultimate attribution revisited. *Journal of Cross-Cultural Psychology, 39*(1), 16–36. https://doi.org/10.1177/0022022107311843

Khandelwal, K., Dhillon, M., Akalamkam, K., & Papneja, D. (2014). The ultimate attribution error: Does it transcend conflict? The case of Muslim adolescents in Kashmir and Delhi. *Psychological Studies, 59*(4), 427–435. https://doi.org/10.1007/s12646-014-0240-3

King, G., Rosen, O., Tanner, M., & Wagner, A. F. (2008). Ordinary economic voting in the extraordinary election of Adolf Hitler. *The Journal of Economic History, 68*(4), 951–996. https://doi.org/10.1017/S0022050708000788

Kinket, B., & Verkuyten, M. (1999). Intergroup relations and social context: A multilevel approach. *European Journal of Social Psychology, 29*(2–3), 219–237.https://doi.org/10.1002/(SICI)1099-0992(199903/05)29:2/3<219::AID-EJSP925>3.0.CO;2-X

Kitschelt, H., & Rehm, P. (2019). Secular partisan realignment in the United States: The socioeconomic reconfiguration of White partisan support since the New Deal era. *Politics and Society, 47*(3), 425–479.

Klandermans, B. (2015). Grievance formation in times of transition: South Africa 1994–2000. *Social Justice Research, 28*(1), 123–142. https://doi.org/10.1007/s11211-014-0232-4

Klautke, E. (2013). Defining the *Volk*: Willy Hellpach's *Völkerpsychologie* between National Socialism and Liberal democracy, 1934–1954. *History of European Ideas, 39*(5), 693–708. https://doi.org/10.1080/03044181.2012.735086

Klautke, E. (2014). *The mind of the nation: Volkerpsychologie in Germany, 1851–1955*. Berghahn.

Klein, O., & Licata, L. (2001). Explaining differences between social groups: The impact of group identification on attribution. *Swiss Journal of Psychology, 60*(4), 244–252. https://doi.org/10.1024//1421-0185.60.4.244

Klein, R. A., Ratliff, K. A., Vianello, M., Adams, R. B., Jr., Bahnik, S., Bernstein, M. J., Bocian, K., Brandt, M. J., Brooks, B., Brumbaugh, C. C., Cemalcilar, Z., Chandler, J., Cheong, W., Davis, W. E., Devos, T., Eisner, M., Frankowska, N., Furrow, D., Galliani, E. M., . . . Nosek, B. A. (2014). Investigating variation in replicability: A "many labs" replication project. *Social Psychology, 45*(3), 142–152. https://doi.org/10.1027/1864-9335/a000178

Kluckhohn, C., & Murray, H. A. (1953). *Personality in nature, society, and culture*. Knopf.

Knowles, E. D., & Tropp, L. T. (2018). The racial and economic context of Trump support: Evidence for threat, identity, and contact effects in the 2016 presidential election. *Social Psychological & Personality Science, 9*(3), 275–284. https://doi.org/10.1177/1948550618759326

Knuckey, J., & Hassan, K. (2020). Authoritarianism and support for Trump in the 2016 presidential election. *The Social Science Journal*. Advance online publication. https://doi.org/10.1016/j.soscij.2019.06.008

Kobak, R. R., & Sceery, A. (1988). Attachment in late adolescence: Working models, affect regulation, and representations of the self and others. *Child Development, 59*(1), 135–146. https://doi.org/10.2307/1130395

Koschate, M., & van Dick, R. (2011). A multilevel test of Allport's contact conditions. *Group Processes and Intergroup Relations, 14*(6), 769–787. https://doi.org/10.1177/1368430211399602

Kotzur, P. E., Tropp, L., & Wagner, U. (2018). Welcoming the unwelcome: How contact shapes contexts of reception for new immigrants in Germany and the United States. *Journal of Social Issues, 74*(4), 812–832. https://doi.org/10.1111/josi.12300

Kovel, J. (1970). *White racism: A psychohistory*. Pantheon.

Kraus, M. W., Onyeador, I. N., Daumeyer, N. M., Rucker, J. M., & Richeson, J. A. (2019). The misperception of racial income inequality. *Perspectives on Psychological Science, 14*(6), 899–921. https://doi.org/10.1177/1745691619863049

Krech, D., & Crutchfield, R. S. (1948). *Theory and problems of social psychology*. McGraw Hill. https://doi.org/10.1037/10024-000

Kristof, N. (2019, July 17). Trump is racist to the bone. *The New York Times*. https://www.nytimes.com/2019/07/17/opinion/donald-trump-racist.html

Krosch, A. R., & Amodio, D. (2014). Economic scarcity alters the perception of race. *Proceedings of the National Academy of Sciences of the United States of America, 111*(25), 9079–9084. https://doi.org/10.1073/pnas.1404448111

Krosch, A. R., Tyler, T. R., & Amodio, D. (2017). Race and recession: Effects of economic scarcity on racial discrimination. *Journal of Personality and Social Psychology, 113*(6), 892–909. https://doi.org/10.1037/pspi0000112

Kruglanski, A. W., Atash, M. N., DeGrada, E., Mannetti, L., Pierro, A., & Webster, D. M. (1997). Psychological theory testing versus psychometric nay-saying: Comment on Neuberg et al.'s (1997) critique of the Need for Closure Scale. *Journal of Personality and Social Psychology, 73*(5), 1005–1016. https://doi.org/10.1037/0022-3514.73.5.1005

Krull, J. L., & MacKinnon, D. P. (2001). Multilevel modeling of individual and group level mediated effects. *Multivariate Behavioral Research, 36*, 249–277. https://doi.org/10.1207/S15327906MBR3602_06

Krumhuber, E. G., Swiderska, A., Tsankova, E., Kamble, S. V., & Kappas, A. (2015). Real or artificial? Intergroup biases in mind perception in a cross-cultural perspective. *PLOS ONE, 10*(9), Article e0137840. https://doi.org/10.1371/journal.pone.0137840

Kteily, N. S., Hodson, G., Dhont, K., & Ho, A. K. (2019). Predisposed to prejudice but responsive to intergroup contact? Testing the unique benefits of intergroup contact. *Group Processes & Intergroup Relations, 22*(1), 3–25. https://doi.org/10.1177/1368430217716750

Kunst, J. R., Dovidio, J. F., & Thomsen, L. (2019). Fusion with political leaders predicts willingness to persecute immigrants and political opponents. *Nature Human Behaviour, 3*, 1180–1189. https://doi.org/10.1038/s41562-019-0708-1

Kunzelman, M., & Galvan, A. (2019, August 7). Trump words linked to more hate crime? Some experts think so. *U.S. News & World Report*. https://www.usnews.com/news/world/articles/2019-08-07/trump-words-linked-to-more-hate-crime-some-experts-think-so

Kurdi, B., Seitchik, A. E., Axt, J. R., Carroll, T. J., Karapetyan, A., Kaushik, N., Tomezsko, D., Greenwald, A. G., & Banaji, M. R. (2019). Relationship between the Implicit Association Test and intergroup behavior: A meta-analysis. *American Psychologist, 74*(5), 569–586. https://doi.org/10.1037/amp0000364

Kurt Lewin. (2020, March 26). In *Wikipedia*. https://en.wikipedia.org/wiki/Kurt_Lewin

Lageson, S., Denver, M., & Pickett, J. T. (2019). Privatizing criminal stigma: Experience, intergroup contact, and public views about publicizing arrest records. *Punishment & Society, 21*(3), 315–341. https://doi.org/10.1177/1462474518772040

Laloggia, J. (2019, May 15). *6 facts about U.S. political independents*. Pew Research Center. https://www.pewresearch.org/fact-tank/2019/05/15/facts-about-us-political-independents/

Langenberg, D. N. (1991). Science, slogans and civic duty. *Science, 252*(5004), 361–363. https://doi.org/10.1126/science.252.5004.361

Latu, I. M. (2011). *Reducing automatic activation: Mechanisms and moderators of situational attribution training*. ProQuest Information & Learning.

Laurence, J., Schmid, K., Rae, J. R., & Hewstone, M. (2018). Prejudice, contact, and threat at the diversity-segregation nexus: A cross-sectional and longitudinal analysis of how ethnic out-group size and segregation interrelate for inter-group relations. *Social Forces, 97*(3), 1029–1066. https://doi.org/10.1093/sf/soy079

Lazarsfeld, P. F. (1962). Introduction. In S. A. Stouffer (Ed.), *Social research to test ideas* (pp. xiv–xxxi). Free Press of Glencoe.

Lea, J., & Young, J. (1993). *What is to be done about law and order?* Pluto Press. (Original work published 1984)

LeBlanc, J., Beaton, A. M., & Walker, I. (2015). The downside of being up: A new look at group relative gratification and traditional prejudice. *Social Justice Research, 28*(1), 143–167. https://doi.org/10.1007/s11211-015-0233-y

LeBon, G. (1896). *The crowd*. Unwin.

Lee, H. (1960). *To kill a mockingbird*. Lippincott.

Lee, H. (2015). *Go set a watchman*. HarperCollins.

Lee, K., & Ashton, M. C. (2013). *The H factor of personality*. Wilfrid Laurier University Press.

Legros, S., & Cislaghi, B. (2020). Mapping the social-norms literature: An overview of reviews. *Perspectives on Psychological Science, 15*(1), 62–80. https://doi.org/10.1177/1745691619866455

Lemmer, G., & Wagner, U. (2015). Can we really reduce ethnic prejudice outside the lab? A meta-analysis of direct and indirect contact interventions. *European Journal of Social Psychology, 45*(2), 152–168. https://doi.org/10.1002/ejsp.2079

Leone, L., Desimoni, M., & Chirumbolo, A. (2014). Interest and expertise moderate the relationship between right-wing attitudes, ideological self-placement and voting. *European Journal of Personality, 28*(1), 2–13. https://doi.org/10.1002/per.1880

Lett, H. A. (1945). Techniques for achieving interracial cooperation. *Proceedings of the Institute on Race Relations and Community Organization*. University of Chicago and the American Council on Race Relations.

Levin, S., Federico, C. M., Sidanius, J., & Rabinowitz, J. L. (2002). Social dominance orientation and intergroup bias: The legitimation of favoritism for high-status groups. *Personality and Social Psychology Bulletin, 28*(2), 144–157. https://doi.org/10.1177/0146167202282002

Levin, S., Van Laar, C., & Sidanius, J. (2003). The effects of ingroup and out-group friendships on ethnic attitudes in college. *Group Processes & Intergroup Relations, 6*(1), 76–92. https://doi.org/10.1177/1368430203006001013

Levine, R. A., & Campbell, D. (1972). *Ethnocentrism: Theories of conflict, ethnic attitudes and group behavior*. Wiley.

Leviston, Z., Dandy, J., Jetten, J., & Walker, I. (2020). The role of relative deprivation in majority-culture support for multiculturalism. *Journal of Applied Social Psychology, 50*(4), 228–239.

Lewin, K. (1948). *Resolving social conflicts: Selected papers on group dynamics*. Harper & Brothers.

Lewis, G. J., & Bates, T. C. (2014). Common heritable effects underpin concerns over norm maintenance and in-group favoritism. Evidence from genetic analyses of right-wing authoritarianism and traditionalism. *Journal of Personality, 82*(4), 297–309. https://doi.org/10.1111/jopy.12055

Leyens, J.-P., Paladino, P. M., Rodriguez-Torres, R., Vaes, J., Demoulin, S., Rodriguez-Perez, A., & Gaunt, R. (2000). The emotional side of prejudice: The attribution of secondary emotions to ingroups and outgroups. *Personality and Social Psychology Review, 4*(2), 186–197. https://doi.org/10.1207/S15327957PSPR0402_06

Lichbach, M. I. (1990). Will rational people rebel against inequality? Samson's choice. *American Journal of Political Science, 34*(4), 1049–1076. https://doi.org/10.2307/2111471

Light, R. J., & Pillemer, D. B. (1984). *Summing up: The science of reviewing research*. Harvard University Press.

Lissitsa, S., & Kushnirovich, N. (2018). Secondary transfer effects of positive and negative online contact between groups involved in high intensity conflict. *International Journal of Intercultural Relations*, *67*, 71–80. https://doi.org/10.1016/j.ijintrel.2018.10.001

Long, S. J. (1975). Malevolent estrangement: Political alienation and political justification among black and white adolescents. *Youth & Society*, *7*(2), 99–129. https://doi.org/10.1177/0044118X7500700201

Lord, C. G., & Saenz, D. C. (1985). Memory deficits and memory surfeits: Differential cognitive consequences for tokens and observers. *Journal of Personality and Social Psychology*, *49*(4), 918–926. https://doi.org/10.1037/0022-3514.49.4.918

Ludeke, S. G., Johnson, W., & Bouchard, T. J., Jr. (2013). "Obedience to traditional authority": A heritable factor underlying authoritarianism, conservatism and religiousness. *Personality and Individual Differences*, *55*(5), 375–380. https://doi.org/10.1016/j.paid.2013.03.018

Ludeke, S. G., Klitgaard, C. N., & Vitriol, J. (2018). Comprehensively-measured authoritarianism does predict vote choice: The importance of authoritarianism's facets, ideological sorting, and the particular candidate. *Personality and Individual Differences*, *123*, 209–216. https://doi.org/10.1016/j.paid.2017.11.019

Ludeke, S. G., & Krueger, R. F. (2013). Authoritarianism as a personality trait. *Personality and Individual Differences*, *55*(5), 480–484. https://doi.org/10.1016/j.paid.2013.04.015

Lynskey, M. T., Ward, C., & Fletcher, G. J. (1991). Stereotypes and intergroup attributions in New Zealand. *Psychology and Developing Societies*, *3*(1), 113–127. https://doi.org/10.1177/097133369100300107

Ma, W., & Karasawa, M. (2006). Group inclusiveness, group identification, and attributional bias. *Psychologia*, *49*(4), 278–290. https://doi.org/10.2117/psysoc.2006.278

Maass, A., Ceccarelli, R., & Rudin, S. (1996). Linguistic intergroup bias: Evidence for in-group protective motivation. *Journal of Personality and Social Psychology*, *71*(3), 512–526. https://doi.org/10.1037/0022-3514.71.3.512

MacInnis, C. C., & Page-Gould, E. (2015). How can intergroup interaction be bad if intergroup contact is good? Exploring and reconciling an apparent paradox in the science of intergroup relations. *Psychological Science*, *10*(3), 307–327. https://doi.org/10.1177/1745691614568482

Madan, S., Basu, S., Rattan, A., & Savani, K. (2019). Support for resettling refugees: The role of fixed versus growth mind-sets. *Psychological Science*, *30*(2), 238–249. https://doi.org/10.1177/0956797618813561

Maguire, P. (2016, January 17). Socially isolated voters more likely to favour Brexit, finds thinktank. *The Guardian*. https://www.theguardian.com/politics/2016/dec/17/socially-isolated-voters-more-likely-to-favour-brexit-finds-thinktank

Main, M., Kaplan, N., & Cassidy, J. (1985). Security in infancy, childhood, and adulthood. *Monographs of the Society for Research in Child Development, 50*(1/2), 66–104. https://doi.org/10.2307/3333827

Major, B., Blodorn, A., & Major Blascovich, G. (2018). The threat of increasing diversity: Why many white Americans support Trump in the 2016 presidential election. *Group Processes & Intergroup Relations, 21*(6), 931–940. https://doi.org/10.1177/1368430216677304

Ma-Kellams, C., Bishop, B., Zhang, M. F., & Villagrana, B. (2018). Using "big data" versus alternative measures of aggregate data to predict the U.S. 2016 presidential election. *Psychological Reports, 121*(4), 726–735. https://doi.org/10.1177/0033294117736318

Mallett, R., Huntsinger, J., Sinclair, S., & Swim, J. (2008). Seeing through their eyes: When majority group members take collective action on behalf of an outgroup. *Group Processes & Intergroup Relations, 11*(4), 451–470. https://doi.org/10.1177/1368430208095400

Mandela, N. (1994). *Long walk to freedom*. Little, Brown.

Mannetti, L., Pierro, A., Kruglanski, A., Taris, T., & Bezinovic, P. (2002). A cross-sectional study of the Need for Cognitive Closure Scale: Comparing its structure in Croatia, Italy, USA and the Netherlands. *British Journal of Social Psychology, 41*(1), 139–156. https://doi.org/10.1348/014466602165108

Marchlewska, M., Cichocka, A., Panayiotou, O., Castellanos, K., & Batayneh, J. (2018). Populism as identity politics: Perceived in-group disadvantage, collective narcissism, and support for populism. *Social Psychological & Personality Science, 9*(2), 151–162. https://doi.org/10.1177/1948550617732393

Marić, N., Kolenović-Đapo, N., & Đapo, N. (2019). Hipoteza zamišljenog kontakta: Uloga radnog pamćenja [The imagined contact hypothesis: The role of working memory capacity]. *Psihologijske Teme, 28*(2), 251–270. https://doi.org/10.31820/pt.28.2.2

Mark, M. M., & Folger, R. (1984). Responses to relative deprivation: A conceptual framework. *Review of Personality and Social Psychology, 5*, 182–218.

Martens, A. L., Stratmoen, E., & Saucier, D. A. (2018). To preserve, protect, and defend: Masculine honor beliefs and perceptions of the 2016 presidential candidates. *Basic and Applied Social Psychology, 40*(5), 308–319. https://doi.org/10.1080/01973533.2018.1500288

Martin, J. (1981). Relative deprivation: A theory of distributive injustice for an era of shrinking resources. In L. L. Cummings & B. M. Staw (Eds.), *Research in organizational behavior* (Vol. 3, pp. 53–107). JAI Press.

Martin, J. (1986). The tolerance of injustice. In J. M. Olson, C. P. Herman, & M. P. Zanna (Eds.), *Relative deprivation and social comparison: The Ontario Symposium* (Vol. 4, pp. 217–242). Erlbaum.

Martin, J., & Harder, J. (1994). Bread and roses: Justice and the distribution of financial and socio-emotional rewards in organizations. *Social Justice Research, 7*, 241–264. https://doi.org/10.1007/BF02334833

Martinez, J., & Smith, G. A. (2016, November 9). *How the faithful voted: A preliminary 2016 analysis*. Pew Research Center. http://www.pewresearch.org/fact-tank/2016/11/09/how-the-faithful-voted-a-preliminary-2016-analysis

Marx, K. (1964). Economic and philosophical manuscripts. In T. B. Bottomore (Ed.), *Early writings* (pp. 63–219). McGraw-Hill.

Marx, P. (2020). Anti-elite politics and emotional reactions to socio-economic problems. Experimental evidence on "pocketbook anger" from France, Germany, and the United States. *British Journal of Sociology*. Advance online publication. https://doi.org/10.1111/1468-4446.12750

McCann, S. J. (2008). Societal threat, authoritarianism, conservatism, and U.S. state death penalty sentencing (1977–2004). *Journal of Personality and Social Psychology, 94*(5), 913–923. https://doi.org/10.1037/0022-3514.94.5.913

McCann, S. J. (2009a). Authoritarianism, conservatism, racial diversity threat, and the state distribution of hate groups. *The Journal of Psychology, 144*(1), 37–60. https://doi.org/10.1080/00223980903356065

McCann, S. J. (2009b). Political conservatism, authoritarianism, and societal threat: Voting for Republican representatives in U.S. Congressional elections from 1946 to 1992. *The Journal of Psychology, 143*(4), 341–358. https://doi.org/10.3200/JRLP.143.4.341-358

McCarthy, T. (2019, July 17). Trump rally crowd chats "send her back" after president attacks Ilhan Omar. *The Guardian*. https://www.theguardian.com/us-news/2019/jul/17/trump-rally-send-her-back-ilhan-omar

McClelland, D. C. (1955). *Studies in motivation*. Appleton-Century-Crofts.

McClelland, D. C. (1961). *The achieving society*. Van Nostrand. https://doi.org/10.1037/14359-000

McConahay, J. B. (1983). Modern racism and modern discrimination: The effects of race, racist attitudes, and context on simulated hiring decisions. *Personality and Social Psychology Bulletin, 9*(4), 551–558. https://doi.org/10.1177/0146167283094004

McCourt, K., Bouchard, T. J., Jr., Lykken, D. T., Tellegen, A., & Keyes, M. (1999). Authoritarianism revisited: Genetic and environmental influences examined in twins reared apart and together. *Personality and Individual Differences, 27*(5), 985–1014. https://doi.org/10.1016/S0191-8869(99)00048-3

McGuire, W. J. (1973). The yin and yang of progress in social psychology. *Journal of Personality and Social Psychology, 26*(3), 446–456. https://doi.org/10.1037/h0034345

Mead, M. (2003). *Sex and temperament in three primitive societies*. HarperCollins. (Original work published 1935)

Measure of America. (2013). *State of the Congress 2013*. https://measureofamerica.org/113-congress-infographic/

Meertens, R., & Pettigrew, T. F. (1997). Is subtle prejudice really prejudice? *Public Opinion Quarterly, 61*(1), 54–71. https://doi.org/10.1086/297786

Meleady, R., & Forder, L. (2019). When contact goes wrong: Negative contact promotes generalized outgroup avoidance. *Group Processes & Intergroup Relations*, *22*(5), 688–707. https://doi.org/10.1177/1368430218761568

Meleady, R., Seger, C. R., & Vermue, M. (2017). Examining the role of positive and negative intergroup contact and anti-immigrant prejudice in Brexit. *British Journal of Social Psychology*, *56*(4), 799–808. https://doi.org/10.1111/bjso.12203

Meleady, R., & Vermue, M. (2019). The effect of intergroup contact on solidarity-based collective action is mediated by reductions in SDO. *Journal of Applied Social Psychology*, *49*(5), 307–318. https://doi.org/10.1111/jasp.12586

Meloen, J. D. (1993). The F scale as a predictor of fascism: An overview of 40 years of authoritarian research. In W. F. Stone, G. Lederer, & R. Christie (Eds.), *Strength and weakness: The authoritarian personality today* (pp. 47–69). Springer. https://doi.org/10.1007/978-1-4613-9180-7_3

Menon, T., Morris, M. W., Chiu, C., & Hong, Y. (1999). Culture and the construal of agency: Attribution to individual versus group dispositions. *Journal of Personality and Social Psychology*, *76*(5), 701–717. https://doi.org/10.1037/0022-3514.76.5.701

Merton, R. K. (1957). *Social theory and social structure* (Rev. ed.). Free Press.

Meuleman, B. (2011). Perceived economic threat and anti-immigration attitudes: Effects of immigrant group size and economic conditions revisited. In E. Davidov, P. Schmidt, & J. Billiet (Eds.), *Cross-cultural analysis: Methods and applications* (pp. 281–310). Routledge.

Meuleman, B., Abts, K., Schmidt, P., Pettigrew, T. F., & Davidov, E. (2020). Group relative deprivation and ethnic threat perceptions in a cross-national perspective. *Journal of Ethnic and Migration Studies*, *46*(3), 593–611. https://doi.org/10.1080/1369183X.2018.1550157

Meuleman, B., Abts, K., Slootmaeckers, K., & Meeusen, C. (2019). Differentiated threat and the genesis of prejudice: Group-specific antecedents of homonegativity, Islamophobia, anti-Semitism, and anti-immigrant attitudes. *Social Problems*, *66*(2), 222–244. https://doi.org/10.1093/socpro/spy002

Meuleman, B., & Billiet, J. (2009). A Monte Carlo sample size study: How many countries are needed for accurate multilevel SEM? *Survey Research Methods*, *3*(1), 45–58. https://doi.org/10.18148/srm/2009.v3i1.666

Meyer, G. J., Finn, S. E., Eyde, L., Kay, G. G., Moreland, K. L., Dies, R. R., Eisman, E. J., Kubiszyn, T. W., & Reed, G. M. (2001). Psychological testing and psychological assessment. *American Psychologist*, *56*(2), 128–165. https://doi.org/10.1037/0003-066X.56.2.128

Middleton, R. (1976). Regional differences in prejudice. *American Sociological Review*, *41*(1), 94–117. https://doi.org/10.2307/2094375

Mikulincer, M., & Shaver, P. R. (2007). *Attachment in adulthood*. Guilford Press.

Milbank, D. (2019, May 26). The calmest of times. *Anchorage Daily News*. https://www.adn.com/opinions/national-opinions/2019/05/26/the-calmest-of-times/

Miles, E., & Crisp, R. J. (2014). A meta-analytic test of the imagined contact hypothesis. *Group Processes & Intergroup Relations, 17*(1), 3–26. https://doi.org/10.1177/1368430213510573

Milgram, S. (1974). *Obedience to authority: An experimental view*. Harper & Row.

Miller, D. A., Smith, E. R., & Mackie, D. M. (2004). Effects of intergroup contact and political predispositions on prejudice: Role of intergroup emotions. *Group Processes & Intergroup Relations, 7*(3), 221–237. https://doi.org/10.1177/1368430204046109

Moghaddam, F. M. (2005). The staircase to terrorism: A psychological interpretation. *American Psychologist, 60*(2), 161–169. https://doi.org/10.1037/0003-066X.60.2.161

Mols, F., & Jetten, J. (2016). Explaining the appeal of populist right-wing parties in times of economic prosperity. *Political Psychology, 37*(2), 275–292. https://doi.org/10.1111/pops.12258

Morris, M. W., Nisbett, R. E., & Peng, K. (1995). Causal attribution and cultures. In D. Sperber & A. J. Premack (Eds.), *Causal cognition: A multidisciplinary debate* (pp. 577–614). Oxford University Press.

Morris, M. W., & Peng, K. (1994). Culture and cause: American and Chinese attributions for social and physical events. *Journal of Personality and Social Psychology, 67*(6), 949–971. https://doi.org/10.1037/0022-3514.67.6.949

Mortensen, C. R., Neel, R. B., Cialdini, R. B., Jaeger, C. M., Jacobson, R. P., & Megan, M. (2019). Trending norms: A lever for encouraging behaviors performed by the minority. *Social Psychological & Personality Science, 10*(2), 201–210. https://doi.org/10.1177/1948550617734615

Moscovici, S. (1993). *The invention of society: Psychological explanations of social phenomena*. Polity Press.

Mullen, B., Brown, R., & Smith, C. (1992). Ingroup bias as a function of salience, relevance and status: An integration. *The Journal of Social Psychology, 22*(2), 103–122. https://doi.org/10.1002/ejsp.2420220202

Murphy, G., Loftus, E. F., Grady, R. H., Levine, L. J., & Greene, C. M. (2019). False memories for fake news during Ireland's abortion referendum. *Psychological Science, 30*(10), 1449–1459. https://doi.org/10.1177/0956797619864887

Murphy, R. (1972, January 29). A Harvard professor and Wallace. *The Atlanta Constitution*, A4.

Mussen, P. H. (1950). Some personality and social factors related to changes in children's attitudes toward Negroes. *Journal of Abnormal and Social Psychology, 45*(3), 423–441. https://doi.org/10.1037/h0056371

Mutz, D. C. (2018). Status threat, not economic hardship, explains the 2016 presidential vote. *Proceedings of the National Academy of Sciences of the United States of America, 115*(19), E4330–E4339. https://doi.org/10.1073/pnas.1718155115

Myrdal, G. (1944). *An American dilemma*. Harper & Row.

Newman, B., Merolla, J. L., Shah, S., Lemi, D. C., Collingwood, L., & Ramakrishnan, S. K. (2020). The Trump effect: Experimental investigation into the emboldening effect. *British Journal of Political Science*. Advance online publication. https://doi.org/10.1017/S0007123419000590

Newport, F. (2013). *In U.S., 87% approve of Black-White marriage vs. 4% in 1958*. Gallup. https://news.gallup.com/poll/163697/approve-marriage-blacks-whites.aspx

Newton, J. W., Mann, L., & Geary, D. (1980). Relative deprivation, dissatisfaction and militancy: A field study in a protest crowd. *Journal of Applied Social Psychology, 10*(5), 384–397. https://doi.org/10.1111/j.1559-1816.1980.tb00718.x

Nier, J. A., Bajaj, P., McLean, M. C., & Schwartz, E. (2013). Group status, perceptions of agency, and the correspondence bias: Attributional processes in the formation of stereotypes about high and low status groups. *Group Processes & Intergroup Relations, 16*(4), 476–487. https://doi.org/10.1177/1368430212454925

Noah, T., Schul, Y., & Mayo, R. (2018). When both the original study and its failed replication are correct: Feeling observed eliminates the facial-feedback effect. *Journal of Personality and Social Psychology, 114*(5), 657–664. https://doi.org/10.1037/pspa0000121

Norman, W. T. (1963). Toward an adequate taxonomy of personality attributes: Replicated factors structure in peer nomination personality ratings. *Journal of Abnormal and Social Psychology, 66*(6), 574–583. https://doi.org/10.1037/h0040291

Norpoth, H. (2016). Primary model predicts Trump victory. *PS, Political Science & Politics, 49*(4), 655–658. https://doi.org/10.1017/S1049096516001323

Northington, D. J. (2016). *An attribution-emotion approach to political conflict* [Doctoral thesis, Loma Linda University]. TheScholarsRepository@LLU.

Nosek, B. A., Smyth, F. L., Hansen, J. J., Devos, T., Lindner, N. M., Ranganath, K. A., Smith, C. T., Olson, K. R., Chugh, D., Greenwald, A. G., & Banaji, M. (2007). Pervasiveness and correlates of implicit attitudes and stereotypes. *European Review of Social Psychology, 18*(1), 36–88. https://doi.org/10.1080/10463280701489053

Obaidi, M., Bergh, R., Akrami, N., & Anjum, G. (2019). Group-based relative deprivation explains endorsement of extremism among western-born Muslims. *Psychological Science, 30*(4), 596–605. https://doi.org/10.1177/0956797619834879

Obaidi, M., Thomsen, L., & Bergh, R. (2018). "They think we are a threat to their culture": Meta-cultural threat fuels willingness and endorsement of extremist violence against the cultural outgroup. *International Journal of Conflict and Violence, 12*, 1–13. https://doi.org/10.4119/UNIBI/ijcv.647

Obschonka, M., Stuetzer, M., Rentfrow, P. J., Lee, N., Potter, J., & Gosling, S. D. (2018). Fear, populism, and the geopolitical landscape: The "sleeper effect" of neurotic personality traits on regional voting behavior in the 2016 Brexit and Trump elections. *Social Psychological & Personality Science, 9*(3), 285–298. https://doi.org/10.1177/1948550618755874

Oesterreich, D. (2005). Flight into security: A new approach and measure of the authoritarian personality. *Political Psychology, 26*(2), 275–298. https://doi.org/10.1111/j.1467-9221.2005.00418.x

Ogorzalek, T., Piston, S., & Puig, L. G. (in press). Nationally poor, locally rich: Income and local context in the 2016 presidential election. *Electoral Studies*.

Oliver, E. J., & Wong, J. (2003). Intergroup prejudice in multiethnic settings. *American Journal of Political Science, 47*(4), 567–582. https://doi.org/10.2307/3186119

Olson, J. M., Herman, C. P., & Zanna, M. P. (Eds.). (1986). *Relative deprivation and social comparison: The Ontario Symposium* (Vol. 4). Hillsdale, NJ: Erlbaum.

Open Science Collaboration. (2015). Estimating the reproducibility of psychological science. *Science, 349*(6251), 943. https://doi.org/10.1126/science.aac4716

Osborne, D., & Sibley, C. G. (2015). Opposing paths to ideology: Group-based relative deprivation predicts conservatism through warmth toward ingroup and outgroup members. *Social Justice Research, 28*(1), 27–51. https://doi.org/10.1007/s11211-014-0227-1

Oswald, F. L., Mitchell, G., Blanton, H., Jaccard, J., & Tetlock, P. E. (2013). Predicting ethnic and racial discrimination: A meta-analysis of IAT criterion studies. *Journal of Personality and Social Psychology, 105*(2), 171–192. https://doi.org/10.1037/a0032734

Oswald, F. L., Mitchell, G., Blanton, H., Jaccard, J., & Tetlock, P. E. (2015). Using the IAT to predict ethnic and racial discrimination: Small effect sizes of unknown societal significance. *Journal of Personality and Social Psychology, 108*(4), 562–571. https://doi.org/10.1037/pspa0000023

Outten, H. R., Schmitt, M. T., Miller, D. A., & Garcia, A. L. (2012). Feeling threatened about the future: Whites' emotional reactions to anticipated ethnic demographic changes. *Personality and Social Psychology Bulletin, 38*(1), 14–25. https://doi.org/10.1177/0146167211418531

Oxley, D. R., Smith, K. B., Alford, J. R., Hibbing, M. V., Miller, J. L., Scalora, M., Hatemi, P. K., & Hibbing, J. R. (2008). Political attitudes vary with physiological traits. *Science, 321*(5896), 1667–1670. https://doi.org/10.1126/science.1157627

Padgett, V. R., & Jorgenson, D. O. (1982). Superstition and economic threat: Germany 1918–1940. *Personality and Social Psychology Bulletin, 8*(4), 736–741. https://doi.org/10.1177/0146167282084021

Page, B. I., & Shapiro, R. Y. (1992). *The rational public: Fifty years of trends in American policy preferences*. University of Chicago Press. https://doi.org/10.7208/chicago/9780226644806.001.0001

Page-Gould, E., & Zhou, S. (in press). A meta-analysis of media contact. *Personality and Social Psychology Review*.

Paluck, E. L. (2009). Reducing intergroup prejudice and conflict using the media: A field experiment in Rwanda. *Journal of Personality and Social Psychology, 96*(3), 574–587. https://doi.org/10.1037/a0011989

Paluck, E. L., Green, S. A., & Green, D. P. (2019). The contact hypothesis re-evaluated. *Behavioural Public Policy*, *3*(2), 129–158. http://doi.org/10.1017/bpp.2018.25

Paolini, S., Harwood, J., Hewstone, M., & Neumann, D. L. (2018). Seeking and avoiding intergroup contact: Future frontiers of research on building social integration. *Social and Personality Psychology Compass*, *12*(12), Article e12422. Advance online publication. https://doi.org/10.1111/spc3.12422

Paolini, S., Harwood, J., Rubin, M., Husnu, S., Joyce, N., & Hewstone, M. (2014). Positive and extensive intergroup contact in the past buffers against the disproportionate impact of negative contact in the present. *European Journal of Social Psychology*, *44*(6), 548–562. https://doi.org/10.1002/ejsp.2029

Payne, K. (2017). *The broken ladder: How inequality affects the way we think, live and die*. Viking.

Pearson, K. (1904). Report on certain enteric fever inoculation statistics. *British Medical Journal*, *2*, 1243–1246. https://doi.org/10.1136/bmj.2.2288.1243

Peitz, L., Dhont, K., & Seyd, B. (2018). The psychology of supranationalism: Its ideological correlates and implications for post-Brexit preferences. *Political Psychology*, *39*(6), 1305–1322. https://doi.org/10.1111/pops.12542

Perry, R., & Sibley, C. G. (2013). Seize and freeze: Openness to experience shapes judgments of societal threat. *Journal of Research in Personality*, *47*(6), 677–686. https://doi.org/10.1016/j.jrp.2013.06.006

Pettigrew, T. F. (1957). Demographic correlates of border-state desegregation. *American Sociological Review*, *22*(6), 683–689. https://doi.org/10.2307/2089198

Pettigrew, T. F. (1958a). The measurement and correlates of category width as a cognitive variable. *Journal of Personality*, *26*(4), 532–544. https://doi.org/10.1111/j.1467-6494.1958.tb02350.x

Pettigrew, T. F. (1958b). Personality and socio-cultural factors in intergroup attitudes. *The Journal of Conflict Resolution*, *2*(1), 29–42. https://doi.org/10.1177/002200275800200104

Pettigrew, T. F. (1959). Regional differences in anti-Negro prejudice. *Journal of Abnormal and Social Psychology*, *59*(1), 28–36. https://doi.org/10.1037/h0047133

Pettigrew, T. F. (1961). Social psychology and desegregation research. *American Psychologist*, *16*(3), 105–112. https://doi.org/10.1037/h0041995

Pettigrew, T. F. (1964a). *Epitaph for Jim Crow*. Anti-Defamation League [This pamphlet provides episodes of the 10-part television series produced by WGBH-TV in Boston]. https://www.thirteen.org/programs/dynamics-of-desegregation/

Pettigrew, T. F. (1964b). *A profile of the Negro American*. Van Nostrand.

Pettigrew, T. F. (1964c). What "White backlash"? *Nieman Reports*, *18*(4), 7–9.

Pettigrew, T. F. (1967a). Social evaluation theory: Convergences and applications. In D. Levine (Ed.), *Nebraska Symposium on Motivation, 1967* (pp. 241–311). University of Nebraska Press.

Pettigrew, T. F. (1967b). SPSSI as honest broker. *Society for the Psychological Study of Social Issues Newsletter*, No. 117.

Pettigrew, T. F. (1969). Gordon Willard Allport, 1897–1967. *Journal of Personality and Social Psychology, 12*(1), 1–5. https://doi.org/10.1037/h0027222

Pettigrew, T. F. (1971). *Racially separate or together?* McGraw-Hill.

Pettigrew, T. F. (1979a). Tensions between the law and social science: An expert witness view. In J. Greenberg, T. F. Pettigrew, S. Greenblatt, W. McCann, & D. A. Bennett (Eds.), *Schools and the courts: Desegregation* (Vol. 1, pp. 23–44). ERIC Clearinghouse for Educational Management, University of Oregon.

Pettigrew, T. F. (1979b). The ultimate attribution error: Extending Allport's cognitive analysis of prejudice. *Personality and Social Psychology Bulletin, 5*(4), 461–476. https://doi.org/10.1177/014616727900500407

Pettigrew, T. F. (1982). Cognitive style and social behavior: A review of category width. In L. Wheeler (Ed.), *Review of personality and social psychology* (Vol. 3, pp. 199–233). Sage.

Pettigrew, T. F. (1986). The contact hypothesis revisited. In M. Hewstone & R. Brown (Eds.), *Contact and conflict in intergroup encounters* (pp. 169–195). Blackwell.

Pettigrew, T. F. (1989). The nature of modern racism in the United States. *Revue Internationale de Psychologie Sociale, 2*, 291–303.

Pettigrew, T. F. (1990). A bold stroke for personality a half-century ago: A retrospective review of Gordon Allport's *Personality: A Psychological Interpretation. Contemporary Psychology, 35*(6), 533–536. https://doi.org/10.1037/028676

Pettigrew, T. F. (1991a). The importance of cumulative effects: A neglected emphasis of Sherif's work. In D. Granberg & G. Sarup (Eds.), *Social judgment and intergroup relations: Essays in honor of Muzafer Sherif* (pp. 89–103). Springer Verlag.

Pettigrew, T. F. (1991b). Normative theory in intergroup relations: Explaining both harmony and conflict. *Psychology and Developing Societies, 3*(1), 3–16. https://doi.org/10.1177/097133369100300102

Pettigrew, T. F. (1991c). Toward unity and bold theory: Popperian suggestions for two persistent problems of social psychology. In C. Stephan, W. Stephan, & T. F. Pettigrew (Eds.), *The future of social psychology* (pp. 13–27). Springer Verlag. https://doi.org/10.1007/978-1-4612-3120-2_2

Pettigrew, T. F. (1997a). Generalized intergroup contact effects on prejudice. *Personality and Social Psychology Bulletin, 23*(2), 173–185. https://doi.org/10.1177/0146167297232006

Pettigrew, T. F. (1997b). Personality and social structure: Social psychological contributions. In R. Hogan, J. A. Johnson, & S. R. Briggs (Eds.), *Handbook of personality psychology* (pp. 417–438). Academic Press/Elsevier. https://doi.org/10.1016/B978-012134645-4/50018-4

Pettigrew, T. F. (1998). Intergroup contact theory. *Annual Review of Psychology, 49*, 65–85. https://doi.org/10.1146/annurev.psych.49.1.65

Pettigrew, T. F. (1999). Gordon Willard Allport: A tribute. *Journal of Social Issues, 55*(3), 415–428. https://doi.org/10.1111/0022-4537.00125

Pettigrew, T. F. (2001). Summing up: Relative deprivation as a key social psychological concept. In I. Walker & H. Smith (Eds.), *Relative deprivation: Specification, development and integration* (pp. 351–374). Cambridge University Press. https://doi.org/10.1017/CBO9780511527753.016

Pettigrew, T. F. (2003). Peoples under threat: Americans, Arabs, and Israelis. *Peace and Conflict, 9*(1), 69–90. https://doi.org/10.1207/S15327949PAC0901_03

Pettigrew, T. F. (2004a). Intergroup contact: Theory, research, and new perspectives. In J. A. Banks & C. A. M. Banks (Eds.), *Handbook of research on multicultural education* (2nd ed., pp. 770–781). Jossey-Bass.

Pettigrew, T. F. (2004b). Justice deferred: A half century after *Brown v. Board of Education*. *American Psychologist, 59*(6), 521–529. https://psycnet.apa.org/doi/10.1037/0003-066X.59.6.521

Pettigrew, T. F. (2006). Commentary: The advantages of multi-level approaches. *Journal of Social Issues, 62*(3), 615–620. https://doi.org/10.1111/j.1540-4560.2006.00477.x

Pettigrew, T. F. (2009a). Post-racism? Putting President Obama's victory in perspective. *Du Bois Review, 6*(2), 279–292. https://doi.org/10.1017/S1742058X0999018X

Pettigrew, T. F. (2009b). Secondary transfer effect of contact: Do intergroup contact effects generalize to non-contacted outgroups? *Social Psychology, 40*(2), 55–65. https://doi.org/10.1027/1864-9335.40.2.55

Pettigrew, T. F. (2010a). Deprovincialization. In D. J. Christie (Ed.), *Encyclopedia of peace psychology*. Wiley-Blackwell. https://doi.org/10.1002/9780470672532.wbepp081

Pettigrew, T. F. (2010b). Herbert C. Kelman: A tribute. *Peace and Conflict, 16*(4), 341–348. https://doi.org/10.1080/10781919.2010.518063

Pettigrew, T. F. (2011). SPSSI and racial research. *Journal of Social Issues, 67*(1), 137–149. https://doi.org/10.1111/j.1540-4560.2010.01688.x

Pettigrew, T. F. (2015a). Gordon Willard Allport. In N. J. Smelser & P. B. Baltes (Eds.), *International encyclopedia for the social and behavioral sciences* (Rev. ed., pp. 401–404). Pergamon. https://doi.org/10.1016/B978-0-08-097086-8.61001-2

Pettigrew, T. F. (2015b). Samuel Stouffer and relative deprivation. *Social Psychology Quarterly, 30*, 1–18. https://doi.org/10.1177%2F0190272514566793

Pettigrew, T. F. (2016). In pursuit of three theories: Authoritarianism, relative deprivation, and intergroup contact. *Annual Review of Psychology, 67*, 1–21. https://doi.org/10.1146/annurev-psych-122414-033327

Pettigrew, T. F. (2017a). Book review of C. B. Dew's *The Making of a Racist*. *The American Journal of Psychology, 103*(4), 521–523. https://doi.org/10.5406/amerjpsyc.130.4.0521

Pettigrew, T. F. (2017b). Social psychological perspectives on Trump supporters. *Journal of Social and Political Psychology*, *5*(1), 107–116. https://doi.org/10.5964/jspp.v5i1.750

Pettigrew, T. F. (2018a). The emergence of contextual social psychology. *Personality and Social Psychology Bulletin*, *44*(7), 963–971. https://doi.org/10.1177/0146167218756033

Pettigrew, T. F. (2018b). Summing up: Did SPSSI answer Dr. King's call? *Journal of Social Issues*, *74*(2), 377–385. https://doi.org/10.1111/josi.12274

Pettigrew, T. F. (2019). The intertwined history of personality and social psychology. In K. Deaux & M. Snyder (Eds.), *Oxford handbook of personality and social psychology* (2nd ed., pp. 11–33). Oxford University Press.

Pettigrew, T. F. (2020, May 29). Intergroup attribution. *Oxford Research Encyclopedia of Psychology*.

Pettigrew, T. F., Allport, G. W., & Barnett, E. (1958). Binocular resolution and perception of race in South Africa. *British Journal of Psychology*, *49*(4), 265–278. https://doi.org/10.1111/j.2044-8295.1958.tb00665.x

Pettigrew, T. F., & Campbell, E. Q. (1960). Faubus and segregation: An analysis of Arkansas voting. *Public Opinion Quarterly*, *24*(3), 436–447. https://doi.org/10.1086/266962

Pettigrew, T. F., Christ, O., Meertens, R. W., Wagner, U., van Dick, R., & Zick, A. (2008). Relative deprivation and intergroup prejudice. *Journal of Social Issues*, *64*(2), 385–401. https://doi.org/10.1111/j.1540-4560.2008.00567.x

Pettigrew, T. F., & Cramer, M. R. (1959). The demography of desegregation. *Journal of Social Issues*, *15*(4), 61–71. https://doi.org/10.1111/j.1540-4560.1959.tb01462.x

Pettigrew, T. F., & Hewstone, M. (2017). The single factor fallacy: Implications of missing critical variables from an analysis of intergroup contact theory. *Social Issues and Policy Review*, *11*(1), 8–37. https://doi.org/10.1111/sipr.12026

Pettigrew, T. F., & Martin, J. (1987). Shaping the organizational context for Black American inclusion. *Journal of Social Issues*, *43*(1), 41–78. https://doi.org/10.1111/j.1540-4560.1987.tb02330.x

Pettigrew, T. F., & Meertens, R. (1992). Subtle racism – its components and measurement. *International Journal of Psychology*, *27*(3–4), 276.

Pettigrew, T. F., & Meertens, R. (1995). Subtle and blatant prejudice in Western Europe. *European Journal of Social Psychology*, *25*(1), 57–75. https://doi.org/10.1002/ejsp.2420250106

Pettigrew, T. F., & Meertens, R. (1996). The *verzuiling* puzzle: Understanding Dutch intergroup relations. *Current Psychology*, *15*, 3–13. https://doi.org/10.1007/BF02686929

Pettigrew, T. F., & Meertens, R. W. (2001). In defense of the subtle prejudice concept: A retort. *European Journal of Social Psychology*, *31*(3), 299–309. https://doi.org/10.1002/ejsp.45

Pettigrew, T. F., & Riley, R. T. (1972). Contextual models of school desegregation. In B. T. King & E. McGinnies (Eds.), *Attitudes, conflict, and social change* (pp. 155–185). Academic Press. https://doi.org/10.1016/B978-0-12-407750-8.50018-2

Pettigrew, T. F., & Tropp, L. (2000). Does intergroup contact reduce prejudice? Recent meta-analytic findings. In S. Oskamp (Ed.), *Reducing prejudice and discrimination: Social psychological perspectives* (pp. 93–114). Erlbaum.

Pettigrew, T. F., & Tropp, L. R. (2005). Allport's intergroup contact hypothesis: Its history and influence. In J. F. Dovidio, P. Glick, & L. P. Rudman (Eds.), *Reflecting on the nature of prejudice* (pp. 262–277). Blackwell. https://doi.org/10.1002/9780470773963.ch16

Pettigrew, T. F., & Tropp, L. (2006). A meta-analytic test of intergroup contact theory. *Journal of Personality and Social Psychology, 90*(5), 751–783. https://doi.org/10.1037/0022-3514.90.5.751

Pettigrew, T. F., & Tropp, L. (2008). How does intergroup contact reduce prejudice? Meta-analytic tests of three mediators. *European Journal of Social Psychology, 38*(6), 922–934. https://doi.org/10.1002/ejsp.504

Pettigrew, T. F., & Tropp, L. (2011). *When groups meet: The dynamics of intergroup contact.* Psychology Press.

Pettigrew, T. F., Wagner, U., & Christ, O. (2010). Population ratios and prejudice: Modeling both contact and threat effects. *Journal of Ethnic and Migration Studies, 36*(4), 635–650. https://doi.org/10.1080/13691830903516034

Pinker, S. (2011). *The better angels of our nature: Why violence has declined.* Viking.

Poore, A. G., Gagne, F., Barlow, K. M., Taylor, J. E., & Wright, S. C. (2002). Contact and the person–group discrimination discrepancy in an Inuit community. *The Journal of Psychology, 136*(4), 371–382. https://doi.org/10.1080/00223980209604164

Portelinha, I., & Elcheroth, G. (2016). From marginal to mainstream: The role of perceived social norms in the rise of a far-right movement. *European Journal of Social Psychology, 46*(6), 661–671. https://doi.org/10.1002/ejsp.2224

Power, R. A., & Pluess, M. (2015). Heritability estimates of the Big Five personality traits based on common genetic variants. *Translational Psychiatry, 5*(7), 604–620. https://doi.org/10.1038/tp.2015.96

Powers, D. A., & Ellison, C. G. (1995). Interracial contact and Black racial attitudes: The contact hypothesis and selectivity bias. *Social Forces, 74*(1), 205–226. https://doi.org/10.2307/2580629

Pratto, F., Sidanius, J., Stallworth, L., & Malle, B. (1994). Social dominance orientation: A personality variable predicting social and political attitudes. *Journal of Personality and Social Psychology, 67*(4), 741–763. https://doi.org/10.1037/0022-3514.67.4.741

Preacher, K. J., Rucker, D. O., & Hayes, A. F. (2007). Addressing moderated mediation hypotheses: Theory, methods, and prescriptions. *Multivariate Behavioral Research, 42*(1), 185–227. https://doi.org/10.1080/00273170701341316

Preacher, K. J., Zhang, Z., & Zyphur, M. J. (2016). Multilevel structural equation models for assessing moderation within and across levels of analysis. *Psychological Methods, 21*(2), 189–205. https://doi.org/10.1037/met0000052

Preacher, K. J., Zyphur, M. J., & Zhang, Z. (2010). A general multilevel SEM framework for assessing multilevel mediation. *Psychological Methods, 15*(3), 209–233. https://doi.org/10.1037/a0020141

Putnam, R. (2007). *E pluribus unum*: Diversity and community in the 21st century. *Scandinavian Political Studies, 30*(2), 137–174. https://doi.org/10.1111/j.1467-9477.2007.00176.x

Ramos, M. R., Bennett, M., Massey, D., & Hewstone, M. (2019). Humans adapt to social diversity over time. *Proceedings of the National Academy of Sciences of the United States of America, 116*(25), 12244–12249. https://doi.org/10.1073/pnas.1818884116

Rattazzi, A. M. M., Bobbio, A., & Canova, L. (2007). A short version of the right-wing authoritarianism (RWA) scale. *Personality and Individual Differences, 43*(5), 1223–1234. https://doi.org/10.1016/j.paid.2007.03.013

Rees, J. H., Rees, Y. P. M., Hellmann, J. H., & Zick, A. (2019). Climate of hate: Similar correlates of far right electoral support and right-wing hate crime in Germany. *Frontiers in Psychology, 10*, 2328. https://doi.org/10.3389/fpsyg.2019.02328

Regan, D. T., & Totten, J. (1975). Empathy and attribution: Turning observers into actors. *Journal of Personality and Social Psychology, 32*(5), 850–856. https://doi.org/10.1037/0022-3514.32.5.850

Reicher, S., & Haslam, S. A. (2016, November 19). The politics of hope: Donald Trump as an entrepreneur of identity. *Scientific American*. https://scientificamerican.com/article/the-politics-of-hope-donald-trump-as-an-entrepreneur-of-identity

Reif, K., & Melich, A. (1991). *Euro-Barometer 30: Immigrants and Out-Groups in Western Europe, October–November 1988*. Inter-University Consortium for Political and Social Research, ICPSR 9321.

Reilly, K. (2016). Racist incidents are up since Donald Trump's election. *Time Magazine*. https://time.com/4569129/racist-anti-semitic-incidents-donald-trump

Reimer, N. K., Kamble, S. V., Schmid, K., & Hewstone, M. (2019). Intergroup contact fosters inclusive social identities. *Proceedings of the National Academy of Science, 116*(25), 12244–12299. https://doi.org/10.31234/osf.io/zcgwt

Reis, H. T., & Holmes, J. G. (2012). Perspectives on the situation. In K. Deaux & M. Snyder (Eds.), *Oxford handbook of personality and social psychology* (pp. 64–92). Oxford University Press.

Reynolds, K. J., Turner, J. C., Haslam, S. A., & Ryan, M. K. (2001). The role of personality and group factors in explaining prejudice. *Journal of Experimental Social Psychology, 37*(5), 427–434. https://doi.org/10.1006/jesp.2000.1473

Ring, K. (1967). Experimental social psychology: Some sober questions about some frivolous values. *Journal of Experimental Social Psychology, 3*(2), 113–123. https://doi.org/10.1016/0022-1031(67)90016-9

Robinson, W. S. (1950). Ecological correlations and the behavior of individuals. *American Sociological Review, 15*(3), 351–357. https://doi.org/10.2307/2087176

Roccato, M. (2008). Right-wing authoritarianism, social dominance orientation, and attachment: An Italian study. *Swiss Journal of Psychology, 67*(4), 219–229. https://doi.org/10.1024/1421-0185.67.4.219

Roccato, M., & Ricolfi, L. (2005). On the correlation between right-wing authoritarianism and social dominance orientation. *Basic and Applied Social Psychology, 27*(3), 187–200. https://doi.org/10.1207/s15324834basp2703_1

Roets, A., & Van Hiel, A. (2011). Allport's prejudiced personality today: Need for closure as the motivated cognitive basis of prejudice. *Current Directions in Psychological Science, 20*(6), 349–354. https://doi.org/10.1177/0963721411424894

Rojahn, K., & Pettigrew, T. F. (1992). Memory for schema-relevant information: A meta-analysis resolution. *British Journal of Social Psychology, 31*(2), 81–109. https://doi.org/10.1111/j.2044-8309.1992.tb00958.x

Rose, M., & Baker, L. (2018, December 6). *No leader, lots of anger: Can France's "yellow vests" become a political force?* Reuters. https://www.reuters.com/article/us-france-protests-future/no-leader-lots-of-anger-can-frances-yellow-vests-become-a-political-force-idUSKBN1O51ON

Rosenfeld, M. J. (2017). Moving a mountain: The extraordinary trajectory of same-sex marriage approval in the United States. *Socius: Sociological Research for a Dynamic World, 3*. Advance online publication. https://doi.org/10.1177/2378023117727658

Rosenfield, D., & Stephan, W. G. (1978). Sex differences in attributions for sex-typed tasks. *Journal of Personality, 46*(2), 244–259. https://doi.org/10.1111/j.1467-6494.1978.tb00178.x

Rosenthal, R. (1991). *Meta-analytic procedures for social research*. Sage. https://doi.org/10.4135/9781412984997

Ross, L. D. (1977). The intuitive psychologist and his shortcomings. Distortions in the attribution process. In L. Berkowitz (Ed.), *Advances in experimental social psychology* (Vol. 10, pp. 173–220). Academic Press. https://doi.org/10.1016/S0065-2601(08)60357-3

Ross, L. D., Amabile, T. M., & Steinmetz, J. L. (1977). Social roles, social control, and biases in social-perception processes. *Journal of Personality and Social Psychology, 35*(7), 485–494. https://doi.org/10.1037/0022-3514.35.7.485

Rothwell, J. T. (2010, July 19). *Trust in diverse, integrated, cities: A revisionist perspective*. https://doi.org/10.2139/ssrn.1358647

Rothwell, J. T., & Diego-Rosell, P. (2016, November 2). *Explaining nationalist political views: The case of Donald Trump*. SSRN. https://doi.org/10.2139/ssrn.2822059

Rozin, P., & Royzman, E. B. (2001). Negativity bias, negativity dominance, and contagion. *Personality and Social Psychology Review, 5*(4), 296–320. https://doi.org/10.1207/S15327957PSPR0504_2

Ruback, R. B., & Singh, P. (2007). Ingroup bias, intergroup contact and the attribution of blame for riots. *Psychology and Developing Societies, 19*(2), 249–265. https://doi.org/10.1177/097133360701900206

Rubin, M., & Hewstone, M. (2004). Social identity, system justification, and social dominance. *Political Psychology, 25*(6), 823–844. https://doi.org/10.1111/j.1467-9221.2004.00400.x

Runciman, W. G. (1966). *Relative deprivation and social justice*. Routledge and Kegan Paul.

Russo, S., Barni, D., Cavazza, N. R., Roccato, M., & Vieno, A. (2019). Political ideology moderates the relationship between outgroup size and prejudice toward immigrants: A longitudinal, multilevel study. *Rivisteweb: The Italian Platform for the Humanities and Social Sciences, 18*(1), 115–128. https://doi.org/10.1482/92930

Rutland, A., Cameron, L., Bennett, L., & Ferrell, J. (2005). Interracial contact and racial constancy: A multi-site study of racial intergroup bias in 3–5-year-old Anglo-British children. *Journal of Applied Developmental Psychology, 26*(6), 699–713. https://doi.org/10.1016/j.appdev.2005.08.005

Ryff, C. D. (1987). The place of personality and social structure research in social psychology. *Journal of Personality and Social Psychology, 53*(6), 1192–1202. https://doi.org/10.1037/0022-3514.53.6.1192

Saguy, T., Tausch, N., Dovidio, J. F., & Pratto, F. (2009). The irony of harmony: Intergroup contact can produce false expectations for equality. *Psychological Science, 20*(1), 114–121. https://doi.org/10.1111/j.1467-9280.2008.02261.x

Sales, S. M. (1973). Threat as a factor in authoritarianism: An analysis of archival data. *Journal of Personality and Social Psychology, 28*(1), 44–57. https://doi.org/10.1037/h0035588

Sales, S. M., & Friend, K. E. (1973). Success and failure as determinants of level of authoritarianism. *Behavioral Science, 18*(3), 163–172. https://doi.org/10.1002/bs.3830180304

Sampson, R. J. (2008). Rethinking crime and immigration. *Contexts, 7*(1), 28–33. https://doi.org/10.1525/ctx.2008.7.1.28

Sampson, R. J. (2019). Neighborhood effects and beyond: Explaining the paradoxes of inequality in the changing American metropolis. *Urban Studies, 56*(1), 3–32. https://doi.org/10.1177/0042098018795363

Sampson, R. J., Morenoff, J., & Gannon-Rowley, T. (2002). Assessing neighborhood effects: Social processes and new directions in research. *Annual Review of Sociology, 28*, 443–478. https://doi.org/10.1146/annurev.soc.28.110601.141114

Sanbonmatsu, D. M., & Johnston, W. A. (2019). Redefining science: The impact of complexity on theory development in social and behavioral research.

Perspectives on Psychological Science, 14(4), 672–690. https://doi.org/10.1177/1745691619848688

Sanford, R. N. (1973). Authoritarian personality in contemporary perspective. In J. N. Knutson (Ed.), *Handbook of political psychology* (pp. 139–170). Jossey-Bass.

Sassenberg, K., & Ditrich, L. (2019). Research in social psychology changed between 2011 and 2016: Larger sample sizes, more self-report measures, and more online studies. *Advances in Methods and Practices in Psychological Science, 2*(2), 107–114. https://doi.org/10.1177/2515245919838781

Saucier, D. A., Miller, C. T., & Doucet, N. (2005). Differences in helping Whites and Blacks: A meta-analysis. *Personality and Social Psychology Review, 9*(1), 2–16. https://doi.org/10.1207/s15327957pspr0901_1

Sawyer, J., & Gampa, A. (2018). Implicit and explicit racial attitudes changed during Black Lives Matter. *Personality and Social Psychology Bulletin, 44*(7), 1039–1059. https://doi.org/10.1177/0146167218757454

Schama, S. (1987). *The embarrassment of riches*. Knopf.

Schelling, T. (2006). *Micromotives and macrobehavior*. Norton. (Original work published 1978)

Schiappa, E., Gregg, P., & Hewes, D. E. (2005). The parasocial contact hypothesis. *Communication Monographs, 72*(1), 92–115. https://doi.org/10.1080/0363775052000342544

Schiappa, E., Gregg, P., & Hewes, D. E. (2006). Can one TV show make a difference? *Will and Grace* and the parasocial contact hypothesis. *Journal of Homosexuality, 51*(4), 15–37. https://doi.org/10.1300/J082v51n04_02

Schlüter, E., & Schmidt, P. (2010). Special issue: Survey experiments. *Methodology: European Journal of Research Methods for the Behavioral and Social Sciences, 6*(3), 93–95. https://doi.org/10.1027/1614-2241/a000010

Schmid, K., Al Ramiah, A., & Hewstone, M. (2014). Neighborhood ethnic diversity and trust: The role of intergroup contact and perceived threat. *Psychological Science, 25*(3), 665–674. https://doi.org/10.1177/0956797613508956

Schmid, K., Hewstone, M., Kuepper, B., Zick, A., & Wagner, U. (2012). Secondary transfer effects of intergroup contact: A cross-national comparison in Europe. *Social Psychology Quarterly, 75*(1), 28–51. https://doi.org/10.1177/0190272511430235

Schmidt, F., & Hunter, J. E. (1995). The impact of data-analysis methods on cumulative research knowledge: Statistical significance, testing, confidence intervals, and meta-analysis. *Evaluation & the Health Professions, 18*(4), 408–427. https://doi.org/10.1177/016327879501800405

Schneider, S. (1994). *Vorurteile gegeneuber ethnichen Minderheiten in Ost und West* [Comparing prejudice against ethnic minorities in the East and West]. Unpublished diploma thesis, Department of Psychology, Bochum University, Bochum, Germany.

Schofield, J. W. (1982). *Black and White in school: Trust, tension, or tolerance*. Praeger.

Schönemann, P. H. (1997). On models and muddles of heritability. *Genetica, 99*(2–3), 97–108. https://doi.org/10.1007/BF02259513

Schultz, P. W., Nolan, J. M., Cialdini, R. B., Goldstein, N. J., & Griskevicius, V. (2007). The constructive, destructive, and reconstructive power of social norms. *Psychological Science, 18*(5), 429–434. https://doi.org/10.1111/j.1467-9280.2007.01917.x

Schultz, P. W., Nolan, J. M., Cialdini, R. B., Goldstein, N. J., & Griskevicius, V. (2018). The constructive, destructive, and reconstructive power of social norms: A reprise. *Perspectives on Psychological Science, 13*(2), 249–254. https://doi.org/10.1177/1745691617693325

Schuman, H., & Presser, S. (1996). *Questions and answers in attitude surveys: Experiments on question form, wording, and context*. Academic Press.

Schwartz, S. (1992). Universals in the content and structure of values. Theoretical and empirical tests in 20 countries. In M. Zanna (Ed.), *Advances in experimental social psychology* (Vol. 25, pp. 1–65). Academic Press. https://doi.org/10.1016/S0065-2601(08)60281-6

Schwarz, N. (2012, January). Open letter re "false-positive findings" symposium at Society for Personality and Social Psychology [Electronic mailing list message]. Society for Personality and Social Psychology.

Sears, D. (1986). College sophomores in the laboratory: Influence of a narrow data-base in social psychology's view of human nature. *Journal of Personality and Social Psychology, 51*(3), 515–530. https://psycnet.apa.org/doi/10.1037/0022-3514.51.3.515

Sears, D. D. (1988). Symbolic racism. In P. A. Katz & D. A. Taylor (Eds.), *Eliminating racism: Profiles in controversy* (pp. 53–84). Plenum. https://doi.org/10.1007/978-1-4899-0818-6_4

Selvanathan, H. P., Techakesari, P., Tropp, L. R., & Barlow, F. K. (2018). Whites for racial justice: How contact with Black Americans predicts support for collective action among White Americans. *Group Processes & Intergroup Relations, 21*(6), 893–912. https://doi.org/10.1177/1368430217690908

Selvin, H. C. (1958). Durkheim's *Suicide* and problems of empirical research. *American Journal of Sociology, 63*(6), 607–619. https://doi.org/10.1086/222356

Sengupta, N. K., Osborne, D., & Sibley, C. G. (2019). On the psychological function of nationalistic "Whitelash." *Political Psychology, 40*(4), 759–775. https://doi.org/10.1111/pops.12563

Shadish, W. R. (1996). Meta-analysis and the exploration of causal mediating processes: A primer of examples, methods, and issues. *Psychological Methods, 1*(1), 47–65. https://doi.org/10.1037/1082-989X.1.1.47

Shah, S. (2019). Does religion buffer the effects of discrimination on distress for religious minorities? The case of Arab Americans. *Society and Mental Health, 9*(2), 171–191. https://doi.org/10.1177/2156869318799145

Shani, M., & Boehnke, K. (2017). The effect of Jewish–Palestinian mixed-model encounters on readiness for contact and policy support. *Peace and Conflict, 23*(3), 219–227. https://doi.org/10.1037/pac0000220

Shelton, J. N., Dovidio, J. F., Hebl, M., & Richeson, J. A. (2009). Prejudice and intergroup interaction. In S. Demoulin, J. P. Leyens, & J. P. Dovidio (Eds.), *Intergroup misunderstandings: Impact of divergent social realities* (pp. 21–38). Psychology Press.

Shepherd, L., Fasoli, F., Pereira, A., & Branscombe, N. R. (2018). The role of threat, emotions, and prejudice in promoting collective action against immigrant groups. *European Journal of Social Psychology, 48*(4), 447–459. https://doi.org/10.1002/ejsp.2346

Sherif, M. (1935). A study of some factors in perception. *Archives of Psychology*, 187.

Sherif, M. (1936). *The psychology of social norms*. Harper.

Sherif, M. (1937). An experimental approach to the study of attitudes. *Sociometry, 1*(1/2), 90–98. https://doi.org/10.2307/2785261

Sherif, M. (1966). *In common predicament: Social psychology of intergroup conflict and cooperation*. Houghton Mifflin.

Sherif, M. (1977). Crisis in social psychology: Some remarks toward breaking through the crisis. *Personality and Social Psychology Bulletin, 3*(3), 368–382. https://doi.org/10.1177/014616727700300305

Sherman, R. A. (2018). Personal values and support for Donald Trump during the 2016 Presidential primary. *Personality and Individual Differences, 128*(1), 33–38. https://doi.org/10.1016/j.paid.2018.02.020

Shook, N. J., Hopkins, P. D., & Koech, J. M. (2016). The effect of intergroup contact on secondary group attitudes and social dominance orientation. *Group Processes & Intergroup Relations, 19*(3), 328–342. https://doi.org/10.1177/1368430215572266

Sibley, C. G., & Duckitt, J. (2008). Personality and prejudice: A meta-analysis and theoretical review. *Personality and Social Psychology Review, 12*(3), 248–279. https://doi.org/10.1177/1088868308319226

Sibley, C. G., & Duckitt, J. (2010). The personality bases of ideology: A one-year longitudinal study. *The Journal of Social Psychology, 150*(5), 540–559. https://doi.org/10.1080/00224540903365364

Sidanius, J., Levin, S., Van Laar, C., & Sears, D. O. (2008). *The diversity challenge: Social identity and intergroup relations on the college campus*. Russell Sage Foundation.

Sidanius, J., & Pratto, F. (1999). *Social dominance: An intergroup theory of social hierarchy and oppression*. Cambridge University Press.

Silver, N. (2016, May 3). The mythology of Trump's "working class" support. *FiveThirtyEight*. https://fivethirtyeight.com/features/the-mythology-of-trumps-working-class-support/

Simmel, G. (1955). *Conflict and the web of group affiliations*. Wiley.

Simmons, J. P., Nelson, L. D., & Simonsohn, U. (2011). False-positive psychology: Undisclosed flexibility in data collection and analyses allows presenting anything as significant. *Psychological Science, 22*(11), 1359–1366. https://doi.org/10.1177/0956797611417632

Simmons, J. P., Nelson, L. D., & Simonsohn, U. (2018). False-positive citations. *Perspectives on Psychological Science, 13*(2), 255–259. https://doi.org/10.1177/1745691617698146

Simonton, D. K. (1977). Eminence, creativity, and geographic marginality: A recursive structural equation model. *Journal of Personality and Social Psychology, 35*(11), 805–816. https://doi.org/10.1037/0022-3514.35.11.805

Simonton, D. K. (2003). Qualitative and quantitative analyses of historical data. *Annual Review of Psychology, 54*, 617–640. https://doi.org/10.1146/annurev.psych.54.101601.145034

Singer, B., & Benassi, V. A. (1981). Occult beliefs. *American Scientist, 69*, 49–55.

Smith, D. N., & Hanley, E. (2018). The anger games: Who voted for Donald Trump in the 2016 election, and why? *Critical Sociology, 44*(2), 195–212. https://doi.org/10.1177/0896920517740615

Smith, E. R. (1993). Social identity and social emotions: Toward new conceptualizations of prejudice. In D. Mackie & D. Hamilton (Eds.), *Affect, cognition, and stereotyping* (pp. 297–315). Academic Press. https://doi.org/10.1016/B978-0-08-088579-7.50017-X

Smith, G. A. (2017, April 26). *Among White Evangelicals, regular churchgoers are the most supportive of Trump*. Pew Research Center. http://www.pewresearch.org/fact-tank/2017/04/26/among-White-Evangelicals-regular-churchgoers-are-the-most-supportive-of-Trump

Smith, H. J., & Pettigrew, T. F. (2014). The subjective interpretation of inequality: A model of the relative deprivation experience. *Social and Personality Psychology Compass, 8*(12), 755–765. https://doi.org/10.1111/spc3.12151

Smith, H. J., & Pettigrew, T. F. (2015). Advances in relative deprivation theory and research. *Social Justice Research, 28*(1), 1–6. https://doi.org/10.1007/s11211-014-0231-5

Smith, H. J., Pettigrew, T. F., & Huo, Y. J. (2019). Relative deprivation theory: Advances and applications. In J. Suls, R. L. Collins, & L. Wheeler (Eds.), *Social comparison, judgment, & behavior* (pp. 495–526). Oxford University Press. https://doi.org/10.1093/oso/9780190629113.003.0018

Smith, H. J., Pettigrew, T. F., Pippin, G. M., & Bialosiewicz, S. (2012). Relative deprivation: A theoretical and meta-analytic review. *Personality and Social Psychology Review, 16*(3), 203–232. https://doi.org/10.1177/1088868311430825

Smith, H. J., Ryan, D., Jaurique, A., Pettigrew, T. F., Jetten, J., Ariyanto, A., Autin, F., Ayub, N., Badea, C., Besta, T., Butera, F., Costa-Lopes, R., Cui, L., Fantini, C., Finchilescu, G., Gaertner, L., Gollwitzer, M., Gómez, Á., González, R., . . . Wohl, M. (2018). Cultural values moderate the impact of relative deprivation. *Journal of Cross-Cultural Psychology, 49*(8), 1183–1218. https://doi.org/10.1177/0022022118784213

Snyder, D., & Tilly, C. (1972). Hardship and collective violence in France, 1830–1960. *American Sociological Review, 37*(5), 520–532. https://doi.org/10.2307/2093448

Soto, C. J. (2019). How replicable are links between personality traits and consequential life outcomes? The life outcomes of Personality Replication Project. *Psychological Science, 30*(5), 711–727. https://doi.org/10.1177/0956797619831612

Southern Poverty Law Center. (2016, November 29). *Ten days after: Harassment and intimidation in the aftermath of the election*. https://www.splcenter.org/20161129/ten-days-after-harassment-and-intimidation-aftermath-election

Sprong, S., Jetten, J., Wang, Z., Peters, K., Mols, F., Verkuyten, M., Bastian, B., Ariyanto, A., Autin, F., Ayub, N., Badea, C., Besta, T., Butera, F., Costa-Lopes, R., Cui, L., Fantini, C., Finchilescu, G., Gaertner, L., Gollwitzer, M., . . . Wohl, M. J. A. (2019). "Our country needs a strong leader now": Economic inequality enhances the wish for a strong leader. *Psychological Science, 30*(11), 1625–1637. https://doi.org/10.1177/0956797619875472

Stark, O., & Taylor, J. E. (1989). Relative deprivation and international migration. *Demography, 26*(1), 1–14. https://doi.org/10.2307/2061490

Statista. (2017). *Reported violent crime in the United States from 1990 to 2015.* http://www.statista.com/statistics/191219/reported-violent-crime-rate-in-the-usa-since-1990

Steele, C. (1997). A threat in the air: How stereotypes shape intellectual identity and performance. *American Psychologist, 52*(6), 613–629. https://doi.org/10.1037/0003-066X.52.6.613

Steele, C. (2010). *Whistling Vivaldi*. Norton.

Stellmacher, J., & Petzel, T. (2005). Authoritarianism as a group phenomenon. *Political Psychology, 26*(2), 245–274. https://doi.org/10.1111/j.1467-9221.2005.00417.x

Stenner, K. (2005). *The authoritarian dynamic*. Cambridge University Press.

Stephan, C. W., Stephan, W. G., & Pettigrew, T. F. (Eds.). (1991). *The future of social psychology: Defining the relationship between sociology and psychology*. Springer Verlag. https://doi.org/10.1007/978-1-4612-3120-2

Stephan, W. G., & Stephan, C. W. (1984). The role of ignorance in intergroup prejudice. In N. Miller & M. B. Brewer (Eds.), *Groups in contact: The psychology of intergroup relations* (pp. 229–255). Academic Press. https://doi.org/10.1016/B978-0-12-497780-8.50017-6

Stephan, W. G., & Stephan, C. W. (1985). Intergroup anxiety. *Journal of Social Issues, 41*(3), 157–175. https://doi.org/10.1111/j.1540-4560.1985.tb01134.x

Stephan, W. G., Ybarra, O., & Morrison, K. R. (2009). Intergroup threat theory. In T. D. Nelson (Ed.), *Handbook of prejudice, stereotyping, and discrimination* (pp. 44–59). Psychology Press.

Stephens, N. M., Townsend, S. S., & Dittman, A. G. (2019). Social-class disparities in higher education and professional workplaces. *Current Directions in Psychological Science, 28*(1), 67–73. https://doi.org/10.1177/0963721418806506

Stewart, T. L., Latu, I. M., Kawakami, K., & Myers, A. C. (2010). Consider the situation: Reducing automatic stereotyping through Situational Attribution

Training. *Journal of Experimental Social Psychology*, *46*(1), 221–225. https://doi.org/10.1016/j.jesp.2009.09.004

Stockemer, D. (2017). The economic crisis (2009–2013) and electoral support for the radical right in Western Europe—Some new and unexpected findings. *Social Science Quarterly*, *98*(5), 1536–1553. https://doi.org/10.1111/ssqu.12374

Stokes, B. (2018). *Populist views in Europe: It's not just the economy*. Pew Research Center. https://www.pewresearch.org/fact-tank/2018/07/19/populist-views-in-europe-it's-not-just-the-economy

Stolle, D., Soroka, S., & Johnson, R. (2008). When does diversity erode trust? Neighborhood diversity, interpersonal trust, and mediating effect of social interactions. *Political Studies*, *56*(1), 57–75. https://doi.org/10.1111/j.1467-9248.2007.00717.x

Stone, J., & Fernandez, N. C. (2008). How behavior shapes attitudes: Cognitive dissonance processes. In W. D. Crano & R. Prislin (Eds.), *Attitudes and attitude change* (pp. 313–334). Psychology Press.

Stössel, K., Kampfe, N., & Riemann, R. (2006). The Jena Twin Registry and the Jena Twin Study of Social Attitudes (JeTSSA). *Twin Research and Human Genetics*, *9*(6), 783–786. https://doi.org/10.1375/twin.9.6.783

Stouffer, S. A. (1955). *Communism, conformity and civil liberties*. Doubleday.

Stouffer, S. A. (1962). *Social research to test ideas*. Free Press.

Stouffer, S. A., Suchman, E. A., DeVinney, L. C., Starr, S. A., & Williams, R. M. (1949). *The American soldier* (Vol. 1). Princeton University Press.

Strack, F., Martin, L. L., & Stepper, S. (1988). Inhibiting and facilitating conditions of the human smile: A nonobtrusive test of the facial feedback hypothesis. *Journal of Personality and Social Psychology*, *54*(5), 768–777. https://doi.org/10.1037/0022-3514.54.5.768

Strong, W. F., Lederer, G., & Christie, R. (Eds.). (1992). *Strength and weakness: The authoritarian personality today*. Springer-Verlag.

Stürmer, S., Benbow, A. E. F., Siem, B., Barth, M., Bodansky, A. N., & Lotz-Schmitt, K. (2013). Psychological foundations of xenophilia: The role of major personality traits in predicting favorable attitudes towards cross-cultural contact and exploration. *Personality and Social Psychology Bulletin*, *105*(5), 832–851. https://doi.org/10.1037/a0033488

Subramanian, S. V., Jones, K., Kaddour, A., & Krieger, N. (2009). Revisiting Robinson: The perils of individualistic and ecologic fallacy. *International Journal of Epidemiology*, *38*(2), 342–360. https://doi.org/10.1093/ije/dyn359

Suls, J. M., & Miller, R. L. (Eds.). (1977). *Social comparison processes*. Halsted Press.

Sumner, W. G. (1906). *Folkways*. Ginn.

Sundie, J. M., Beal, D. J., Neuberg, S. L., & Kenrick, D. T. (2019). Moving beyond unwise replication practices: The case of romantic motivation. *Journal of Experimental Psychology: General*, *148*(4), e1–e11. https://doi.org/10.1037/xge0000527

Swart, H., Hewstone, H., Christ, O., & Voci, A. (2011). Affective mediators of intergroup contact: A three-wave longitudinal study in South Africa. *Journal of Personality and Social Psychology, 101*(6), 1221–1238. https://doi.org/10.1037/a0024450

Tajfel, H., Billig, M. G., Bundy, R. P., & Flament, C. (1971). Social categorization and intergroup behavior. *European Journal of Social Psychology, 1*(2), 149–178. https://doi.org/10.1002/ejsp.2420010202

Tankard, M., & Paluck, E. L. (2017). The effect of a Supreme Court decision regarding gay marriage on social norms and personal attitudes. *Psychological Science, 28*(9), 1334–1344. https://doi.org/10.1177/0956797617709594

Tausch, N., Hewstone, M., Kenworthy, J. B., Psaltis, C., Schmid, K., Popan, J. R., Cairns, E., & Hughes, J. (2010). Secondary transfer effects of intergroup contact. *Journal of Personality and Social Psychology, 99*(2), 282–302. https://doi.org/10.1037/a0018553

Taylor, T. (Director). (2011). *The help* [Film]. Walt Disney Studios.

Techakesari, P., Barlow, F. K., Hornsey, M. J., Sung, B., Thai, M., & Chak, J. L. Y. (2015). An investigation of positive and negative contact as predictors of intergroup attitudes in the United States. Hong Kong, and Thailand. *Journal of Cross-Cultural Psychology, 46*(3), 454–468. https://doi.org/10.1177/0022022115570313

Tierney, J., & Baumeister, R. F. (2020). *The power of bad*. Penguin Press.

Tilley, J., & Hobolt, S. B. (2011). Is the government to blame? An experimental test of how partisanship shapes perceptions of performance and responsibility. *The Journal of Politics, 73*(2), 316–330. https://doi.org/10.1017/S0022381611000168

Trawalter, S., Adam, E. K., Chase-Lansdale, P. L., & Richeson, J. A. (2012). Concerns about appearing prejudiced get under the skin: Stress responses to interracial contact in the moment and across time. *Journal of Experimental Social Psychology, 48*(3), 682–693. https://doi.org/10.1016/j.jesp.2011.12.003

Trawalter, S., Richeson, J. A., & Shelton, J. N. (2009). Predicting behavior during interracial interactions: A stress and coping approach. *Personality and Social Psychology Review, 13*(4), 243–268. https://doi.org/10.1177/1088868309345850

Triandis, H. C. (1994). *Culture and social behavior*. McGraw-Hill.

Trickett, E. J. (1972). *Handbook of community mental health*. Prentice-Hall.

Triplett, N. (1898). The dynamogenic factors in pacemaking and competition. *The American Journal of Psychology, 9*(4), 507–533. https://doi.org/10.2307/1412188

Tropp, L. R. (2008). The role of trust in intergroup contact: Its significance and implications for improving relations between groups. In U. Wagner, L. R. Tropp, G. Finchilescu, & C. Tredoux (Eds.), *Improving intergroup relations: Building on the legacy of Thomas F. Pettigrew* (pp. 91–106). Blackwell. https://doi.org/10.1002/9781444303117.ch7

Tropp, L. R. (2019). Adaptation to diversity: Individual and societal processes. *Proceedings of the National Academy of Sciences of the United States of America, 116*(25), 12,131–12,133. https://doi.org/10.1073/pnas.1907380116

Tropp, L. R., Hawi, D. R., O'Brien, T. C., Gheorghiu, M., Zetes, A., & Butz, D. A. (2017). Intergroup contact and the potential for post-conflict reconciliation: Studies in Northern Ireland and South Africa. *Peace and Conflict, 23*(3), 239–249. https://doi.org/10.1037/pac0000236

Tropp, L. R., & Pettigrew, T. F. (2004). Intergroup contact and the central role of affect in intergroup prejudice. In L. Tiedens & C. W. Leach (Eds.), *The social life of emotion* (pp. 246–269). Cambridge University Press. https://doi.org/10.1017/CBO9780511819568.014

Tropp, L. R., & Pettigrew, T. F. (2005a). Differential relationships between intergroup contact and affective and cognitive dimensions of prejudice. *Personality and Social Psychology Bulletin, 3*(8), 1145–1158. https://doi.org/10.1177/0146167205274854

Tropp, L. R., & Pettigrew, T. F. (2005b). Relationships between intergroup contact and prejudice among minority and majority status groups. *Psychological Science, 16*(12), 951–957. https://doi.org/10.1111/j.1467-9280.2005.01643.x

Tropp, L. R., Smith, A. E., & Crosby, F. J. (2007). The use of research in the Seattle and Jefferson County desegregation cases: Connecting social science and the law. *Analyses of Social Issues and Public Policy, 7*(1), 93–120. https://doi.org/10.1111/j.1530-2415.2007.00149.x

Tryon, R. C. (1964). Psychology in flux: The academic-professional bipolarity. *Applied Psychology, 13*(1), 134–143. https://doi.org/10.1111/j.1464-0597.1964.tb00507.x

Tucker, P. D., Torres, M., Sinclair, B., & Smith, S. S. (2019). Pathways to Trump: Republican voters in 2016. *Electoral Studies, 61*, Article 102035. https://www.sciencedirect.com/science/article/pii/S0261379418303032

Tupes, E. C., & Christal, R. E. (1961). *Recurrent personality factors based on trait ratings* (USAF ASD Tech. Rep. 61-97). United States Air Force.

Turner, R. N., Crisp, R. J., & Lambert, E. (2007). Imagining intergroup contact can improve intergroup attitudes. *Group Processes & Intergroup Relations, 10*(4), 427–441. https://doi.org/10.1177/1368430207081533

Turner, R. N., & West, K. (2012). Behavioral consequences of imagining intergroup contact with stigmatized outgroups. *Group Processes & Intergroup Relations, 15*(2), 193–202. https://doi.org/10.1177/1368430211418699

Tyler, T. R., & Smith, H. J. (1998). Social justice and social movements. In D. Gilbert, S. T., Fiske, & G. Lindzey (Eds.), *Handbook of social psychology* (4th ed., Vol. 2, pp. 595–629). McGraw Hill.

Ungaretti, J., Etchezahar, E., & Barreiro, A. (2018). Validation of the subtle and blatant prejudice scale towards indigenous people in Argentina. *Current Psychology, 37*. https://doi.org/10.1007/s12144-018-9844-4

Urbanska, K., & Guimond, S. (2018). Swaying to the extreme: Group relative deprivation predicts voting for an extreme right party in the French presidential election. *International Review of Social Psychology, 31*(1), 26. https://doi.org/10.17605/OSF.IO/C3K9Y

Useem, B. (1980). Solidarity model, breakdown model and the Boston anti-busing movement. *American Sociological Review, 45*(3), 357–369. https://doi.org/10.2307/2095171

Uslaner, E. M. (2011a). Does diversity drive down trust? In P. Selle & S. Prakash (Eds.), *Civil society, the state, and social capital: Theory, evidence, policy*. Routledge.

Uslaner, E. M. (2011b). Trust, diversity, and segregation in the United States and the United Kingdom. *Comparative Sociology, 10*(2), 221–247. https://doi.org/10.1163/156913311X566571

Uslaner, E. M. (2012). *Segregation and mistrust: Diversity, isolation, and social cohesion*. Cambridge University Press. https://doi.org/10.1017/CBO9781139026758

Van Assche, J., Dhont, K., & Pettigrew, T. F. (2019). The social-psychological bases of far-right support in Europe and the United States. *Journal of Community and Applied Social Psychology, 29*(5), 385–401. https://doi.org/10.1002/casp.2407

Van Assche, J., Dhont, K., Van Hiel, A., & Roets, A. (2018). Ethnic diversity and support for populist parties: The "right" road through political cynicism and lack of trust. *Social Psychology, 49*(3), 182–189. https://doi.org/10.1027/1864-9335/a000340

Van Assche, J., Van Hiel, A., Dhont, K., & Roets, A. (2019). Broadening the individual differences lens on party support and voting behavior: Cynicism and prejudice as relevant attitudes referring to modern-day political alignments. *European Journal of Social Psychology, 49*(1), 190–199. https://doi.org/10.1002/ejsp.2377

Van den Bos, K., Van Veldhuizen, T. S., & Au, A. K. C. (2015). Counter-cross-cultural priming and relative deprivation: The role of individualism-collectivism. *Social Justice Research, 28*(1), 52–75. https://doi.org/10.1007/s11211-014-0230-6

Van Hiel, A. (2012). A psycho-political profile of party activists and left-wing and right-wing extremists. *European Journal of Political Research, 51*(2), 166–203. https://doi.org/10.1111/j.1475-6765.2011.01991.x

Van Hiel, A., & Brebels, L. (2011). Conservatism is good for you: Cultural conservatism. *Personality and Individual Differences, 50*(1), 120–123. https://doi.org/10.1016/j.paid.2010.09.002

Van Hiel, A., Cornelis, I., Roets, A., & De Clercq, B. (2007). A comparison of various authoritarianism scales in Belgian Flanders. *European Journal of Personality, 21*(2), 149–168. https://doi.org/10.1002/per.617

Van Hiel, A., & Mervielde, I. (2002). Explaining conservative beliefs and political preferences: A comparison of social dominance orientation and authoritarianism. *Journal of Applied Social Psychology, 32*(5), 965–976. https://doi.org/10.1111/j.1559-1816.2002.tb00250.x

Van Hiel, A., Pandelaere, M., & Duriez, B. (2004). The impact of need for closure on conservative beliefs and racism: Differential mediation by authoritarianism submission and authoritarian dominance. *Personality and Social Psychology Bulletin*, *30*(7), 824–837. https://doi.org/10.1177/0146167204264333

Van IJzendoorn, M. H. (1997). Attachment, emergent morality, and aggression. *International Journal of Behavioral Development*, *21*(4), 703–727. https://doi.org/10.1080/016502597384631

Vanneman, R. D., & Pettigrew, T. F. (1972). Race and relative deprivation in the urban United States. *Race*, *13*(4), 461–486. https://doi.org/10.1177/030639687201300404

Van Oudenhoven, J. P., Groenewoud, J. T., & Hewstone, M. (1996). Cooperation, ethnic salience and generalization of interethnic attitudes. *European Journal of Social Psychology*, *26*, 649–661. https://doi.org/10.1002/(SICI)1099-0992(199607)26:4<649::AID-EJSP780>3.0.CO;2-T

Vargas-Salfate, S., Paez, D., Oriol, X., da Costa, S., Gondim, S., & Techio, E. (2020). Nationalistic collective rituals, intergroup relations, and legitimization of national social systems. *Revue Internationale de Psychologie Sociale*, *33*(1), 1–12. https://doi.org/10.5334/irsp.291

Varshney, A. (2002). *Ethnic conflict and civil life: Hindues and Muslims in India*. Yale University Press.

Velasco González, K., Verkuyten, M., Wessie, J., & Poppe, E. (2008). Prejudice towards Muslims in the Netherlands: Testing integrated threat theory. *British Journal of Social Psychology*, *47*(4), 667–685. https://doi.org/10.1348/014466608X284443

Verkuyten, M. (2011). Assimilation ideology and outgroup attitudes among ethnic majority members. *Group Processes & Intergroup Relations*, *14*(6), 789–806. https://doi.org/10.1177/1368430211398506

Verkuyten, M., & Brug, P. (2004). Multiculturalism and group status: The role of ethnic identification, group essentialism and Protestant ethic. *European Journal of Social Psychology*, *34*(6), 647–661. https://doi.org/10.1002/ejsp.222

Verkuyten, M., Thijs, J., & Bekhuis, H. (2010). Ingroup contact and ingroup reappraisal: Examining the deprovincialization thesis. *Social Psychology Quarterly*, *73*(4), 398–416. https://doi.org/10.1177/0190272510389015

Vezzali, L., Capozza, D., Stathi, S., & Giovannini, D. (2012). Increasing outgroup trust, reducing infrahumanization, and enhancing future contact intentions via imagined intergroup contact. *Journal of Experimental Social Psychology*, *48*(1), 437–440. https://doi.org/10.1016/j.jesp.2011.09.008

Vezzali, L., Capozza, D., Stathi, S., Giovannini, D., & Pettigrew, T. F. (2020). *Optimal conditions for intergroup contact in and out of the workplace* [Manuscript in preparation]. Department of Education and Humanities, University of Modena and Reggio Emilia, Italy.

Vezzali, L., Di Bernado, G. A., Stathi, S., Visintin, E. P., & Hewstone, M. (2019). Using intercultural videos of direct contact to implement vicarious contact:

A school-based intervention that improves intergroup attitudes. *Group Processes & Intergroup Relations, 22*(7), 1059–1076. https://doi.org/10.1177/1368430218809885

Vezzali, L., & Giovannini, D. (2012). Secondary transfer effect of intergroup contact. *Journal of Community & Applied Social Psychology, 22*(2), 125–144. https://doi.org/10.1002/casp.1103

Vezzali, L., Hewstone, M., Capozza, D., Giovannini, D., & Wölfer, R. (2014). Improving intergroup relations with extended and vicarious forms of indirect contact. *European Review of Social Psychology, 25*(1), 314–389. https://doi.org/10.1080/10463283.2014.982948

Vezzali, L., Turner, R., Capozza, D., & Trifiletti, E. (2018). Does intergroup contact make you a better person? A longitudinal study on the bidirectional relationship between intergroup contact and personality traits. *European Journal of Social Psychology, 48*(2), 159–173. https://doi.org/10.1002/ejsp.2313

Visintin, E. P., Green, E. G. T., Falomir-Pichastor, J. M., & Berent, J. (2019). Intergroup contact moderates the influence of social norms on prejudice. *Group Processes & Intergroup Relations*. Advance online publication. https://doi.org/10.1177%2F1368430219839485

Vollhardt, J. R. (2010). Enhanced external and culturally sensitive attributions after extended intercultural contact. *British Journal of Social Psychology, 49*(2), 363–383. https://doi.org/10.1348/014466609X459899

Vorauer, J. D., Main, K. J., & O'Connell, G. B. (1998). How do individuals expect to be viewed by members of lower status groups? *Journal of Personality and Social Psychology, 75*(4), 917–937. https://doi.org/10.1037/0022-3514.75.4.917

Wagenmakers, E. J., Beek, T., Dijkhoff, L., Gronau, Q. F., Acosta, A., Adams, R. B., Jr., Albohn, D. N., Allard, E. S., Benning, S. D., Blouin-Hudon, E.-M., Bulnes, L. C., Caldwell, T. L., Calin-Jageman, R. J., Capaldi, C. A., Carfagno, N. S., Chasten, K. T., Cleeremans, A., Connell, L., DeCicco, J. M., . . . Zwaan, R. A. (2016). Registered replication report: Strack, Martin & Stepper (1988). *Perspectives on Psychological Science, 11*(6), 917–928. https://doi.org/10.1177/1745691616674458

Wagner, U., Christ, O., Pettigrew, T. F., Stellmacher, J., & Wolf, H. (2006). Prejudice and minority proportion: Contact instead of threat effects. *Social Psychology Quarterly, 69*(4), 380–390. https://doi.org/10.1177/019027250606900406

Wagner, U., van Dick, R., Pettigrew, T. F., & Christ, O. (2003). Ethnic prejudice in East and West Germany: The explanatory power of intergroup contact. *Group Processes & Intergroup Relations, 6*(1), 22–36. https://doi.org/10.1177/1368430203006001010

Waldzus, S., Mummendey, A., Wenzel, M., & Weber, U. (2003). Towards tolerance: Representations of subordinate categories and perceived ingroup prototypicality. *Journal of Experimental Social Psychology, 39*(1), 31–47. https://doi.org/10.1016/S0022-1031(02)00507-3

Walker, I., & Mann, L. (1987). Unemployment, relative deprivation and social protest. *Personality and Social Psychology Bulletin, 13*(2), 275–283. https://doi.org/10.1177/0146167287132012

Walker, I., & Pettigrew, T. F. (1984). Relative deprivation theory: An overview and conceptual critique. *British Journal of Social Psychology, 23*(4), 301–310. https://doi.org/10.1111/j.2044-8309.1984.tb00645.x

Walker, I., & Smith, H. (Eds.). (2002). *Relative deprivation: Specification, development and integration*. Cambridge University Press.

Walker, I., Wang, N. G., & Kretzschmar, K. (2001). Relative deprivation and attribution: From grievance to action. In I. Walker & H. Smith (Eds.), *Relative deprivation: Specification, development and integration* (pp. 288–312). Cambridge University Press. https://doi.org/10.1017/CBO9780511527753.013

Wang, G., & McKillip, J. (1978). Ethnic identification and judgments of an accident. *Personality and Social Psychology Bulletin, 4*(2), 296–299. https://doi.org/10.1177/014616727800400226

Ward, C., & Masgoret, A. (2006). An integrative model of attitudes toward immigrants. *International Journal of Intercultural Relations, 30*(6), 671–682. https://doi.org/10.1016/j.ijintrel.2006.06.002

Watson, G. (Ed.). (1942). *Civilian morale: Second yearbook of the Society for the Psychological Study of Social Issues*. Houghton Mifflin.

Weber, C., & Federico, C. M. (2007). Interpersonal attachment and patterns of ideological belief. *Political Psychology, 28*(4), 389–416. https://doi.org/10.1111/j.1467-9221.2007.00579.x

Weber, J. G. (1994). The nature of ethnocentric attribution bias: Ingroup protection or enhancement? *Journal of Experimental Social Psychology, 30*(5), 482–504. https://doi.org/10.1006/jesp.1994.1023

Weber, M. (1930). *The Protestant ethic and the spirit of capitalism*. Scribner.

Weber, M. (1968). *Economy and society: An outline of interpretive sociology* (G. Roth & C. Wittich, Eds.). University of California Press.

Webster, D. M., & Kruglanski, A. W. (1994). Individual differences in cognitive closure. *Journal of Personality and Social Psychology, 67*(6), 1049–1062. https://doi.org/10.1037/0022-3514.67.6.1049

West, K., Turner, R. N., & Levita, L. (2015). Applying imagined contact to improve physiological responses in anticipation of intergroup interactions and the perceived quality of these interactions. *Journal of Applied Social Psychology, 45*(8), 425–436. https://doi.org/10.1111/jasp.12309

Westland, J. C. (2015). *Structural equation modeling: From paths to networks*. Springer.

White, F. A., Abu-Rayya, H. M., & Weitzel, C. (2014). Achieving twelve-months of intergroup bias reduction: The dual identity-electronic contact (DIEC) experiment. *International Journal of Intercultural Relations, 38*, 158–163. https://doi.org/10.1016/j.ijintrel.2013.08.002

Williams, R. M., Jr. (1947). *The reduction of intergroup tensions*. Social Science Research Council.

Wilner, D. M., Walkley, R. P., & Cook, S. W. (1955). *Human relations in interracial housing: A study of the contact hypothesis.* University of Minnesota Press.

Wilson, T. C. (1996). Prejudice reduction or self-selection? A test of the contact hypothesis. *Sociological Spectrum, 16*(1), 43–60. https://doi.org/10.1080/02732173.1996.9982119

Winterich, K. P., & Zhang, Y. (2014). Accepting inequality deters responsibility: How power distance decreases charitable behavior. *The Journal of Consumer Research, 41*(2), 274–293. https://doi.org/10.1086/675927

Wölfer, R., Christ, O., Schmid, K., Tausch, N., Buchallik, F. M., Vertovec, S., & Hewstone, M. (2019). Indirect contact predicts direct contact: Longitudinal evidence and the mediating role of intergroup anxiety. *Journal of Personality and Social Psychology, 116*(2), 277–295. https://doi.org/10.1037/pspi0000146

Wölfer, R., Schmid, K., Hewstone, M., & van Zalk, M. (2016). Developmental dynamics of intergroup contact and intergroup attitudes: Long-term effects in adolescence and early adulthood. *Child Development, 87*(5), 1466–1478. https://doi.org/10.1111/cdev.12598

Womick, J., Rothmund, T., Azevedo, F., King, L. A., & Jost, J. T. (2019). Group-based dominance and authoritarian aggression predict support for Donald Trump in the 2016 presidential election. *Social Psychological & Personality Science, 10*(5), 643–652. https://doi.org/10.1177/1948550618778290

Works, E. (1961). The prejudice–interaction hypothesis from the point of view of the Negro minority group. *American Journal of Sociology, 67*(1), 47–52. https://doi.org/10.1086/223049

Wright, J. D., & Esses, V. M. (2019). It's security, stupid! Voters' perceptions of immigrants as a security risk predicted support for Donald Trump in the 2016 U.S. Presidential election. *Journal of Applied Social Psychology, 49*(1), 36–49. https://doi.org/10.1111/jasp.12563

Wright, S. (1921). Correlation and causation. *Journal of Agricultural Research, 20*, 557–585.

Wright, S. (1960). Path coefficients and path regressions: Alternative or complementary concepts? *Biometrics, 16*(2), 189–202. https://doi.org/10.2307/2527551

Wright, S. C., Aron, A., McLaughlin-Volpe, T., & Ropp, S. A. (1997). The extended contact effect: Knowledge of cross-group friendships and prejudice. *Journal of Personality and Social Psychology, 73*(1), 73–90. https://doi.org/10.1037/0022-3514.73.1.73

Wright, S. C., & Lubensky, M. E. (2009). The struggle for social equality: Collective action versus prejudice reduction. In S. Demoulin, J.-P. Levens, & J. F. Dovidio (Eds.), *Intergroup misunderstandings: Impact of divergent realities* (pp. 291–310). Psychology Press.

Yitzhaki, S. (1979). Relative deprivation and the Gini coefficient. *The Quarterly Journal of Economics, 93*(2), 321–324. https://doi.org/10.2307/1883197

Yucel, D., & Psaltis, C. (2019). Intergroup contact and willingness for renewed cohabitation in Cyprus: Exploring mediating and moderating mechanisms. *Group Processes & Intergroup Relations*. Advance online publication. https://doi.org/10.1177%2F1368430219845053

Yung, Y.-E., & Chan, W. (1999). Statistical analysis using bootstrapping: Concepts and implementation. In R. Hoyle (Ed.), *Statistical strategies for small sample research* (pp. 82–108). Sage.

Zajonc, R. B. (1968). Attitudinal effects of exposure. *Journal of Personality and Social Psychology*, *9*(2), 1–27. https://doi.org/10.1037/h0025848

Zell, E., & Krizan, Z. (2014). Do people have insight into their abilities? A meta-synthesis. *Perspectives on Psychological Science*, *9*(2), 111–125. https://doi.org/10.1177/1745691613518075

Zhang, H., Tian, Y., Lei, B., Shuo, Y., & Man, L. (2015). Personal relative deprivation boosts materialism. *Basic and Applied Social Psychology*, *37*(5), 241–259. https://doi.org/10.1080/01973533.2015.1072090

Zhou, S., Page-Gould, E., Aron, A., Moyer, A., & Hewstone, M. (2019). The extended contact hypothesis: A meta-analysis on 20 years of research. *Personality and Social Psychology Review*, *23*(2), 132–160. https://doi.org/10.1177/1088868318762647

Zick, A., Wolf, C., Küpper, B., Davidov, E., Schmidt, P., & Heitmeyer, W. (2008). The syndrome of group-focused enmity: The interrelation of prejudices tested with multiple cross-sectional and panel data. *Journal of Social Issues*, *64*(2), 363–383. https://doi.org/10.1111/j.1540-4560.2008.00566.x

Zitek, E. M., & Hebl, M. R. (2007). The role of social norm clarity in the influenced expression of prejudice over time. *Journal of Experimental Social Psychology*, *43*(6), 867–876. https://doi.org/10.1016/j.jesp.2006.10.010

Zmigrod, L., Rentfrow, P. J., & Robbins, T. W. (2018). Cognitive underpinnings of nationalist ideology in the context of Brexit. *Proceedings of the National Academy of Sciences of the United States of America*, *115*(19), E4532–E4540. https://doi.org/10.1073/pnas.1708960115

Zubielevitch, E., Sibley, C. G., & Osborne, D. (2019). Chicken or the egg? A cross-lagged panel analysis of group identification and group-based relative deprivation. *Group Processes & Intergroup Relations*. Advance online publication. https://doi.org/10.1177/1368430219878782

Zyzniewski, L. E. (2002). *Strategic linguistic bias in intergroup processes* (AAI3055316). ProQuest Information and Learning.

Index

A

B

F

G

M

N

S

T

U

V

W

Y

Z

About the Author

Thomas F. Pettigrew, PhD, is a research professor of social psychology at the University of California, Santa Cruz. He received his BA from the University of Virginia and his MA and PhD in social psychology from Harvard. Professor Pettigrew has spent more than 6 decades studying intergroup relations, prejudice, meta-analyses of intergroup contact and relative deprivation while publishing more than 400 journal articles and books. Alongside Kenneth Clark, he was responsible for inviting Martin Luther King Jr. to speak at the American Psychological Association meeting in 1967, a landmark event in the association's history. Professor Pettigrew has received dozens of honors and awards, including an honorary doctorate from Philipps University in Marburg, Germany, a Center for the Advanced Study in the Behavioral Sciences Fellowship, a Guggenheim Fellowship, a Senior Fulbright Fellowship, the University of California's Distinguished Emeriti Panunzio Award, and Harvard Graduate School's Centennial Medal. From psychology, he was awarded the Lewin Prize, lifetime achievement awards from four organizations, two Allport Intergroup Research awards, and the Scientific Impact Award. From sociology, he has been awarded the Cox–Johnson–Frazier Award for race relations research, the Cooley-Mead Award for social psychology, the Spivack Award for Race Research, and the Whyte Career Award.